EMPOWERING
COMMUNITIES

Empowering Communities

How
Electric Cooperatives
Transformed
Rural South Carolina

LACY K. FORD AND
JARED BAILEY

Foreword by James E. Clyburn

THE UNIVERSITY OF
SOUTH CAROLINA PRESS

Cooperatives around the world operate according to the same set of core principles and values, adopted by the International Co-operative Alliance. Cooperatives trace the roots of these principles to the first modern cooperative founded by a group of craftsmen and entrepreneurs in Rochdale, England, in 1844. These principles are a key reason that electric cooperatives operate differently from other electric utilities, placing the needs of their members first.

THE SEVEN COOPERATIVE PRINCIPLES

1. Open and Voluntary Membership

2. Democratic Member Control

3. Members' Economic Participation

4. Autonomy and Independence

5. Education, Training, and Information

6. Cooperation Among Cooperatives

7. Concern for Community

© 2022 University of South Carolina

Published by the University of South Carolina Press
Columbia, South Carolina 29208

www.uscpress.com

Manufactured in the United States of America

31 30 29 28 27 26 25 24 23 22
10 9 8 7 6 5 4 3 2 1

Library of Congress Cataloging-in-Publication Data
can be found at http://catalog.loc.gov/.

ISBN: 978-1-64336-268-7 (hardcover)
ISBN: 978-1-64336-269-4 (paperback)
ISBN: 978-1-64336-270-0 (ebook)

CONTENTS

FOREWORD

Throughout my career in public service, electric cooperatives in South Carolina have been important players in the development of rural communities in the state. I did not appreciate the breath of their significance, however, until 1968, when I became Executive Director of the South Carolina Commission for Farm Workers (SCCFW), a community action program created under Title III-B of the 1964 Economic Opportunity Act.

It was in that capacity that I began working with communities throughout the Sea Islands of South Carolina and rural communities in several other counties in the state's Lowcountry. It became clear to me that their mission went beyond getting electricity to underserved areas. They were committed to improving the quality of life for their members. Currently, a quarter of South Carolinians are served by an electric cooperative, and many of them are my constituents.

I met Lieutenant Governor John West on August 16, 1969, when he accepted my invitation to speak at a groundbreaking ceremony for a Self-Help housing program SCCFW was launching in Adams Run on Yonge's Island, South Carolina. I remember the date very well because my second daughter Jennifer was born earlier that morning about six hours before that 11:00 AM ceremony. When I explained SCCFW's programs to John West, he told me that he was going to run for governor the next year, and if elected, he wished I would consider becoming a part of his staff and bringing those kinds of creative efforts with me. He ran and was elected. He extended the invitation and I accepted.

Several things grew out of that. Two of them were, the South Carolina Housing and Finance Commission, and "John's Johns." Creation of the Housing and Finance Commission had a rocky start. It took three trips to the State Supreme Court for it to pass legal muster.

John's Johns had a much smoother launch. I worked with the electric cooperatives as they installed scores of John's Johns; prefabricated bathrooms that were attached to homes in rural communities that were without indoor plumbing. Just like the co-ops' efforts to turn on lights in homes throughout rural communities, this initiative to provide indoor bathroom facilities to rural homeowners was lifechanging. This would be the beginning of my collaborations with the co-op movement.

Since being sworn into Congress in 1993, I have worked closely with Mike Couick and the state's electric cooperatives to create other measures to improve the quality of life for rural residents of South Carolina. I worked with them to design the Rural Energy Savings Program to enable homeowners and businesses to take out loans through their electricity provider to make energy-efficient improvements to their homes. These loans are paid back on their monthly electric bills and the savings they realize because of the improvements often cover the cost of their loan re-payments. The extraordinary success of this South Carolina electric co-op initiative has enabled me to expand the program and provide energy and cost savings to millions of homeowners nationwide.

In recent years, my work with the co-ops has expanded to focus on universal access to broadband. Many of the communities impacted by the electrification efforts of the co-ops eighty years ago are digital deserts today. Internet providers, much like electricity providers of the twentieth century, have determined that it is not cost effective to build out the infrastructure needed to deliver high-speed broadband in sparsely populated areas. Fortunately, the electric cooperatives have already demonstrated that they can be very effective in meeting this challenge. Just as they electrified rural America in the twentieth century, South Carolina electric co-ops are demonstrating that they are willing and able to be partners in today's efforts to make broadband accessible and affordable to all.

Growing up in a parsonage, I learned at an early age that we are all called to lead by precept and example. It is not enough to express our faith with our words, we must demonstrate our faith through our actions. The electric cooperatives were built on this same principle.

I not only work closely with the co-ops in our shared mission of improving the quality of life for those we serve, but I am also a member of the Tri-County Electric Cooperative which is the utility provider at my home in Santee, South Carolina. I am a beneficiary of the creative and cooperative service they provide and the sense of community they build in their service areas throughout the state.

One of the themes that author, Dr. Lacy Ford, discusses in this important story of the birth, growth, and contributions of electric cooperatives in South Carolina, is that these organizations are an integral part of the social fabric of the communities they serve. They reflect their communities, and they have weathered the challenges that these communities have faced during their eighty-year history. It pleases me that this book takes an unvarnished look at that history, because it is only through the lessons that our history teaches that we can work productively towards a better future.

Through my long association with South Carolina's electric cooperatives, I have found them to be forward-looking and mission-driven. They are an extraordinary asset to our rural communities and serve as an important partner in our efforts to ensure that the promise of America is just as accessible and affordable to their members as it is to those living in non-member areas.

I am confident our co-ops will continue to provide innovative leadership on behalf of our rural communities and fight to help make these communities viable and vibrant for many generations to come. And I thank Dr. Lacy Ford and Jared Bailey for this memorialization of their efforts.

JAMES E. CLYBURN

ACKNOWLEDGMENTS

A small community produced this book. Mike Couick, CEO of The Electric Cooperatives of South Carolina (the trade association serving eighteen of the state's twenty individual electricity distribution cooperatives along with materials supply, generation and transmission, and transmission service cooperatives), conceived of the project and set it in motion. ECSC, together with the robust cooperation of the individual electric cooperatives, which serve parts of every county in the state, made the telling of this story possible. From the outset, the goal of the team working on the volume was to tell the story of the electric cooperatives in South Carolina rather than present a formal history. That story is a powerful and suggestive one, and to a significant degree, the story is told through the words of cooperative members and cooperative publications.

Giving cooperative members the opportunity to tell their stories required the support and coordination of all the electric cooperatives across the state as well as ECSC. Rachel Despres, Campbell Shuford, Jackson Shuford, and Blake Ward worked as student interns on the project. Without those interns helping with the interviews, as well as with research, this would have been a much less compelling volume. As the book neared completion, Jillian Hinderliter provided valuable research, editing, and copyediting skills to the project, and the final product is much the better for her efforts.

Throughout the process, the staff at ECSC and at the local cooperatives have been amazingly helpful, patient, and cooperative. Walter Allread of ECSC, Muriel Gouffray of Aiken Electric Cooperative, and Sheila Rivers of Tri-County Electric Cooperative played key roles in organizing and conducting the early interviews. Mark Quinn of ECSC also helped in the early stages. Special appreciation must be extended to Van O'Cain for spearheading the interview process, and to Lindsey Smith and Lou Green for their guidance and help at critical moments during the process. Just as the inspiration and support of Mike Couick launched the project, it would never have been completed without his patience and insight.

To an unusual extent, even the authorship of this volume has been a cooperative effort. Lacy Ford and Jared Bailey served as lead authors. Eric Plaag and David Dangerfield, contributing authors, made essential research and writing contributions in the earlier stages of the project. Suzanne Nagy served as managing editor, charged with working to keep the team effort on track, a challenge as rewarding as herding cats, but one that needed doing.

And last but far from least, we need to thank all the members and supporters of South Carolina's electric cooperatives through all the cooperatives' years of existence. Without their need for service, without their willingness to form a local cooperative and seek not only to improve their own quality of life but also that of the communities in which they lived and live, there would be no story to tell. Instead, a remarkable story is there to tell, one of neighbors helping neighbors which, while as old as the sacred texts that encourage such efforts, remains vital to the collective future of all our communities. And the story gains power with the telling.

LACY FORD

INTRODUCTION

An important South Carolina story has never been told. It is the story of the role of the Palmetto State's electric cooperatives bringing electricity to the rural population of the state and their ongoing efforts over decades to enhance the quality of life in the state's rural areas. From the moment the lights came on, South Carolina's electric cooperatives have played a major, if often overlooked, role in ushering rural South Carolina into the modern world through making not simply electricity but also labor-saving electric appliances and modern conveniences available to rural people, serving as a center of community experience, and, at the present moment, leading the effort to bring high-speed broadband service to currently underserved rural households in South Carolina. This volume tells the story of rural electrification and electricity's impact on rural living from the perspective of the electric cooperatives. It seeks to tell the story that has never been told as the state's electric cooperatives enter their ninth decade of their service to communities around the Palmetto State.[1]

Early in the twentieth century, evolving coalitions of South Carolinians with an eye for progress sought three key drivers of social and economic improvement in the state: public education, a state highway system, and electric power. In the political vernacular of the era, Palmetto State progressives talked about getting rural South Carolinians "out of the mud, out of the dark, and into good schools." From 1900 to 1930, various progressive coalitions brought these essentials of modernity to portions of South Carolina and some segments of the state's population. Yet throughout the 1920s, rural areas of the state lagged well behind towns and cities in access to education, roads, and electricity. By the late 1920s, however, progress appeared at hand in terms of public education and roads, as the state assumed a larger role in providing more funding for educating students and building more highways than ever before. The 6-0-1 Education Reform Law of 1924 brought more educational opportunity to rural citizens, or at least to white children in rural areas, by increasing the length of the school year through guaranteeing that the state would pay for six months of teacher salaries if the local district would pay for one. Five years later, the passage the Highway Bond Bill of 1929 promised a system of state roads financed by state bonds that served rural areas and urban centers, with the promised funding valued at nearly $30 million, an amount that represented several times the size of the annual state budgets of the era.[2]

Yet even at the end of the decade, as the promise of more school days and better roads was nearing fulfillment, the curse of darkness still fell heavily across most of rural South Carolina. Cities and most towns in the state had electric lights by the 1920s, with electricity provided by investor-owned utilities and municipal corporations which depended on population density to make their efforts financially feasible. But most rural South Carolinians, white and Black, remained without electricity because they lived in areas where the lack of population density rendered it unprofitable for utilities such as Duke Power (or its forerunners) or South Carolina Electric and Gas to serve. It took the emergence of electric cooperatives and the availability of "public power" to bring electricity to the previously unserved areas, fulfilling a dream shared by many rural people across the South Carolina countryside during the 1930s, 1940s, and 1950s.

Today, South Carolina's electric cooperatives serve over a quarter of South Carolina's citizens and seventy percent of the state's land area. From their inception, the electric cooperatives have been a social movement, more like the Farmer's Alliance cooperatives of 1890s than private enterprises. Cooperative members were their owners, and their customers were their members. Working together, rural South Carolinians formed cooperatives and brought electricity, one of the great modernizing essentials of the twentieth century, to the countryside. Led by the organizing efforts of farmers, teachers, agricultural extension agents, pastors and others, rural communities drew on their modest resources to become members, and cooperatives, with federal financial support, brought electricity to portions of the still unserved countryside.

The rise of electricity transmitted, delivered, and serviced by member-owned cooperatives and sanctioned by federal and state legislation is a complicated saga, one that takes its students and readers into matters of politics, law, finance, business, territorial competition, environmental concerns, the technology of electrical generation and transmission, and rural economic development. Each of these matters will be touched on in this short book, but this volume's focus will remain on the dramatic and continuing changes driven by the electricity and sense of community the cooperatives brought to rural areas across the Palmetto State. While it can tell only a portion of the story, this book focuses on how, across decades, the cooperatives helped bring dramatic, fundamental, and transformational change to the lives of rural people in South Carolina. To be sure, it was an era of dramatic change across much of South Carolina as owner-ship of automobiles and other modern improvements lessened the isola-tion of the countryside, but without question rural electrification changed the daily routines and life experiences of rural people—Black and white, men and women—repeatedly across the decades after the "lights came on" in rural South Carolina.

By the time electricity reached rural households, most country people had seen electric lights in visits to towns and cities or in the homes of rela-tives and friends who lived in areas with electric utility service. But when electric power came to their own households and they saw their own lives transformed by the convenience and comfort of electricity, many rural South Carolinians felt their own sense of awe and amazement. No longer left out or left behind, tens of thousands of rural South Carolinians grasped that rural life was changing—chiefly for the better in their view—in very tangible ways as the cooperatives began to deliver electricity to previously unserved areas. As cooperative member Hubert Waldrop of Laurens de-clared: "It was just a modern miracle when the lights came on."[3]

The familiar saying that the electric cooperatives were "born in poli-tics" and will live their life "in politics" is another theme of this book. A product of active local organizing efforts, the cooperatives enjoyed suc-cess in no small part because of their input and influence on the passage of state and national policies which facilitated the generation, distribu-tion infrastructure, and service providers that brought electricity to ru-ral citizens. But both state and federal political support grew contested at various moments in cooperative history, and the political energy of co-operative members often proved critical to the continuing success of the cooperatives.

Nationally, the rural electrification movement in the United States gained great energy from the election of Franklin D. Roosevelt in 1932 and his desire to launch a "New Deal" that would revive a depression-ridden national economy. FDR's ideas included bringing new life to rural areas seemingly being left behind as the nation grew more urban and indus-trial, a point affirmed by the 1920 census revelation that over half of all Americans lived in towns and cities for the first time. The New Deal's em-phasis on rural electrification gave rise, both directly and indirectly, to the electric cooperative movement in South Carolina. With New Deal sup-port for federal loan funding to help finance the building of a distribu-tion infrastructure, the dream of rural electrification was indeed realized, however slowly, following passage of the Rural Electrification Act in 1936. In January 1935, only 744,000 of seven million farms in the nation had access to electricity, but by 1940 some 1,700,000 farms nationwide had access to electricity. Federal loans, made available to rural cooperatives, financed the infrastructure—particularly the running of electric lines through sparsely populated rural areas—needed to bring light to the countryside.

Moreover, in the decades following the establishment of electric service by the cooperatives, political battles at the state and national level continued with regularity and vigor. Some presidential administrations often made efforts to reduce, if not fully eliminate, funding for electric cooperatives and generally opposed funding the major hydroelectric dam projects needed to supply cooperatives with electricity. National politics had state-level repercussions. At the state level, the South Carolina legislature remained generally supportive of cooperatives and their members, but constant vigilance was required to preserve public power coalitions against the continued efforts of investor-owned utilities in the state to either purchase the cooperatives outright or encroach on cooperative territory as population densities and opportunities to serve industrial customers increased in those areas. This volume even provides a glimpse into the colorful world of South Carolina politics as it examines political controversies and their implications to illustrate the level of social and political organization the cooperatives needed to protect their mission.

A different dimension of this book examines the electric cooperatives' role as part of the social fabric of the communities they served. Chapters discuss the changing roles of women in the cooperatives as customers, employees, and board members as the roles of women changed in their communities. The strong sense of family that emerged among members of the cooperatives' workforce, whether working the lines or the offices, becomes clear through testimony of workers themselves. As a retired employee who spent some thirty-seven years on the job, Theresa Hicks expressed a sentiment common among cooperative employees, past and present, "It's not your blood family, but it's your family. . . ."[4]

At the same time, while the cooperatives served portions of the African American population in their service regions and employed African American workers as laborers from their earliest days, the desegregation of cooperative supervisory and management-level employment as well as board membership came slowly and much later. Initially, the strong sense of family among cooperative workers made it hard for African American employees to gain entrance into the community, but as desegregation proceeded across southern society, African Americans came to experience that same family sentiment within the cooperatives, even if such sentiment evolved with painstaking slowness.

The concluding section of the volume explores the ongoing efforts of the cooperatives to fulfill three critical areas of their mission: providing the safe, efficient, and affordable energy to their members, serving their members in new and innovative ways, and addressing directly, and in a transparent and democratic manner, controversies over questionable actions of local boards.

Inspired by US senator Ernest F. "Fritz" Hollings' so-called poverty tours, which called state and national attention to the extent of deep poverty and deprivation in the Palmetto State, South Carolina governor John West, who served from 1971 to 1975, found an eager partner in the state's electric cooperatives when he launched his "Privy Project" (informally known among West's aides as "John's Johns"). West's project sought to bring indoor plumbing to as many South Carolina homes as possible. The electric cooperatives identified members who were candidates for the improvements and helped find funding to bring indoor plumbing to more homes in poor rural areas in the 1970s. Some years later, in 2011, the state's electric cooperatives launched the "Help My House®" program, a pilot-project for reducing energy use by making residences more energy efficient. Supported by low-interest loans, the program turned residences into energy efficient homes, reducing overall carbon emissions and lowering power bills for low-income homeowners.

Mindful of the climate-change implications of long-term use of fossil fuel–powered generation facilities, the cooperatives launched their own solar-power farm to advance the cause of sustainable energy and worked consistently to find ways to prevent higher energy costs from being passed down to its customers.

South Carolina's electric cooperatives also performed a valuable service to its veterans, a significant population among the cooperative membership, by sponsoring "Honor Flights" to Washington, DC. These flights allowed veterans a chance to visit national memorials and shrines and share the experience and the company of each other as they did so.[5] Very recently, cooperatives statewide supported an aggressive movement to replace local board members who violated the cooperative members' trust, as Tri-County Electric Cooperative in the state's Midlands changed its leadership in a resounding display of member participation and voting rights, suggesting once again that a "free media and . . . a working ballot box" are critical to effective governance.[6]

Finally, the book covers the current resolution of the ongoing controversy over the future of Santee Cooper, the state-owned electric utility which generates and sells some 65 percent of its electricity to its leading customer, South Carolina's electric cooperatives. Moreover, Santee

Cooper is the cooperatives' largest single provider of electricity. The leadership of state-owned Santee Cooper invested heavily as a junior partner in the construction of a new nuclear facility in Fairfield County. The project suffered from serious cost overruns that ran the project into bankruptcy, ultimately resulting in the sale of South Carolina Electric & Gas Company (SCE&G), the leading investor in the project, and leaving a heavy debt to Santee Cooper. The legislature's decision on Santee Cooper's future role will have a significant impact on its major customer: South Carolina's electric cooperatives. As this book goes to press, the South Carolina legislature has decided that now is the time to reform Santee Cooper rather than sell it.[7]

When the Lights Came On

COOPERATIVES POWER THE COUNTRYSIDE

n the first decades of the twentieth century, nightfall still meant the coming of a deep darkness across most of rural South Carolina. Cities and most towns had electric lights by the 1920s, but most rural South Carolinians, white and Black, remained without electricity. It took the emergence of electric cooperatives to bring these previously unserved rural households out of darkness into the light, fulfilling a dream of many rural people across the state of South Carolina countryside during the 1930s, 1940s, and early 1950s.[1]

Understanding those changes electricity brought to the countryside and the dramatic way rural life was transformed begins with exploring what rural life was like before electrification—and the difficult daily labors that are easily forgotten amid today's modern conveniences. When asked about their lives before electricity, rural Carolinians almost universally remember the same daily tasks and chores: tending kerosene lanterns, chopping wood, pumping (or worse, carrying) water, hand-washing laundry, and bathing weekly in tin tubs. "We thought it was tough," Frank Hart, a member of Broad River Electric Cooperative, reflected. "Everyone was assigned a chore, and you had to do it."[2] Lynches River Electric member William F. Robinson remembered "everything was primitive. We had to cut wood with an axe. We heated with wood, we cooked with wood."[3] Edisto Electric member Jack Morris put it simply: "Everything was cutting wood. Everything was wood. Wood in the winter for heat and wood year-round for cooking; it was a labor that never stopped."[4]

Sons in rural families were often assigned the jobs of carrying water and cutting wood. F. E. Hendrix of Laurens Electric remembered rising each morning to draw water up from a well for livestock and then more water for his mother to wash laundry. "A fourteen-year-old boy, he can really appreciate electricity today because of what he went through in those first fourteen years," Hendrix reflected.[5] Marlboro Electric member Sammie McKinley, related that as a child he "used to have to pump water for the livestock, before we had electricity, it was hand pumps, and I felt like [the livestock were] ... drinking too much and I'd get tired of pumping and I'd just get me a stick and run 'em off."[6]

Beyond the house and farm work that was incumbent on rural sons and daughters before electrification, good hygiene and bathing posed its own challenges without electric water pumps, indoor plumbing, and electric water heaters. Rather than carry or pump water for daily tub-baths, many described taking sponge baths out of a basin on most days and a soaking bath in a tin tub maybe once per week. Arthur James of Black River Electric described his family's weekly ritual that he shared with his parents and seven brothers and sisters. "On Saturday, everybody would take a bath and you would use an old tin tub. ... And we would put that tin tub in front of the fireplace 'cause [sic] that was your heat and one side of that tin tub would get real hot and burn you almost, because of the fire. You would put the tub as close as you could to stay warm." James' family took turns, the boys waited in another room while the girls bathed, and they carried new water for each family member.[7] Others who remembered weekly baths, like Gary Roberts of Fairfield, might have seen clean water as a luxury. He reported that in his household "a lot of times [we] used the same water." Of course, Roberts also confessed that "in the summertime [the boys] .... would take the soap down to the creek."[8] The impracticality of hauling and heating water for each family member was the same in Eunice Spilliards's family in Tillman. "We had to take our baths in a wash tub on the back porch. And I was the baby of six, so sometimes I got the last bath. And you can imagine the fussing and the fighting. 'I don't want to take a bath after that one. I don't want to take a bath when that one gets through.'"[9]

Electricity eased some of the workload and brought more modern conveniences, but of all the changes that electricity brought to rural South Carolinians, the most obvious change was also the most symbolic of rural transformation: lights. Before, "it was all dark," recalled Pee Dee Electric member Henry Norris.[10] Many households used kerosene lamps which produced dark smoke and relatively dim light. According to Dargan Hodge of Black River Electric Cooperative, "if you went outside you used a lantern. Couldn't see much. We didn't know any better. ... It was dark at night, it was dark everywhere. In the community-no lights no-where, no night lights, road lights, nothing."[11] Inside the home was not much better as Marion Caldwell of Fairfield Electric recalled, "Most people, when it got dark, they went to bed."[12] Little River member Bob Parker, recalled having to complete his homework by kerosene lantern as a seven-year-old child.[13] Madge Strickland of Fairfield had electricity as a girl living in Charleston before moving to the Blaney community, near Elgin, where she no longer had lights. She described her excitement when the lights came on in Blaney. "But, ah . . . when electricity came, I remember thinking, oh my, no more studying by that smoky kerosene lamp. That was something, you just couldn't see to study. . . . I enjoyed reading and that was a big thing for me."[14] Electric lights brought warmth and security, they lengthened the restful evenings, and lights were symbols of electricity's force in rural change. Dargan Hodge of Black River summarized what many cooperative members called electricity, light: "That's what we called it. The light line."[15]

When that change came, lights represented a dramatic moment, "like something from another planet," claimed William Robinson when recalling the day that the lights came on in the rural Pee Dee. The Lynches River member remembered the moment "like it was yesterday."[16] Clover's Dick Burrell remembered clearly that his family did not get electricity until 1949. "When York Electric Co-op . . . came our way and we got power. I remember the exact day it was turned on," Burrell reflected. "It was on Saturday," he continued.

> They had put the meter base on and the power to the meter base. We had gone to the picture show, me and my brother. We rode our bicycles up to Clover, a couple miles. And the two gentlemen that wired our house, they came on Saturday, and they were wiring the house. When I came back that afternoon from the picture show about five o'clock and went in, the prettiest little light cord was hanging up there. We had one light bulb and a light cord . . . that was on a Saturday in 1949 that we turned the lights on. It was a memorable day.

"It was daytime when the lights came on," Burrell recalled, "but that didn't make any difference! We wanted to see what that power looked like."[17]

Fairfield's Madge Strickland remembered that her family anticipated the lights coming on "from early dawn" on the day electricity arrived. "[W]e didn't get anything accomplished that day. . . . they came. And . . . when they flipped the switch and did the final things, we were ready! We had the bulbs already installed and when the lights came on, I think we burned the lights for twenty-four hours because we just couldn't get enough of seeing the light! It was just wonderful!"[18] Billy Catoe, a Lynches

River Electric member, recalled that community leaders had "tried to get Duke [Power] to extend the line down to where we were at, but they couldn't get anything out of them," so then they turned to the Lynches River cooperative for assistance. "[I]t made a big difference when we did get electricity," Catoe insisted.[19] Tri-County Electric member Gene Carson recalled that before the arrival of electricity in his community south of Columbia: "It was dark." He remembered how the power of darkness prompted Carson to awaken at daylight in order to get all of his work done before sundown. Old kerosene lamps did little to illuminate the darkness, but when the electric lights came on, they were "so bright," Carson remarked, that you were "nearly blind . . . they were so bright." The arrival of electricity in rural areas of the lower Midlands, in Carson's view, marked "one of the biggest changes I've ever seen in my lifetime: from darkness to light."[20]

The change that electricity brought to the countryside, at least in the minds of those who remember its arrival, lay in its time-freeing and labor-saving capacity. Electric light itself both extended the workday and made it more flexible. Those who recalled the arrival of electricity in their homes as children and youth focused specifically on the ways the change affected their lives directly. Electricity reached William Good's house outside of Great Falls, located in an area he termed (without intent of exaggeration) "real country," when he was eleven. To Good, its arrival meant chiefly the end of having to carry water pulled by hand from a deep well "all the way to the house." Not long after the lights came on, a new electric water pump drew water out of the well and pumped it to the Good house, allowing the washing of clothes in the house rather than in the nearby spring. According to Good, the arrival of electricity relieved him of "a whole lot of duties." Lula Mathews, born and raised in Dorchester County, remembered that before Edisto Electric brought electricity to her area, washing clothes required much hard work. Mathews had to draw water from wells by hand and then wash clothes by hand on a scrub board.[21]

For most rural young people, electrification alleviated some of their household chores, but also became an integral part of precious childhood memories. In Black River Electric territory, Leslie Tindal recalled that his family's electricity was connected just before the Christmas holidays in 1937. Tindal remembered that 1937 was still "horse and buggy days" because so many of his neighbors still used that mode for traveling. When his family's power was turned on, his parents brought electric, colored Christmas lights from Sumter to decorate a small cedar tree in their front yard. "And the wagons and the buggies kept passing by in front of the house to look at the Christmas tree," Tindal recalled. Hubert Waldrop of Laurens shared a similar holiday memory when his family's home received electricity in the fall of 1939, and instead of lighting their tree with candles that they could only burn for a short time, it was lit with real lights. "That was something for an eleven-year-old," remembered Waldrop.

For families, electricity also meant the advent of modern conveniences. Electric refrigerators facilitated cool and cold storage (meaning more frequent ice cream treats to children and teenagers) and electric stoves reduced the labor of cutting and chopping wood and simplified cooking. After lights, refrigerators were often the first appliances that families acquired. Kirk Roberts of Fairfield Electric reported that some families could not afford to buy the appliance, but their co-op would help them finance a refrigerator while paying their monthly electric bill. "That's how we got our first refrigerator, and it had four little cubes of ice up at the top," Roberts remembered. "Of course that was a gift; we didn't have to buy ice anymore."[22] Just having ice was a great luxury. Lou Carson of Broad River Electric remembers that her family, like most, had to buy blocks of ice and keep them as long as possible in a chest.[23] Dick Burrell, a member of York Electric who grew up outside Clover, remembered his family driving their Model A Ford into Clover for a fifty-pound block of ice. "You'd hang it on the back bumper, between the back bumper and the fender on that Model A Ford. We'd drive home and half of it, sometimes, would be melted," Burrell recalled.[24] Keeping the ice once at home was another challenge. Some, like Winona Peagler's family in Moncks Corner or Walter Sanders in White Oak, covered their twenty-five- or fifty-pound blocks with sawdust to insulate them and slow the melting. Sanders even recalled that his grandparents would dig holes to store the ice blocks in the ground.[25] With electricity came the possibility for refrigeration and ice at home. Lou Carson remembered that when her family finally got electricity, they bought a refrigerator and "we really had a family celebration when we got our power because we could cook and have ice tea. . . . My daddy wouldn't let us drink [soft drinks]. So we had tea. Sweet tea. I will never forget how good it tasted with our own homemade ice. It was really exciting."[26]

Other modern amenities including electric pumps and running water changed the nature of personal hygiene and washing clothes after rural electrification. Carrying and pumping water was replaced by electric pumps, and soon, indoor plumbing. According to Fairfield's Marion Caldwell, "the biggest thing is that everybody got electric pumps, [so they] had water in the house, and bathrooms, and stoves." Arthur James of the Rembert community said those pumps were "a tremendous thing, saving time and extra work."[27] LaVern Polk of Islandton noted the change it brought about on his family's farm. "We ran water lines back in the fields where we had pens and things for cattle and livestock. Instead of hauling water all the time, you were able to pump it. It was much easier."[28] Running water in the home was another blessing, for members like Nancy Heustess of Marlboro Electric. She recalled, "Before we had electricity, we had hand pumps in the kitchen and that was the way we had to get the water from the well, but I was so glad when we got running water in the house so we didn't have to pump that pump and we had some hot water."[29] Scottie Plummer of Williamsburg recalled that running water encouraged some families to build dedicated bathrooms onto their existing homes, while others converted their storage closets.[30] Little River's Cleland Manning also fondly remembered when his family acquired electricity and, after World War II, an electric water pump. "When that [pump] was put in, it saved that drawing the water for wash day. It was such a blessing," Manning recalled. "And more than that, then came indoor plumbing. People are often saying, 'I enjoy the old days.' Well, I don't enjoy some old days. I don't want to go back to some old days that we had. That bathroom was just wonderful."[31]

Electricity also facilitated the use of radios and, in later years, television. Louise Clark, who grew up outside of Leesville in the Traffic Circle community of Saluda County, remembered that her father replaced his battery-powered radio with an electric model that brought programming and connected them to the news. She enjoyed listening to "a variety of programs."

"There was one in the morning and I don't know what the program was, but I know how they started the program. 'It's a beautiful day in Chicago, and I hope it's more beautiful wherever you are.' . . . There was one called Dr. I. Q. They asked questions to the audience and people tried to answer them and they got candy bars as prizes if they answered so many of the questions. . . . Then they had some kind of like soap opera stories. They had one they called Just Plain Bill. [And The] Lone Ranger."

Clark remembered that the radio brought them not only entertainment, but a connection with the world outside of their rural community. "We could get the news. And I remember well, of course we had had electricity for a while, when Pearl Harbor was bombed. We listened to the radio all day that day. If we had not had electricity, we wouldn't have known about it."[32]

Like the radio, televisions eventually connected rural families with regional and even national broadcasts of news, entertainment, and sporting events. Frequently, some of the first homes to get televisions became gathering places for family and friends to enjoy the broadcasts. Sammie McKinley of Marlboro Electric remembered, "When they would have the boxing matches on television, we would have company from everywhere to come watch the fight." Frances Freeland of Little River noted her family may have been the first in their community to get a television. Family would gather to watch "fights and all that stuff." Freeland had "an uncle and aunt that lived down in Plum Branch, and she loved the fights. She would just be . . . she couldn't be still when they were up there fighting."[33] Jessie Mae Jordan of Lynches River related that her family had electricity for some time and her "children were way on up over half grown" before buying a television. "All the family would sit around at night and watch that television when we got through with supper," Jordan remembered. "That television would come on and we'd watch television until it was time to go to bed."[34] Eunice Spilliards also remembered her own family gathering around their radio and later their television to watch *the Lawrence Welk Show*. "Oh, we were Uptown. We were really Uptown," she recalled.[35]

Harry Slattery, a member of President Franklin Roosevelt's cabinet and an avid supporter of rural electrification, published a study in 1940 on the New Deal's Rural Electrification Act (REA) and the early growth of rural electrification. Slattery found that "the menfolk want to know how electricity can profitably be used in dairying, stock raising, truck and fruit farming, in short, all branches of agriculture." But, Slattery observed, "When wiring time comes, inquiries begin to pour into REA from housewives asking about wiring, plumbing, lighting, the most efficient and economical appliances, and what not."[36] Indeed, while some older cooperative members highlighted the benefits of electricity to farm work, especially as a boon to dairy farming, men and women alike agreed that it was rural women in particular who had their lives transformed and their work burdens reduced by the arrival of electricity and the conveniences that became available to them once electricity arrived. Edisto's Bob Smith remembered that his wife cried tears of "joy" and "unbelief" when the lights came on. "People talk about the good ole days," Smith observed, "I'll tell you, anybody that says that wasn't there. Because it wasn't good. It was tough on particularly the women, more than anybody. Particularly on the lady folks, the mothers."[37] Mildred Allen, another Edisto member, also maintained that the women of the household benefited from the arrival of electricity "more than anyone else did because it made her work a lot easier when you had electrical things to use." She specified refrigerators, electric stoves and other kitchen appliances that made keeping house much less labor intensive. "I declare I hate to think if something [had] happened and we didn't have power because this made life easier for the housewife," Allen insisted. "I think . . . especially for the housewife[—]the one that keeps house and does cooking and cleaning and so forth."[38]

In interview after interview, longtime cooperative members identified eliminating dependence on the wood stove for cooking, heat and hot water, and reducing the labor of washing clothes through electric water pumps and washing machines as key improvements made possible by electricity. Dick Burrell recalled that his mother's life improved dramatically just by electricity "taking that load of washing clothes off of her." Before electricity, he explained, the Burrell household "had to go down and draw the water out of the well with a bucket." That "was our job on Monday morning, and then go to school," Burrell reflected. "When wintertime came, the clothes still had to be washed," but "you didn't bring them into the house to be washed, you washed them out in the cold. So Mom and sister had a pretty rough time in the wintertime. . . ." Burrell also remembered that "the old wood stove . . . would be awfully hot in that kitchen," especially in the summertime, but "when the electric stove came in" it "really made a big difference in cooking." Burrell declared that his mother "loved" the electric stove because "She didn't have to fool with that old hot stove, putting the wood in it and stuff like that."[39] Willie Mae Wood of Little River remembered that her mother also had to battle summertime heat and the wood-fired stove while preparing family meals. Wood's family "had another room that we ate in in the summertime because the wood stove was so hot" and that her mother, trying to prevent firing the stove more than once a day, "cooked enough for dinner that we had something left over for supper."[40]

Lynches River's Eugene Robinson recalled that electricity transformed his mother's life, first with an electric water pump and then wringer washing machines which allowed her to avoid washing clothes by hand. Later, with the purchase of an electric range, Robinson recalled, she could "just turn the knob" on the range and begin cooking rather than cutting wood and firing up the wood stove. "[I]t absolutely took a load off my mother," Robinson recalled.[41] Palmetto Electric Cooperative's Jerry Vaigneur thought the purchase of an electric, wringer-style washing machine represented the single biggest improvement in the quality of life for his mother after the coming of electricity. Before electricity, Vaigneur recalled, "You had a scrub board. . . [and] of course you boiled your water in a big pot in the yard and then you could get that water into a big number three wash tub and then put your clothes in there and scrub 'em and rinse 'em and rinse 'em." That new washing machine "just made all the difference in the world to her." The new machines washed clothes and "then after a while, you let the water out and then you took those clothes and you run 'em through a wringer up at the top and it would wring the water out of 'em. And they was ready to go to the clothesline."[42]

Bobby Edmonds of Little River insisted that "the woman had a much harder life [before electricity] than the man." He remembered that his mother "would go to the farm with dad in the morning" and "work hard in the field" and then leave around 11 o'clock, walk home, and "fire up the wood stove, cook," and serve the family lunch "shortly after 12 noon." Moreover, "while the men were taking a little break after lunch she was in there doing dishes and ready to go back."[43] Laurens's Hubert Waldrop remembered that prior to electricity arriving, "Momma did the washing outside by the old wash pot with the scrub board, and when she got the ringer type washing machine, she put it on the back porch. She was tickled to death; it saved her a lot of work."[44] Mary Spigner of Tri-County Electric recalled that she "washed outside in a washpot" before electricity. "You would build your fire outside, make your hot water, had a wash pot, a rub board, put your clothes in there and rub them out, rinse them," she explained, adding that "you had to draw your water from the well" first. "We had it tough, really. Those days were tough. Tough," Spigner reflected, "But we got electricity—That was a blessing."[45] And the visible evidence of that blessing was a washing machine.

Jessie Mae Jordan of Lynches River Electric told the story of her first washing machine with emphasis. When a local salesman with a pick-up truck full of washing machines came to her house, she had "done wash that day with scrub boards and he wanted to sell me that washing machine. Well, I couldn't buy it 'cause I didn't know what to do. My husband wasn't there, he was working." The salesman told her, "Well I'm going to leave it. I'm going to put it right here on your front porch and I'll be back in a week and you can decide what you want to do about it." Jordan declared, "Well you know what I decided. I said I'm going to keep that washing machine. Well, my husband came in. Of course I told him. I don't remember what he said, but it wouldn't have made no difference what he said. I would have fought him a duel over that washing machine."[46]

Another type of satisfaction, psychological satisfaction, accompanied the arrival of electricity in the countryside. With electricity common in towns and cities and present in some rural areas served by investor-owned utilities, many rural residents felt stigmatized by town people as isolated, backward, behind the times, or even simply inferior South Carolinians. Mildred Allen of Jasper County remembered the sense of inadequacy she felt before electricity arrived. She recalled that people "who lived in town felt more important than the country kids because they had those conveniences." And, she added, "I think they felt like they were better than we were" until "our time finally came."[47] Allen's suspicions were partially confirmed by the testimony of Charles Banks, who admitted that it was "quite a shock to me that the country had no electricity." Banks had moved as a fourteen-year-old from the town of Chester where he had electricity to a rural community near the Fairfield County line that had no service. He reported struggling to study by kerosene lamps and having to get near the fireplace for extra light as well as heat. Even more of a shock to Banks was the lack of indoor plumbing in rural areas and nothing pleased him more than the purchase of electric water pumps that facilitated the installation of indoor plumbing in many rural households.[48] In the view of Bill Gibbons of Broad River Electric, the cooperatives "changed the whole concept of who these [rural] people were. You see, people up town were fine-they had water and lights-ironed their own clothes. And all this kind of stuff. And these people out here—I don't think they felt inferior . . . Their surroundings were inferior." But, Gibbons continued, "When the co-op came and they got everything that the other crowd had, they were a little prouder. We did it. This is ours. We did this. You folks got it, but we got our own. It made a real difference in the way people felt their standing in the community was."[49]

From its genesis, the cooperative movement helped foster that sense of community among rural South Carolinians as they worked with one another to organize local cooperatives and build membership. Jerry Vaigneur of Jasper County represented this spirit when explaining his own father's role signing up neighbors so that lines could be run to their community.

> On the road that we lived on, which is about six miles north of Ridgeland, in order for Dad to get the power company to come, he needed to get some more people on the road above us signed up. The membership was five dollars. So, Dad went on up and talked with some of the other neighbors above us and they all or some of them agreed they all wanted electricity, so they paid their five dollars up front and of course, it didn't come over night. In other words, it took them awhile to get to work their way to our farm and then on beyond our farm.

Vaigneur continued, "And I remember my mama telling me that on Sunday mornings she would hear a knock on the door. Dad would go to the door and it would be some of those neighbors above us inquiring about their five dollars because their electricity hadn't gotten to 'em and it had been a month or two or three. So, he kind of had to talk 'em into just holding on and eventually it would come."[50] When the lines were connected, their community outside of Ridgeland became part of Palmetto Electric Cooperative.

Helping to organize for their own electrical power and progress undoubtedly cultivated a sense of pride within these communities. Like Vaigneur, F. E. Hendrix of Laurens remembers his father taking part in early efforts to bring light to his family and their neighbors. They believed that Duke Power would connect them and were disappointed to learn that Duke did not believe there were enough customers. "But my father and others in the community did a campaign trying to get others to sign up that they would use their electric lights, and electric stove, and a refrigerator. They got a lot to sign up," Hendrix remembered. Despite their campaign, Duke refused them again. But the community found hope in learning that "Laurens Electric [Cooperative] was close to running power in our area. That brought new life to the people." "'Hey, we're going to get electricity.'" Hendrix further recalled, "It was not too long after that, in 1939, that Laurens Electric Cooperative ran power down our road. I understand that Duke came back and said, 'Well, we think we can do it now.' We said, 'No, we've already signed with Laurens Electric, and we're gonna let them do it.' That was a great day that we connected to the Laurens Electric Co-op."[51] Persistence and organization met with the accomplishment of electrification in their own communities.

Perhaps nowhere was the feeling of community more evident among members than at annual cooperative fairs that each cooperative held to conduct business. They were an opportunity for these rural communities to come together, to visit, and to have a voice in their cooperative organization. Mammie Jones of Lynches River Electric reported that she did not miss an annual meeting until she was ninety-one years old—and she enjoyed going because it allowed for "seeing everyone, getting together, it was really nice."[52] Eunice Spillards of Tillman related that, for her family, annual cooperative meetings could not be missed.

> Every year we had to go up to the annual co-op meeting. It was *big stuff.* . . . It didn't matter if you had homework at school, you had to go to the co-op meeting. Because they had given us electricity, we had to go to the business meeting. To Daddy, it was most important that he be there. . . . But for the families that I can remember—my aunts and uncles, mom and dad—you did not miss that meeting. It wasn't because you got a prize, or it wasn't because you were in the beauty contest, it was because Palmetto, the electric company, had given us something that was so valuable to our way of life. . . .[53]

Frank Hart of Broad River echoed this appreciation for the transformations and opportunities that the cooperatives brought to rural South

Carolinians. In Hart's appraisal, "the co-ops were really the salvation of farming and the rural areas of America. Industry would have never moved into the rural areas without that. . . . [T]he co-ops were the salvation of bringing rural America forward. And we should be grateful for that."[54]

On balance, the story of the arrival of electricity in unserved rural households from the 1930s through the early 1950s unfolds as one of rural communities pulling together and forming cooperatives and signing up enough households to bring electricity to rural communities across the state. Yet the early story of electric cooperatives was also shaped, like all else in the South Carolina of that era, by racial segregation and unequal opportunity. Despite strong support for the cooperative movement from the New Deal, the cooperatives were launched during the years when Jim Crow laws and attitudes held a vice-like grip on South Carolina. Lacking political influence, African Americans found themselves on the outside looking in as decisions were made by whites (and almost always white men) who were in control. Backed by federal money and driven by economics that showed that the more households served the cheaper the service, the electric cooperatives in every part of the state willingly served African American households who subscribed. Yet disparate income levels made this process even more challenging for typical Black households than for typical white ones, and it was challenging enough for many whites as well as Blacks as rural South Carolina struggled to climb out of the Great Depression. For example, Louise Nichols, an African American woman, explained that when she first learned about rural electricity in the Pee Dee around 1939, "no one out here and on the surrounding areas had a full-time job or salary." Instead, all the "men worked in the fields" or cut timber or cleaned yards. The women worked "in the homes of the white people" where "they cleaned house, they cared for their kids, they helped with the food, sometimes even did all the cooking. . . ." Nichols recalled hearing her father and his friends "talking about the idea of a cooperative" and how it might prove "quite a hard sell" at five dollars for a membership, though the Nichols family became members and electricity soon came to their home.[55]

But there were other obstacles for potential African American subscribers. Tenant farming households, which were disproportionately Black, needed their landlord's permission, and often financial assistance, to have their houses wired and to have power lines run on the landlord's property to their houses. One example of how tenant farmers faced difficulty in getting such permission illustrates the larger point. In October 1950, David Junious, a Black tenant on a large Clarendon County farm owned by Irvine F. Belser, a native of Summerton and a prominent Columbia lawyer who argued cases before the US Supreme Court, contacted his landlord with a plea for assistance in getting Black River Electric to bring electricity to his and other tenant homes on Belser's land near Rimini. In his efforts "trying to get the light connected," Junious explained, he learned that Belser was the "hold up."[56] In September, Black River Electric Cooperative had informed Belser that it would not be economically feasible to run lines to tenants on his Hickory Hill plantation unless more of them signed up for service. Without Belser's help, many tenants could not afford to have their houses wired, and without enough households, David Junious noted, "they can't turn the power on."[57] Urging Belser to get involved, Junious reminded his landlord that without his help, "it looks very much like we lose our money in wiring this house up, and . . . we will not have light." Junious emphasized that, "our money could have been used for some other good."[58]

Belser claimed that the delay was a misunderstanding of the role he needed to play and within two weeks of receiving Junious's letter, Belser contacted Black River explaining his confusion. "I am very anxious for David Junious to get service and would appreciate it very much if you could furnish him with service at once," Belser added.[59] Shortly thereafter, Belser communicated with other tenants at his Hickory Hill plantation and offered to pay half the cost of wiring their homes to support the effort. But even with Belser's offer of assistance, some of his tenants at Hickory Hill could still not afford electric service.[60] Not all landlords were as forthcoming, as financially able, or as willing to help their tenants get electric service. Given the high tenancy rate among South Carolina farmers, the challenge of extending electric service to tenant populations proved difficult, and this challenge had a differentially greater impact on rural African Americans than rural whites, though both groups were affected.

Nonetheless, despite the continued presence of discrimination against African Americans and the hardships faced by rural households of both races, the initial reception of electricity in rural South Carolina remained one of joy and amazement. For rural households on the back end of two decades of agricultural recession and one full decade of the economic collapse we know as the Great Depression, patience had become a rural watchword, and the days the lights came on heralded new beginnings of unknown dimensions. Lynches River member Laylon Davis recalled that when the lights came on "we thought we had died and gone to heaven. You know after being in the dark for so long. Then the houses you could see . . . you could see a little light on which we had never seen before at night. It was just amazing."[61] Randolph Mackey of the same cooperative recalled that on the day the lights came on, his family "had a sort of little gathering when we got that first light switch put into that one room because everybody was filled with a lot of joy and everything just switching it on and off. . . . [We] didn't know exactly what was taking place, but that was a moment in our lives that we never will forget. Something happened different to us."[62] When the lights came on in McCormick County in 1950, resident Bobby Edmonds, whose family had "no conveniences" previously, recalled that "it just meant everything to rural people."[63] Eunice Spilliards of the Palmetto Electric service area in the Lowcountry called the day her household "actually got electricity" in 1949 or 1950 "a great day." It "was celebration *everywhere*," she recalled, "And of course it changed *completely* the way that we lived."[64]

The Origins of Electric Cooperatives

LEADING THE WAY FOR RURAL ELECTRIFICATION IN SOUTH CAROLINA

The emergence of the textile industry in the late nineteenth and early twentieth century created pockets of development in cities (Spartanburg, Greenville, Anderson, Columbia, and Rock Hill) and towns (Gaffney, Lancaster, Clinton, Florence, Greenwood, and Honea Path) across South Carolina, leading to a pattern of uneven development across the state. As a general rule, the Upstate was more developed than the Lowcountry, and cities and towns raced ahead of rural areas across much of the state. The pressing challenge for state leaders at the time, as per capita income in the state of South Carolina still lurked around 50 percent of the national average, remained bringing the underdeveloped areas into the twentieth century mainstream.[1] Central to this effort loomed three areas of advancement: improving all South Carolina schools, building more and better highways, and bringing electricity to unserved areas. In the daily language of Palmetto politics, state leaders talked about getting more students in the classroom, getting families "out of the mud," and "turning the lights on" in the homes of rural South Carolinians."

In the early twentieth century, investor-owned, state-regulated utilities, such as Duke Power, South Carolina Electric & Gas Company (SCE&G), and Carolina Power & Light (CP&L) brought electricity to areas with dense populations and industrial customers, but bringing affordable electric service to rural areas with widely scattered populations and little industry to generate around-the-clock demand was more challenging. When Franklin Roosevelt assumed the presidency in 1933 and launched his "New Deal," South Carolina leaders looked to Washington for assistance in addressing the challenge of rural electrification. In fact, the rural electrification movement across the United States gained great energy from President Roosevelt's desire to revive a Depression-ridden national economy and bring new life to rural areas seemingly being left behind as the nation grew more urban and industrial. Moreover, many supporters of the New Deal saw rural development and agricultural renewal as essential components of ending the Depression. Among progressive New Dealers, reviving and modernizing the southern agricultural economy loomed as a key component of bringing the South out of the Depression and into a new American economic mainstream. Aware of the human and environmental suffering caused by the Dust Bowl, these New Dealers saw hydroelectric dams as crucial to both the rural electrification and natural resource management.[2] At the heart of the New Deal effort lay an emphasis on creating a federal agency that could provide funding to facilitate rural electrification. These national efforts gave rise, both directly and indirectly, to the electric cooperative movement in South Carolina.

Commenting on proposed legislation to establish the New Deal's original ad hoc Rural Electrification Administration as a permanent federal agency, George W. Norris, senator from Nebraska, declared that "experience shows that nothing can be more beneficial to the farmer and that nothing will add more to the comfort, satisfaction, and happiness of the rural population than the electrification of farm homes."[3] Norris pointed out that farms needed and would use much electricity because of the special uses that farmers had for electricity that city dwellers did not, such as grinding feed, pumping water for livestock, and performing other difficult farm work. In a report addressed to South Carolina's Ellison D. "Cotton Ed" Smith, chairman of the US Senate Committee on Agriculture and Forestry, the first administrative head of the Rural Electrification Administration (REA) revealed that "only about 1 farm in 10 from the United States ha[d] electric service." By comparison, in France, as a result of national rural electrification programs, nine out of every ten rural communities had electric service. In Germany, approximately 90 percent of the farms were electrified.[4] In addition to comparing the poor American rural electrification rates to those of other countries, the director noted that "rural residents in all parts of the country are demanding electric service, many are quite able to pay a reasonable price for it." Moreover, "they are looking to the federal government to provide the service which private companies have in such large part withheld."[5] The dream of rural electrification was indeed realized, and realized with reasonable speed, due largely to the New Deal's Rural Electrification Act passed in 1936 and its aggressive financing strategies. The 1936 act provided for the federal government to extend long-term loans to local electric cooperatives to build distribution lines for electricity across the nation's vast countryside to serve farmers and other potential rural customers. These federal funds made possible the construction of far-flung electricity grids and established a distribution system that could bring electricity to more thinly populated rural areas that investor-owned utilities could not profitably serve.

A separate, but closely related New Deal initiative and one critical to the success of rural electrification involved building hydroelectric facilities to help supply affordable electricity to rural consumers. Even before the Rural Electrification Act gained congressional approval in 1936, the New Deal's Public Works Administration, an agency designed to provide work for the unemployed and stimulate much-needed income growth through the circulation of wages, planned to spend nearly half of its funds designated for South Carolina on the development of two hydro-electric facilities in the state.[6] While paling in scope to the vast Tennessee Valley Authority (TVA) project approved by the Roosevelt administration in 1933, one South Carolina facility was on the Saluda River at Buzzard's Roost near Greenwood, and the second, a much larger and more ambitious project in the rural Lowcountry, proposed diverting water from the powerful Santee River down a seventy-five-foot gradient into the Cooper River to generate electric power for the largely rural Lowcountry region inland from Charleston. Both of these projects promised to generate electricity for previously unserved areas, and the Santee Cooper project in particular had the potential to generate electricity that could bring electric service to much of the rural South Carolina Lowcountry.

Fortuitously for South Carolina advocates of federally assisted electricity, a 1933 survey of rivers conducted by the Army Corps of Engineers designated Buzzard's Roost on the Saluda River as a prime site for the construction of a hydroelectric dam. Once the Army Corps of Engineers approved the Buzzard's Roost project, Greenwood applied to the Public Works Administration (PWA) for $2.8 million to fund construction of the hydroelectric facility. The planned facility would generate and sell electricity to municipalities in nearby counties (Greenwood, Laurens, and Newberry) since electric cooperatives did not yet exist and, in turn, those municipalities would resell the electricity to users. Charlotte-based Duke Power, which supplied most of the electricity in South Carolina's Piedmont, immediately expressed opposition to the Buzzard's Roost project. Duke's opposition to the project first emphasized the company's philanthropic contribution to the Piedmont, noting that the Duke Endowment's financial support for schools and hospitals in the area were subsidized by

Duke Power and would suffer from federally subsidized competition, even though the Duke Endowment owned only one-eighth of all Duke Power stock. Duke Endowment president George Allen called the potential project "unfair competition" for Duke Power. When Harold Ickes, President Roosevelt's Head of the PWA, heard of Duke's argument, he noted wryly, that apparently "charity covers a multitude of sins."[7]

Duke Power also applied subtle pressure on US senator James F. Byrnes, South Carolina's most influential New Dealer and a key ally of President Roosevelt, in an effort to stall the Buzzard's Roost project. Byrnes's Spartanburg law firm, Wyche, Nichols and Byrnes, had been on retainer for Duke Power since 1931. When the president of Furman College, Bennette E. Geer, informed Byrnes that support of the Buzzard's Roost project could endanger a $350,000 gift to the college from the Duke Endowment, the senator replied, disingenuously, that "he knew little of the matter," and pledged to have his staff look into it. At the same time, the "sly and able" Byrnes also quietly assured PWA director Harold Ickes that he supported the Buzzard's Roost project. When Greenwood state senator W. H. Nicholson asked Byrnes to testify on behalf of the project at a public hearing in the district, Byrnes's office, eager to keep the senator's support for the project quiet, cagily responded that the senator was "away for a much-needed rest." Duke also turned its public relations guns on other local luminaries. It argued that most of the electricity generated at Buzzard's Roost would serve Greenwood Mills, owned by James C. Self, a prominent supporter of the hydroelectric project. Later, when the PWA gave the project full approval, Byrnes cleverly advised Nicholson to take all the credit.[8]

The PWA approved the Buzzard's Roost project in 1934. Duke Power, having lost the battles of public opinion and political influence, immediately challenged the project in court. In bitter and prolonged legal battles that tied the project up in the courts until 1938, Duke argued that government-funded electricity proffered "unfair competition" against the private power companies and challenged the constitutionality of the federal legislation which created the PWA.[9]

While the legal battle over Buzzard's Roost and other potential hydroelectric sites around the nation raged, controversy also enveloped South Carolina's other major hydroelectric project of the era: Santee Cooper. The Santee Cooper project was a much larger project than Buzzard's Roost, and, as it turned out, much more critical to the future of the electric cooperatives in South Carolina. After several efforts by private companies to develop a hydroelectric facility using the Santee Cooper opportunity failed, and none seemed likely to revive during the Great Depression, public champions of Santee Cooper hydroelectric development scrambled for public funds. Charleston mayor Burnett Maybank and powerful state senator Richard Jeffries of Colleton lobbied Franklin Roosevelt even before he was elected, arguing that the Santee Cooper project would enhance rural electrification, attract industry to the state, and stimulate employment. The idea intrigued Roosevelt, but the president was reluctant to commit public money to a project confined to one state (a concern that lingered throughout the project's development) and previously associated with private investors.

In November 1933, the private Columbia Railway and Navigation Company applied for $24 million in PWA funds for a similar project and Governor Ira Blackwood led a delegation to Washington to lobby for the funds. The PWA promptly declined the company's request, noting that it funded only public projects, not private ones. South Carolina's congressional delegation quickly called for the formation of a public corporation similar to the TVA to develop the Santee Cooper project. While Senator Byrnes cautioned the rest of the delegation that such a request faced an uphill battle, chiefly due to the fact the project was confined to one state, he also began urging the state legislature to set up a public service authority that could qualify to receive PWA funds.[10]

In 1934, with continued encouragement from Byrnes in Washington, state senator Richard Jeffries of Colleton and state representative James Glymph of Oconee proposed the creation of the S.C. Public Service Authority (PSA). The PSA was a state body designed to receive federal money to improve river navigation and generate electricity in South Carolina. The PSA faced ferocious opposition from investor-owned utilities, the timber industry, those hoping to market old plantations as hunting or vacation retreats, and some large landowners still operating "New South" plantations using large numbers of mostly African American tenant farmers as a workforce. Given Jim Crow–era suffrage restrictions, these African American tenants had virtually no direct say in the matter. The private power companies operating in South Carolina could flex significant political and public relations muscle as could wealthy northern sportsmen and absentee plantation owners, who vacationed and hunted on abandoned South Carolina plantations retooled as private clubs and hunting preserves in the Santee area. In addition, state legislator and future gubernatorial candidate Wyndham Manning of Sumter, epicenter of the state's postbellum timber industry, complained that the Santee Cooper project would destroy the Lowcountry timber industry, while others charged that the project would serve as "a vast political machine" for Byrnes and his political allies.[11]

The legislative push for a PSA that could facilitate the Santee Cooper development brought to the forefront once again the problem of unbalanced growth and development in the state. By and large, the more densely populated Piedmont had built industry, roads, and generated electricity since the 1890s, and these advantages over the Lowcountry and the Pee Dee region helped them garner new advantages moving forward due to a larger population, higher incomes, a stronger tax base, and hence better schools and roads. By the late 1920s, this pattern of unbalanced growth was clear. But given the political landscape of South Carolina in the 1930s, which allowed one state senator from each county regardless of population, Lowcountry and Pee Dee counties and their senators worked together to counter the established economic and population advantages of the Piedmont, and increasingly, non-Piedmont legislators sought to use their clout in the state General Assembly to bring more balance to growth and development in South Carolina.

The situation with the generation and transmission of electricity was especially striking by the early 1930s. In 1905, the Southern Power Company (later Duke Power), founded with the considerable capital of James Buchanan Duke and guided by the engineering genius of William States Lee, began to build a truly regional power system based on a series of dams located along the Catawba River in North and South Carolina. The activity of these dams was coordinated for maximum power generation and efficiency, and the Duke Power transmission lines were tied in with other major power generation companies in the South, including Carolina Power & Light (CP&L). Locating to meet existing and prospective demand, the Duke system served chiefly the Piedmont of the two Carolinas. For private utilities, the key to profit and economic success was the so-called load factor, or the company's need for a high ratio of average to maximum demand for electricity, allowing companies to avoid having too much under-utilized capacity needed for peak demand but not needed to meet average demand. Favorable load factors were facilitated by around-the-clock users, usually industry such as the textile mills of the Piedmont. Likewise, the region's high population density also reduced cost of transmission per square mile.[12]

By 1931, high voltage electric transmission lines (over 100,000 volts) crisscrossed much of the Piedmont, but only one line of more than 100,000 volts moved through the Lowcountry, and it was a CP&L line primarily designed to move South Carolina-generated electricity to North Carolina consumers. The frustrated Lowcountry and Pee Dee regions held 60 percent of the seats in the legislature as a whole and nearly three-fourths of seats in the Senate (where there was one senator from each county at the time). Thus, Lowcountry and Pee Dee leaders forged a pro-development coalition and began to fight back against Piedmont dominance. This coalition was led by three men prominent in the advocacy of the Santee Cooper project: state senator Richard M. Jeffries of Colleton, state senator Edgar Brown of Barnwell, and Mayor Burnet Maybank of Charleston.

Legislative opposition to the creation of the new Public Service Authority came mostly from the Piedmont. Over three-fifths of Piedmont representatives voted against the measure while representatives from the Pee Dee and the Lowcountry voted 51–14 in favor of the PSA. When the measure reached the Senate, an intense lobbying effort from Duke Power forced the inclusion of a proviso that limited the PSA's service region to areas south and east of Columbia (effectively protecting the Duke Power service area in the Piedmont).[13]

Even after the legislature approved the PSA in April 1934, debate over the Santee Cooper project raged on. Mayor Maybank argued that public power was essential to pull the state out of the Great Depression. Jeffries, who was now serving as General Counsel of the state PSA as well as state senator, applied for a Public Works Administration grant of nearly $36 million, while Senator Byrnes worked hard to convince skeptical New Deal officials in Washington that Santee Cooper was a worthwhile project. Byrnes continued to lobby for PWA funding for the project, but his efforts encountered significant reservations. A skeptical PWA director Harold Ickes, who liked smaller public projects, thought Santee Cooper was too expensive, too environmentally destructive, and offered geographic benefits that were too narrow. Byrnes countered that the Santee Cooper project would bring a "fair share" of the relief and recovery money to South Carolina and that the state's loyal support of the New Deal justified it receiving a fair share of federal funding. Byrnes also cautioned Ickes not to confuse legitimate opposition to the Santee Cooper project with the complaints of wealthy hunt club members who "fear that as a result of this great development, there will be fewer ducks for them to kill." Opposition to dam projects, labelled as environmental opposition in South Carolina in the 1930s, usually came from advocates of what we would now call "conservation," championing the protection of existing land uses, including their use as hunting preserves. Byrnes witty remark about dividends looming as a much larger concern than ducks was doubtless on target.[14]

Chiefly through the Charleston press, CP&L emerged as a strong opponent of the PSA, threatening legal action against the authority. Taking up the cudgels for CP&L, Charleston newspapers mounted an editorial campaign against the Santee Cooper project, calling it a "bluff" and all a part of Byrnes's political machinations. Other interests also opposed the Santee Cooper development. Some national advocates of rural electrification complained that the Santee Cooper project served chiefly as a bailout for the Columbia Railway and Navigation Company, which sold its license to construct a hydroelectric complex on the site, while others objected that the project would upset the delicate ecological balance of the Lowcountry. Garden clubs nationwide complained to President Roosevelt about the project's ecological implications; some engineers questioned the project as geologically untenable.

Inside New Deal circles, the project received criticism as a bailout for private interests, for its expense, and as a setback to conservation. Together this litany of complaints prompted Roosevelt to appoint a board to study the various concerns in late September 1934. A frustrated Byrnes reminded Roosevelt that the apparent conservationist push against the project owed much to "members of the Santee Gun Club who are more deeply interested in public utilities than they are in the gun club." Dividends rather than ducks were their concerns. Ultimately, a worried and exasperated Byrnes appealed to his friend, New Deal pragmatist Harry Hopkins, to press Roosevelt for approval of the project. In the meantime, the PWA held a hearing in Columbia at which "sportsmen" insisted that Santee Cooper would "imperil every fish in and every duck on the Santee River." On November 4, 1935, the board finally released its report and concluded that Santee Cooper was feasible from a financial standpoint and that its effect on wildlife would not be sufficient to justify a refusal. In December 1935, Byrnes learned that Ickes had approved $5.5 million for the project.

As debate and discussion over the merits of the Santee Cooper project proceeded within the Roosevelt administration, other New Deal initiatives gave a much-needed push to the movement for rural electricity and the organization of electric cooperatives. Once Congress authorized the REA as an independent federal agency in 1936, Morris Cooke, an aggressive champion of rural electrification, was named head of the REA and advocated the creation of non-profit electric cooperatives. Cooke offered low-cost government loans to cooperatives to string miles of electric lines through the countryside. Earlier, in February 1935, the South Carolina state legislature had created the South Carolina Rural Electrification Authority (SCREA) to construct and operate electric distribution systems. The legislation empowered the SCREA to purchase electricity from private power companies at a wholesale rate set by the state Public Service Commission and resell this electricity to rural customers at a rate adequate to cover the SCREA's debt for construction and distribution.

In November 1935, the investor-owned South Carolina Power company questioned the constitutionality of the state's rural electrification program—specifically complaining that a public service commission could not require them to sell electricity to the state for its rural electrification program—especially not at what they termed a low and "discriminatory" rate. South Carolina Power "alleged the proposed rate [averaged] approximately one cent per kilowatt hour."[15] With litigation pending that threatened to limit the generation of electricity to investor-owned companies, from which cooperatives would have to purchase electricity at ten cents per kilowatt hour, a comparatively high price, the formation of cooperatives proceeded with agonizing slowness under the state's first authorizing law. Public concern about the membership dues and the concept of a monthly electric bill in the middle of the Great Depression persisted and contributed to the cooperatives' slow starts. Thus, some of the first rural lines in the state were built by the South Carolina Public Service Authority—a total of 2,400 miles of line using an initial loan of $100,000. Over the next few years, the legislature began to authorize the sale of these "lines to recently organized REA projects."[16] In 1936, the national REA approved $40 million for in-home wiring, which almost all rural homes required.

In South Carolina, Aiken Electric Cooperative was initially the most successful cooperative organized under the 1935 legislation, though it did not get off the ground until 1938. In fact, between 1935 and 1939 under the SCREA, Aiken Electric Cooperative and the Greenwood County board were the only organizations to actually receive a loan from the federal program for their own lines. Reflecting on their early days, Aiken Electric Cooperative president Monson Morris published a letter in *The State* on March 12, 1939, that reported Aiken Co-op was formed "by the farmers of Aiken County after waiting a number of months for lines which the State Rural Electrification Authority said they would build for us." According to Morris, they were informed by administrators in Washington that "South Carolina was the only state in the United States that had a state authority that built and operated lines." Morris attributed Aiken's early success to their initiative in trying to speed up the process of getting rural lines and to the help and guidance they received from Washington.[17]

Late in 1937, Aiken held a number of local organizational meetings driven by the activity of the county's agricultural extension agent. In December of that year, a national REA official attended one of these meetings in Aiken. By February 1938, rural people from all over Aiken County attended a meeting at the county agricultural building on a Saturday to hear more about organizing a cooperative. Nearly all those in attendance pledged to join at $5 per family and put down a $1 deposit. On February 15, 1938, Aiken Electric Cooperative was formed. Aiken's Tom Craig remembered the hard work building transmission lines for the local cooperative. "Stakin' out the line, hackin' through the woods, wadin' in the swamp, pikin' up those polls, that's what we were doin'," Craig recalled. Looking back on his work later in life, Craig observed, "I feel like maybe I contributed a little to this area."[18] According to Morris's 1939 letter to *The State*, 267 miles of lines stood in Aiken County, with "the farmers of Edgefield, Saluda, Orangeburg, Bamberg, and Allendale counties [all asking] . . . if we would not extend our lines in their county and with the consent of the Washington authorities, we are now doing so, and are daily awaiting news from Washington that about 285 miles of electric lines have been approved for building by the Washington authority in these counties."[19] By the end of 1939, Aiken Electric Cooperative had enrolled more than one thousand members. Some 570 of these members were already being served and another 500 were enrolled and waiting for service.

All of these steps toward rural electrification and the formation of cooperatives took place while the political and legal battle over Santee Cooper roiled. In December 1935, South Carolina Electric & Gas and Carolina Power & Light challenged the project in federal court arguing against the constitutionality of government funding for public hydroelectric projects. They secured an injunction prohibiting construction while agreeing to delay the Santee Cooper case until the results of the earlier TVA and Buzzard's Roost cases wound their way through federal courts. Even after an early 1937 court decision upheld the constitutionality of the Tennessee Valley Authority, South Carolina's investor-owned power companies still felt comfortable pressing their suit against Santee Cooper. Finally, in January 1938, the United States Supreme Court decided in the case brought by Alabama Power Company that federally funded power did not constitute unfair competition with existing investor-owned utilities. The same logic clearly applied in the Duke Power case against Buzzard's Roost, so the project gained the authority to proceed.[20]

The 1938 court decision triggered celebration in Greenwood. Sirens sounded far and wide in the city, bells rang, and the popping of firecrackers could be heard from neighborhood to neighborhood. Some 1,500 citizens jammed into the local high school auditorium to celebrate to the tune of Roosevelt's signature song "Happy Days Are Here Again." Governor Olin D. Johnston congratulated the crowd on its success. Charleston Mayor Maybank, who also served as chair of the state's Public Service Authority from 1935 to 1938, called the court decision a defeat for the "power trusts," and Greenwood's state senator Floyd Nicholson heralded the court's ruling as a "new day for those who love freedom and the rights of individuals." Ultimately the Roosevelt administration agreed to provide over $37 million to the state through a grant of nearly $17 million and loans of over $20 million to support the state's two public hydroelectric projects.

The end of litigation gave new energy to the electric cooperative movement. On May 4, 1939, Governor Johnston signed into law the South Carolina Rural Electric Cooperative Act, now commonly known as the "Enabling Act," which became law and sparked the spread of electricity to the rural areas of the state. The statute established the process and requirements for an electric cooperative to be formed and be recognized by the state by permitting "five or more persons to organize a rural electric cooperative, which would have the authority to borrow funds direct from Washington for power line construction in the area which is proposed to serve," independent of the state rural electrification authority.[21] The statute defined "rural area" as "any area not included within the boundaries of any incorporated or unincorporated city, town, village, or borough having a population in excess of twenty-five hundred (2,500) persons."[22] The statute also enumerated all the powers that are specifically granted to electric cooperatives in addition to the general powers granted to all private corporations. Under the statute, an electric cooperative had the power to "generate, manufacture, purchase, acquire, accumulate, and transmit electric energy and to distribute, sell, supply, and dispose of electric energy to its members, to governmental agencies and political subdivisions, and to other persons not in excess of ten per centum (10%) of the number of its members." The act also granted the cooperatives the important power of eminent domain which enabled them to run electric lines through privately owned property.[23]

The electric cooperatives were given the statutory power "to make loans to persons to whom electric energy is or will be supplied by the cooperative for the purpose of, and otherwise to assist such person in, wiring their premises and installing therein electric and plumbing fixtures, appliances, apparatus, and equipment of any and all kinds and character."[24] The ability to loan money for the wiring of houses was important because the potential rural customers often could not afford to have their homes wired properly; without properly wired homes, the electric cooperatives would have served no purpose.

The Enabling Act was a significant boon to the growth of South Carolina's electric cooperatives—in fact, Senator J. M. Lyles of Fairfield, the chairman of the joint legislative committee on rural electrification, said the act would "do more than anything else 'to speed up rural power development.'"[25] Aiken Electric Cooperative had been "formed under a special legislative act" and was therefore "a pioneer in the field of cooperative rural electrification." Months before the Enabling Act was passed, Aiken Electric's president, Monson Morris, was lobbying the legislature to allot one thousand dollars to each county to "assist in the formation of cooperatives," a sort of seed money to be used while seeking loans from the national REA.[26] While Morris's exact plan did not come to fruition, it was clear that, for people like Morris, the Enabling Act represented the General Assembly opening the doors for rural South Carolinians to take their own initiative and improve their communities through electrification. Now, just days after Governor Maybank, who won the gubernatorial election of 1938 against a crowded field, signed the new act into law, communities began to do just that.

Laurens Electric Cooperative was incorporated on May 15, 1939, and immediately received approval from Washington for a loan of $224,000 to serve 939 members along 265 miles of lines in Laurens, Greenville, Spartanburg, and Newberry counties.[27] Laurens immediately began to construct lines and just as quickly faced opposition from private utilities. By June, Senator Cromer of Laurens requested the Public Service Commission "make an actual survey before granting permits to construct lines competing with any state or county rural electrification authority or electric cooperative project already authorized, under construction or in operation."[28] This was in response to customers in the Trinity Ridge section of Laurens County, which had been surveyed by the state REA as part of the Laurens Electric Cooperative project. Thirty residents later "indicated they wanted the Duke Power company to build the six-mile line instead of the county cooperative."[29] In August, the Public Service Commission ruled for Duke Power due to the number of residents who wanted their service from Duke.[30]

Not surprisingly, such conflicts occurred frequently. After the REA or local cooperatives conducted surveys to find the optimal routes for the distribution of electricity, the investor-owned companies would often seek to construct private lines to serve the most profitable rural areas. The conflict caught the attention of national REA leaders, particularly Robert E. Craig, the assistant administrator for the federal REA. In a letter to the state's Public Service Commission before its decision, Craig wrote that it would be setting precedent for "all problems of this kind. It is a principle which will have vital effect upon the question as to whether the farmers of South Carolina receive the full measure of benefit from the national rural electrification program."[31] Federal REA director Harry Slattery railed against similar turf wars between cooperatives and Duke Power in North Carolina the following year, alleging that Duke and other private power companies were working to "wreck the cooperatives by cutting off their best territory through the construction of spite lines."[32] Laurens Electric Cooperative's scrimmage over Trinity Ridge was not the end of investor-owned electricity's efforts to limit the service areas of the cooperatives, but it was certainly not a deterrent to the cooperatives' growth. In fact, it may have strengthened the resolve to organize cooperatives and hastened their formation.

Following South Carolina's Enabling Act, new cooperatives formed and began capitalizing on the available REA loans from Washington. On May 22, 1939, just days after Laurens Electric Cooperative was chartered, Lynches River Electric Cooperative emerged and "on June 9, 1939, Fairfield Electric Cooperative received its charter." Edisto Electric Cooperative followed suit on June 26.[33] By late June and July, all three of these cooperatives were preparing to raise lines. In its early organizing, on June 21, Edisto Electric Cooperative reported 300 miles of planned power lines and, on July 13, boasted a $149,000 loan from the REA for construction of 185 miles serving "500 families in Bamberg, Orangeburg, Dorchester, and Allendale Counties."[34] On June 23, the Lynches River board announced it had begun surveying for 250 miles of lines, and on July 28, Fairfield Electric Cooperative announced that construction had commenced on 150 miles of its original projected lines and had gotten approval for ninety additional miles of lines in Kershaw and Lee Counties.[35]

September 1939 revealed some of the first statewide fruits of the rural electrification effort. Archibald "A. J." Beattie, the secretary of the state's Rural Electrification Authority, reported that on September 15, "over 200 rural families in three South Carolina counties enjoyed the use of electricity for the first time." These new lines were electrified in Orangeburg, Fairfield, and Newberry counties—bringing the number of rural customers served by the REA to 5,400 served on 1,600 miles of line.[36] Not surprisingly, later in the month, state business news touted that refrigerator sales had risen 54 percent statewide compared with the first half of the previous year.[37] Clearly, rural electrification paved the way for progress.

By November, Governor Maybank implored the state's Public Service Commission to work in favor of the cooperatives. "I want to say to you that, in my opinion, the federal government favors the cooperative associations," Maybank stated. He noted, "There was in Washington 'waiting for us in South Carolina a large sum of money' to be expended in construction of rural electric power lines." He was careful in his statements not to blame any single person or entity but remarked on the differences between South Carolina and its neighbors. "We all just did not keep up with the times," said Maybank. "In Georgia, they have spent over $8,000,000 on rural power lines; in South Carolina, they have spent approximately $2,500,000." Maybank went on to raise questions about Public Service Commission permits to Heath Springs Light and Power Company, as well as to Duke Power. While not directly criticizing these permits, Maybank spoke of the power companies which could not build lines where customers were few but added that he "would like to see lines over all of South Carolina." The governor expressed the hope that nothing would be done which might be interpreted as evidence that South Carolina was against a program that could enhance "the future welfare of the fellow at the bottom of the ladder in South Carolina." Federal REA money was readily available for the cooperatives, Maybank observed, encouraging the Public Service Commission to offer its full support.[38]

In the 1940 legislative session, efforts emerged within the General Assembly to transition lines owned and operated by the state's REA from the state agency to the local electric cooperatives. By the summer of 1940, the state was facilitating the transfer of rural lines to emerging electric cooperatives throughout the state.[39] The Enabling Act and the transfer of extant rural lines from the state REA to cooperatives helped produce a period of rapid growth among rural cooperatives. Between May 1939 and August 1940, twenty-one separate electric cooperatives filed for incorporation with the South Carolina secretary of state. By then, the state was beginning to transfer more than five hundred miles of line serving more than 1,800 customers to the Pee Dee, Santee, Marlboro, and Marion cooperatives.[40] South Carolina's rural residents had good reason to appreciate the REA. In 1934, only 2 percent of Palmetto State farmers had electricity. By 1940, that figure had risen to 14.5 percent.

TABLE 2.1: Electric Distribution Cooperative Formation in New Deal Era

COOPERATIVE	DATE CHARTERED OR INCORPORATED
Aiken	January 6, 1938
Laurens	May 15, 1939
Lynches River	May 22, 1939
Fairfield	June 9, 1939
Edisto	June 26, 1939
Marion	July 7, 1939
Santee	December 14, 1939
Marlboro	December 15, 1939
Pee Dee	December 18, 1939

Berkeley	January 10, 1940
Black River	February 5, 1940
Coastal	February 13, 1940
Horry	April 25, 1940
Broad River	June 10, 1940
Tri-County	June 15, 1940
Newberry	June 20, 1940
Little River	June 18, 1940
Mid-Carolina	June 20, 1940
Salkehatchie	August 1, 1940
Palmetto	August 23, 1940
Richland	August 9, 1940
Blue Ridge	August 10, 1940
York	March 12, 1941

Source: Records of the South Carolina Secretary of State.

The newly formed cooperatives offered a means for electric transmission to rural Carolinians, but they were not generating their own power. While the cooperatives were developing, another state agency—Santee Cooper—was in its own genesis and, some years later, it would supply the lion's share of electricity to South Carolina's rural cooperatives and their members. In 1939, some five years after the legislature had created the PSA, the Authority was able to issue contracts to initiate construction on the Santee Cooper project, but due to the scope of construction, the facility did not go into operation until 1942. Yet as early as August 1941, well before the United States entered World War II over five months later, the war had begun to increase demand for American production. As a result, the US government declared the Santee Cooper project a national defense project even before it began operation because the project could supply power to the Charleston Navy Yard and to McAlloy, a Charleston-area manufacturer of armor plating. During the war, demand for electricity generated by Santee Cooper remained steady, but when World War II ended, Santee Cooper struggled because the Navy Yard and McAlloy did not use nearly as much electricity in peacetime. Lower demand proved a problem because Santee Cooper was still required to recover all of its costs from its sales.

With excess power on hand, Santee Cooper faced the prospect of doubling or even tripling the rates to the retail clients it served. A team of consulting engineers from Southern Engineering Company, a firm that was doing all of Santee Cooper's engineering work, came to the rescue with the idea of forming the Central Electric Power Cooperative. Their vision was for Central to build the transmission system from Santee Cooper's generating resources to the distribution substations owned by the emerging electric cooperatives.[41]

Previously, the electric cooperatives were purchasing the bulk of their power from investor-owned utility companies on an individual basis and being charged about ten cents per kilowatt hour at wholesale, which resulted in high prices for the cooperative consumers. By law, Santee Cooper could not build or own any facilities outside of the three counties it served. As a result, an entity was needed to build the transmission lines from Santee Cooper to the cooperative substations. The creation of Central Electric Power Cooperative allowed the electric cooperatives other than those serving the Upstate to purchase their wholesale power generated by Santee Cooper through Central, which made lower rates available to electric cooperatives.[42] The electric cooperatives purchased wholesale power through Central at a rate of two to three cents/kWh (down from the ten cents/kWh the investor-owned utilities were charging them).

The idea worked like a charm. Throughout the 1950s and '60s and into the '70s, Central built four thousand miles of the backbone transmission system that was operated by Santee Cooper. The growth of the generation and transmission system was funded by either Central or Santee Cooper depending on who could obtain the lower interest rate on the funding. Once built, the system became the property of Santee Cooper, which as a state-owned entity, did not have to pay property taxes. Santee Cooper's long-term impact on South Carolina proved dramatic. By 1959, more than 74 percent of all farms in South Carolina received electricity generated by Santee Cooper.[43]

The confluence of federal money available from the REA, the state's Enabling Act, and the availability of cheaper electricity via Santee Cooper all hastened rapid growth among South Carolina's electric cooperatives during the 1940s and 1950s. World War II itself presented extraordinary challenges and opportunities amid this growth. On one hand, line construction slowed significantly as materials for building were scarce or rationed for the war effort. Conversely, the electrification project, especially for rural farmers, represented an opportunity to increase farming efficiency and, therefore, food production during the war. Despite the difficulty of acquiring building materials for lines during the war, by late 1946, South Carolina's cooperatives had more than 20,595 miles of rural lines and served 105,131 customers. Much of this was due to the more than $16 million dollars that had already been allotted to the state by the REA and the cooperatives that emerged to apply this money to rural electrification.[44]

But the construction and implementation of the electric power grid in rural South Carolina took boots, hardhats, machinery and safety gear, not simply political success. It required skill, determination, courage, and just plain hard labor by the dedicated people who worked the lines.

3

Working the Lines

DUTY AND DANGER

While South Carolina's electric cooperatives brought electricity to and helped modernize homes in rural areas, they also dramatically changed the lives of members and changed the communities they served. Part of that change emerged from the creation of a new workforce composed of people who lived in communities served by the cooperatives and whose careers would be devoted to sustaining a new electrical grid and serving the needs of cooperative members. In their early days, cooperatives were relatively small employers, but in a short period of time, a host of new jobs emerged: line worker, meter reader, engineer, service worker, billing clerk, customer service representative, manager, and board member. While early cooperative offices may have employed a half-dozen employees or fewer, inside and out, today a single cooperative may employ one hundred or more people.

The challenges faced by those who worked for the cooperatives were multiple and they evolved over the years. Initially, the construction of the grid—pole by pole and line by line—presented significant physical and environmental challenges. Building the delivery system house by house required hard, time-consuming labor. Moreover, the dangers associated with working closely with electricity made worker safety a key issue. The emergence of new technologies to facilitate efficient delivery, worker and customer safety, and rigorous training programs helped make the work environment much safer, but the presence of electricity always demanded respect. Moreover, the growing density of cooperatives' service area population in parts of the state and the need to diversify the cooperative workforce presented new challenges. The now eighty-year-old saga of South Carolina's electric cooperatives involves the contributions of workers, managers, leaders, and customers of the state's electric cooperatives.

In the early days, just raising sufficient money from an interested member base loomed as the greatest challenge for cooperative organizers. Arthur James, a long-time member in Black River Electric Cooperative, remembered that Robert V. Dinkins, who became the local cooperative manager, drove over the region to sign up new members for the fee of five dollars before poles could be lifted and wires strung. According to James, Dinkins "took his personal car, and I never have known for sure whether he was paid to take his car."[1] "I think he told me it was 125 customers he had to get before the federal government would come in and finance the cooperative," James recalled. Nevertheless, the rural part of any given county was filled with customers who did not yet have electricity and saw little hope of receiving it. "Carolina Power and Light, all they would do was they ran [electricity] down [Highway] 521," James remembered, "But if it was a house over two blocks away from the highway, they would not put [the electric] current there because it was too expensive for them. That's why the Cooperative was formed, because it would go several miles out into the country."[2] Those stories played out again and again in every cooperative territory as they came online.

The difference between that five-dollar fee and what the for-profit power companies were seeking was enormous, according to the memories of members. "My father wanted lights," Dargan Hodge remembered of his family's decision to connect in 1940. "And we went up to town, to Sumter, to Carolina Power & Light to talk to those people, and they wanted $500 to run a line from [Route 15] to our house. And $500 was impossible. I couldn't imagine what $500 was." Later, "someone came through there signing you up for the power line. . . . I think my daddy signed up for five dollars because . . . he wanted those lights."[3]

Eager new customers often hurriedly wired their houses in anticipation of the coming electric access, often failing to check with the cooperatives about specifics. As Kirk Roberts from Fairfield Electric Cooperative remembered, his family hired someone to wire the house, but because it was a log cabin, and they did not want to disrupt the log walls, they had their neighbor install sockets in the floor. "Then when [the cooperative employees] came in and inspected, of course, it didn't pass inspection because things were in the floor of the house," Roberts said. "We had to move them and put them up on the wall."[4]

Cooperative workers also often did the wiring in houses themselves during the early years. Jack Morris, an Edisto Electric Cooperative member, who was eleven years old when his family first got electricity in 1941, remembered the name of the worker who brought light to their home.

"Do you remember Mr. J. B. Moody?" Morris asked his interviewer in 2014. "He's the one who wired the house, put everything on one circuit. All the lights were on one circuit, and the receptacles were on one. . . . Back then the cooperative furnished the meter box, the meter, and the wire, and a cooperative man did the wiring, charged you for it, and you paid by the month for the bill. . . . Thirty-five dollars to wire the house." So memorable was the experience for Morris's family that he still retained one of their first bills from June 1941, when the family was charged $1.34 for that month's installment on the wiring. The 1.5KVA transformer, Morris insisted, serviced the house until 1996.[5]

Part of the joy of the job for some early line workers was having lived without electricity and understanding its significance for peoples' lives when it was finally connected. N. L. "Shorty" Caprell, a line worker from Wagener, South Carolina, remembered keenly what life was like without electricity and how the cooperatives treated farmers differently from the investor-owned electric companies:

> We were only a mile from Wagener, and SCE&G, the people that owned the power system in Wagener, just refused to bring power out. . . . We were just a mile out of town, but there were probably six or eight homes between Wagener and where we lived. [Caprell believed that] the power company didn't think we'd have sense enough to use it. . . . The power company just couldn't see that if they had brought the power, it would have been certainly appreciated and used. In their mindset, they figured that we were country farmers, and we were not able to comprehend what electricity could do for us. . . . [When the local cooperative did bring electricity to his rural area, Caprell recalled,] it was well-received when the REA came through the countryside. I can tell you that.[6]

"It's almost impossible to believe that we ever had to do without lights," explained Ray Derrick, a retired Aiken Electric Cooperative line worker. "I cannot see how you could get by. You could tell the customers that had lived through that time. They were so much more appreciative, when their lights went out, of you getting them back on for them. That's one thing that made the job so good. You had a feeling that you were really doing something great."[7]

Work was often dangerous for those installing the lines to the residences of new members, especially since that work often involved starting from scratch in areas that had never seen electrification. Both the range and seriousness of those dangers were great, and even following all known safety precautions, workers still knew they were putting themselves at risk. Falling was a very significant danger, and even state-of-the-art safety equipment in the early days often offered only modest protection to line workers. "It's dangerous work, always," Derrick remembered.

> Climbing a pole now is "fall-safe." They have belts that will not let you fall. For us, [we] had a safety belt, but the only thing, it was there for you to halfway sit in [it] while you were doing your work up there. If your feet cut out, as we called it, you'd come straight to the ground. The belt followed you. It just made sure you didn't fall two or three yards back away from the pole.[8]

Peggy Dantzler, who started her career working for four years on the lines for the Mid-Carolina Electric Cooperative before becoming vice president of Loss Control and Training at the state level, ultimately left line work because of her issues with heights. "I realized that I was going to have a problem with heights," Dantzler explained: "I did cut out. I did fall. I was not seriously injured, but it made me realize, 'Am I going to be able to do this?' If I have one of my brothers up the pole, can I go up there and get him down? . . . And after I fell, it got to where I just realized, you know what, I'm going to struggle. I don't know if I can do this. So why stay? If you're not qualified to do it, you don't just stay there. You need people that can do the job."[9]

Problems with early equipment and the risk of electrocution were never far from line workers' minds, especially considering that workers rarely wore insulated gloves in the early years, relying instead on sticks to move wires into place. Faulty poles could also be the end of a worker's life. Ray Derrick, who started working the lines in the 1950s, remembered how he was brought into service. "When I was coming along, [a lot of] the poles had been set back in the 1930s and 1940s. They weren't treated well, . . . and a lot of the poles were breaking," Derrick recalled. "The guy I replaced—I didn't actually replace him. He was in the town of North, and a pole broke with him. He rode it all the way to the ground. The wire stayed on the pole, and when the pole came down, it kicked back with the pressure of the wire; 7,200 volts caught him across the neck." When Derrick started, he was assigned the tools that had belonged to the man who had fallen with that pole. When Lenelle "Red" Johnson, the employee who trained Ray Derrick, learned that Derrick had been assigned those tools, superstition kicked in, and Johnson declared: "I'm not going out with that boy with those tools. No way." Then he found a new set of tools for Derrick to use.[10]

Electrocution stood as a very real danger for cooperative workers. Dickie Walker, who worked for Berkeley Electric Cooperative, remembered an experience early in his career that made a stark and lasting impression on him. "Was running the road," Walker recalled, "and got a radio call about picking the ambulance up . . . to take them to this house. And I get there, and this is one of the boys that worked out at Goose Creek on the service truck. He was my age, and you could see him on the ground—dead. That was the worst experience I ever could've imagined, because I had only been here about six months or a year, but we were both fairly new. . . . I never want to see that again."[11]

Helen Martin, who worked in the office at Edisto Electric Cooperative, remembered the serious accident that befell a line worker, I. W. Roundtree, and the ways in which coworkers cared for the well-being of one another. "The high voltage wire hit him in the back," Martin recalled:

> Beck [a coworker] was a person that kind of stood back, but he was the person who went up the pole to get I. W. He was just hanging up there . . . [and] they called me, and I got to the hospital a little after he had gotten there. It burned a hole in his shoulder. You could have put a bottle in that hole. It burned a hole through into his lung and then his leg. He stayed in the burn unit for a long time. He was crippled and couldn't work anymore. That was a really sad time because we had worked together so long.[12]

Billy Catoe, who lived in the Lynches River Electric Cooperative area, remembered his brother's electrocution on September 1, 1955. As with so many similar stories, the death stemmed from a combination of freak occurrence and carelessness. "They were setting a fire pole," Catoe recalled, "and the highway department was having them move a fire line. Three fellows were supposed to be guiding the pole and were supposed to turn the power off. I don't know what happened, but the grass and weeds were about knee high, and they couldn't tell. Two of the fellows turned the pole loose. It charged the trucks and set the wheels on fire. One of the fellows holding the poles—it electrocuted him and my brother, too."[13]

The dangers of electrocution also came in other forms. Vic Wilform of York Electric Cooperative called thunderstorms, common in South Carolina during the summer months, the greatest risk. "Get out there with that lightning," Wilform said, "the thunderstorm might catch you when you're finishing up the job. . . . I would say summertime lightning storms is about the worst part."[14] Michael Dupree, who started as a lineman with Berkeley Electric Cooperative in 1958, remembered his greatest fear was electrocuting a fellow worker, given that the slightest mistake could be the end. "I cut a wire, and it went up and hit the energized wire, and my line-man was on the next pole," Dupree recalled. "The only thing that saved him is he had his rubber gloves on, and I had mine on, too.... And it burnt me and him a little bit on our legs. It wasn't bad. We went to the hospital, and they just did a routine check. That was my last and closest call."[15]

Dupree's early career had been marked by several incidents. Once he bumped his head—while wearing a helmet—on an energized fuse jack, but nothing happened. On another occasion in the rain, while working trouble calls, the circumstances required that Dupree temporarily give three-phase service to a line that didn't have three phases to it. "[It] was not a very safe situation," Dupree explained:

And I climbed up that pole, and it had wires from the transformer going up to that wire. Climbed right by it, put my safety around the pole. And the Lord must have told me something. He said, "Touch that wire with your screwdriver." I thought I saw something kind of spark as I was climbing up that pole, and it was supposed to be dead. [So] I took my screwdriver out of my pouch, and I touched that thing, and boy, it knocked the living fool out of me 'cause my gloves and all were wet because it was raining. And I come down off that pole, and I was one nervous, thankful guy. The Lord had saved my life that day. Or more than one day. Three times. Four times.[16]

Members of the cooperative boards were just as aware of the electro-cution risks. Leslie Tindal, who served more than fifty-four years on the board of Black River Electric Cooperative Board, highlighted this concern. "I've always known that electricity is a deadly thing," Tindal said. "It can be very good but can kill you in a second, and we stress safety programs. We don't want our linemen and others working with them to get out there and be exposed to high voltage and not know exactly what they are do-ing." Maintenance was also essential. "Safety first and secondly, keeping lines clear from trees, overhanging limbs, and that sort of thing," Tindal continued. "Keeping the lines clean underneath as well as above.... Our maintenance bill is pretty high, but with the rainfall that we have in South Carolina, vegetation grows rapidly, and you have to stay behind it."[17]

Poles could sometimes be just as treacherous as the lines themselves. Hoisting poles often proved especially dangerous as early teams often used mules to haul the poles into the field and lift them into place, but the work was hard on the animals, who were often stubborn and occasionally unreliable.[18] Setting the pole was a six-man job in the 1940s, in large part because there was still no mechanized equipment to assist with the lifting of the pole into its hole. Instead, the line crew typically consisted of two men on a service truck, along with a line foreman and three workers. "If you look at pictures," Ray Derrick recalled, "you can see the guys [in the old days] setting the poles by hand. None of them had safety gear on— hard hats or anything. This one guy's up under the pole with a stick that had a fork on top of it, and the pole lay in it. [That fork] was called the 'dead man.' So, if the four or five people on the outside who had the pike poles let the thing slip, the guy with the [fork] was a dead man. That's where it got its name."[19] Marion Caldwell, a line worker with Fairfield Electric Cooperative starting in 1947, remembered that digging the hole for a pole alone could take an hour and a half under even the most favorable conditions.[20]

Walter Baker worked on the lines as a teenager in the late 1940s in Lynches River Electric Cooperative territory. The hazards of hoisting poles were numerous, starting with the use of dynamite to blast through rock. More torturous for Baker, though, was hauling lines by hand across a right of way that might be a half mile long. "They'd give you the wire and say, 'Alright, right through yonder,'" Baker explained. "And we'd go through there, and every once in a while, we knew about how far we could pull it pretty easy, and it wouldn't get too heavy on us. So, then another man would just take a hold and just line up and come on and pull it across however far it was across there. Then the linesman would come by and lay it up on the post on the insulators."[21] Lewis Ringer, the very first lineman to serve with Newberry Electric Cooperative, remembered putting poles in near the lake [Lake Murray] as the worst. "If you got it down three feet you were doing good, especially around the lake," Ringer said. "We would get as far as we could go with a crowbar, chipping and chipping. Sometimes [it would take] a day, all day, and maybe you would have to go back the next day to finish it off. Sometimes a day and a half [for one hole]."[22]

In fact, the varied terrain of South Carolina also presented problems for those working the lines. In the upper portions of the state, rolling hills created "uphill" journeys with power poles and equipment, but it was in the Lowcountry and the Pee Dee region, areas in which swamps, marshes, and floodplains made running lines difficult and dangerous. Getting lines across swamps and marshes was especially tricky. Dickie Walker, a Berkeley Electric Cooperative veteran who retired as a superintendent of field engineering, remembered the challenges of working the marshes. "Before we learned how to use the transistor to go across a marsh. . . . I was a bit smaller [then]," recalled Walker as he described their strategy for navigating marshes. "And then Robert, he was a little bit on the plump side. And you had Clayton. I don't think he weighed a hundred pounds, but we would send Clayton in the marsh first to see how hard it was. And Clayton would yell, 'Come on, it's hard!' And we'd walk out there and boom, we'd go down to our knees in that plough mud. And the only thing you could do was a belly flop, kick your legs out, and crawl back."[23]

The rough edges of male work culture in the early decades also revealed themselves at times. Ray Derrick remembered that another of the hazards of line work during the 1950s was the coworkers themselves. "It was rough here the first years," he explained. "It was all muscle and brawn, with a lot of cussing and hollering and going on—things you'd be fired for doing today." Derrick's first foreman, "Punk" Ready, doubted Derrick's ability from the start. "Bubba, you too damn little to be a lineman," Ready told him. "So, I had a chore then to prove that I could do it," Derrick added. "Occasionally, he'd walk by and say, 'You not gonna be with us long.'"[24] One of the most taxing parts of the job—a deal breaker for some—was the long shift hours. "The hardest thing," Derrick recalled, "was to work 30 hours and be on your way in and get a call from dispatch: 'We've got one more job for you.' That one more job would turn into another job. I guess adrenaline just kicked in, and you just kept going. . . . One thing a lineman will do is work his hiney off as long as you feed him. You feed him and give him four hours of sleep, [and] he doesn't think about stopping."[25]

The hazing behavior that Derrick remembered remained prevalent well into the 1990s, when Peggy Dantzler started as a line worker. "There was still a lot of that around whenever I went out on the line crew," Dantzler recalled. "When I was there, my Lord, the stuff that would get done. Rubber snakes in bins, putting glove powder in the [trucks' air conditioning] vents, putting water cups over the [windshield sun] visors, just stuff constantly happening out there. And you know, it's all in good fun until someone gets hurt. And then it's a problem." Managing that behavior, Dantzler insisted, was not easy for supervisors, especially given the nature of the work and the long hours that line workers spend together. "There's always going to be some form of rite of passage for these line workers," Dantzler observed.

Over time, however, the importance of training of workers on safety and other matters became paramount, and with it, the degree of professionalism among workers grew to match their dedication to the work. "What I would say now, though," Peggy Dantzler concluded, "is that the linemen are more professional. What I see now, I see crew leaders who are put in positions not because of seniority, but because of knowledge, experience, and professionalism. And the ability to do a supervisor's job, not just be 'Hey, you're a good lineman. You've been here the longest. We're going to put you in this crew leader job.' That is going away . . ." Dantzler saw this trend as a positive development for on-the-job training, as well. "We're hiring better supervisors, better mentors, which puts your trainees in a much better position to receive better education, better training. Safety is rolled into that."[26]

Staying mentally acute on the job was and remains essential for line workers, Dantzler continued. "People think it's just a physical job. It's not just physical. It is very much a mental job. . . . There's a certain process that you have to go through. You can't skip over 'C' to get to 'F.' If you do, it can hurt you. It can bite you. So there are certain things that you have to do. That's why we do repetition in training. That's why we have those training manuals."[27] As a result, workers who are keenly focused on their training and their professionalism have gradually populated the line worker ranks and rounded off the rough edges of male work culture previously common in the 1950s and '60s. "These young guys," Dantzler added, "they pay a lot of attention to their studies, and they work really hard because they want those leadership roles. So, I would say probably within the last fifteen to twenty years, line work has really developed from . . . a laborer's job. These guys are highly skilled. . . . They have to be educated. So, instead of in years past, where 'You do it this way because that's the way I was shown, and that's the way we're always going to do it'—that's out the window."[28]

In spite of the antics of the early years, safety was always on their minds in the early days. "It was a top priority, safety," Michael Dupree remembered. "You looked out and you tried to plan each thing as you were gonna do and make sure it was a safe situation."[29] As the cooperatives became more focused on worker training and emphasizing the importance of worker safety, not all workers were pleased with changes in technology and safety requirements, or with demographic changes in the workforce, noted Peggy Dantzler:

> When I got there, we still had quite a few of the older linemen there, and I trained with one specifically, and he very much did not appreciate any of the newer technology. Also, right about the time I got there, safety had become a really big issue with linemen, and there was a lot of emphasis put on safety. At the time, the Loss Control Coordinator was very, very thorough with what she did . . . so it also required the crew to implement a lot of personal protective equipment. There were a lot of procedures they had to follow,

so a lot of the older linemen [weren't okay with that] because it made them change, and they didn't want to. They didn't want to have to do things differently. So, I was very fortunate that whenever I went out on a line crew, I had a younger crew leader that got put with me because I was with one of the older linemen, and he . . . didn't want me out there because I was female. And he was not the only one that felt that way.[30]

For several decades after the inception of the cooperatives, race loomed as a determinative factor in employment decisions. During the Jim Crow era, which lasted into the 1960s, whites exclusively held the supervisory and managerial positions. But due to the amount of physical labor required in building distribution systems (clearing ground, setting poles, and running lines) African American workers were often hired by electric cooperatives as laborers, especially in areas with large Black populations, from the beginning. But their chances of climbing the employment ladder were essentially nonexistent. By the late 1960s, these patterns began to change, though sometimes with agonizing slowness. The employment patterns changed with the success of the civil rights movement, first by opening the door for more Black women to join the clerical staffs in cooperative offices, and slowly, very slowly, African Americans began to receive promotion to supervisory and managerial positions, though board membership came even later, as discussed in a later chapter.

Women seeking jobs outside the office also faced barriers. Even in the early 1990s, the seniority system of promotion often led to a top-down command based on old, passed-on habits rather than high-skills training—a pattern that many within the cooperatives realized needed to change. "Whenever I was out there," Dantzler explained, "it was 'You don't ask questions, you just do what I tell you to do.' Some of that still exists, but for the most part, I think a lot of that has gone away. It's more of a crew effort. If you've got a better way to do it, let's do it this way. Let's talk about it first, because there's always safety considerations that you have to take into account." Creativity became central to doing the job well, Dantzler added. "They can come up with some really crazy ways to get things done. If they have a tool break or if . . . something goes wrong . . . , you've still got to get the pole back up, get the lines back up. Linemen can be very creative."[31]

Training from younger leaders willing to embrace the new changes probably saved lives. "From the very beginning, with [a young crew leader] training me, I got some of the newer methods—using actual connectors instead of just splicing things together or . . . whenever you're going to hook something up to an energized conductor, the proper order of con-nection. Making sure that you're wearing all of your personal protective equipment, and why we do things that we do and in what order that we do them," Dantzler recalled. "It wasn't just 'go over there and dig that hole.'"[32] The introduction of on-the-job training manuals also made a huge differ-ence in the 1990s. "I was also fortunate working at Mid-Carolina," Dant-zler added. "They had a very developed training program for their younger line workers. . . . Those manuals were filled with tasks that you had to perform repeatedly, and you had to show proficiency in those tasks. You could not progress to the next level of being a line worker without having completed that as well as written tests—a practical test—and you had to go to school at [the state association's training center]. . . . Prior to then, nobody had that kind of training."[33] As Dantzler describes the rapidly evolving nature of the cooperative work culture into one of profession-alism, cooperation, and respect (and away from "doing things as we have always done them") gradually took hold.

Later, around 2009 or 2010, the statewide office added a full line worker curriculum through Northwest Linemen College, while cooperatives be-gan modifying their manuals to meet the needs and concerns of line work-ers throughout the state. "We took those manuals from Mid-Carolina," Dantzler explained, "and we altered them and added certain tasks. We had a committee of various line workers around the state. . . . The line work-ers would go over every task. 'Is this something we want to keep? Is this something we all do? Let's keep it in there. . . .' Prior to that, there was no consistent, on-the-job training manual that every co-op in this state used. Now they do."[34]

While the work itself was dangerous, sometimes the threats came from forces outside the control of the cooperatives. Occasionally the custom-ers themselves were the hazard for cooperative workers. Walter Baker re-membered that some farmers were insistent that the lines not touch their crops when they were being laid across farmland. "One time, a man told us, ' . . . I don't want this wire to touch that cotton,'" Baker remembered. "So the farmer said we got to hold this wire up all the way across this field. He said we've got to hold it up out of the way and not let it touch this man's cotton. . . . So we got out, and we manhandled it. Held it up, and the next man would catch it somewhere over yonder, somewhere he could do his part. And we held it up and put it up and got it in there for him."[35] On another occasion, a worker on Baker's crew made the mistake of ca-sually reaching down to thump on a watermelon in a farmer's field to see if it was ripe. The farmer confronted them with a shotgun, insisting on being compensated for any loss of his crop if the cooperative workers were to try to steal any of his watermelons. "A man that mad," Baker said. "You don't know what that joker's going to do with his gun in his hand! He had a shotgun, and that kind of got my nerves stirred up, but I made it, and he didn't shoot us. He let us out. We didn't take none of his watermelons neither. Nobody did, because he meant business."[36]

Other customers sometimes grew frustrated with tree trimming to keep the lines safe, but as Bill Gibbons from Broad River Electric Cooperative pointed out, talking down those customers was usually a bit easier. "One of the best things I think they have done is coming in and getting these trees out of the way," Gibbons explained. "That was a good move. People have told me, 'That was a beautiful tree. I wish they wouldn't have done what they've done.' I say, 'Would you [rather] have that big tree or electricity?' I'd rather have electricity."[37]

While most consumers were grateful for the work of the line workers and the electricity it brought into their homes, others prioritized their wallets over the safety of cooperative workers. Joe Gibbs from Berkeley Electric Cooperative remembered the problems meter readers might encounter. "We had some problems . . . with some of the consumers . . . because, as you know, if your bill is not paid for so long, we disconnect your services." Gibbs recalled one customer who tried "shooting the meter reader off the post when a co-op crew tried to disconnect the electricity. Other customers had vicious dogs in their yards, so they couldn't come in there to turn the power off at the meter."[38]

Indeed, many delinquent customers kept dogs near the meter in an effort to dissuade meter readers from doing their work. Gene Carson, a meter reader with Tri-County Electric Cooperative, remembered, "Those dogs were bad. They would come after you. I remember another time a dog came out. I got out to read the meter, and the dog came at me, and I backed up. I couldn't get the car door open, and he caught me by the leg, and I was kicking him with my other leg. Finally, I stepped on his head, and he turned me loose, and I got in the car."[39]

Delinquent customers sometimes pulled other tricks that endangered line workers, often by installing substandard equipment to circumvent the controls of the cooperative. Helen Martin remembered that sometimes service workers "would go back to check," on homes with delinquent bills only to find that customers "had connected themselves back." "They were taking a big chance, Martin concluded, "They didn't know it."[40] In at least one situation, a customer followed through on his threats. In the Edisto Electric Cooperative territory, a disgruntled customer with a delinquent bill shot and killed one of the Edisto employees as he left the billing office.[41]

Storms were a frequent feature of the job for line workers. But few storms left as memorable an impact as Hurricane Hugo in 1989 and the ice storm of the winter of 2014. Bill Murray, an engineer at Berkeley Electric Cooperative, remembered waiting out Hurricane Hugo at home through the night in 1989, and then starting the two-mile walk to work because it was impossible to drive. Soon, a neighbor came by on his four-wheeler and gave Murray a lift. For many other line workers, though, going home at the end of the day during the aftermath of Hugo was not possible, so they stayed at the local cooperative. "One of the guys that worked for me lived in Summerville," Murray remembered. "He couldn't get home because the drive to Summerville from Moncks Corner was not possible for days." Murray recalled the sheer scope of the damage. "You can't put your head around that much damage and how long it'll take you to get [the power] back. So, it was traumatic."[42] Buddy Harvey, a lineman also from Berkeley, agreed. "We've had hurricanes before, and they were bad, but Hugo was the worst thing we ever had. I don't think we had a meter turning after Hugo hit and left." "Trees was down," Harvey continued, "lines everywhere." Harvey left home that morning and "rode some lines, and you just couldn't get through the highway. . . . I had to walk [to my family in Monck's Corner] to check on them and make sure everything was all right."[43]

Even cooperative workers who were not out working on the lines were trapped at cooperative offices when Hugo hit. Hilda Lewis, who worked as a cashier for Berkeley Electric Cooperative, remembered spending the night at the cooperative, then being stunned by the scene in the morning. "We looked around and all the trees were gone everywhere," Lewis remembered. "Buildings torn down and everything. It was a rough night. . . . It was a mess . . . chaos." But the days that followed also brought hope. "It brought tears to your eyes [to] see all of these trucks in a line from other states coming to help you. It was such a blessing to see people so cooperative like that. And of course, we've done the same for other states, too." Lewis remembered power being out for two weeks in most of the Berkeley Electric Cooperative territory, and a month or more in some places. That chaos also meant that employees often performed other tasks outside of their normal roles. "You did anything that came along," Lewis added. "Everybody did something different, even the women in the office. We all did different things and helped out any way we could."[44]

That different type of work included preparing meals for one's coworkers. Jerry Brewer, also with Berkeley Electric Cooperative, remembered that the cooperative took over a local restaurant for six weeks in the wake of Hugo. "We came in about five o'clock in the morning and fixed breakfast for the whole crew, and you probably had over a hundred people," Brewer explained. "Had one crew that would make sandwiches that the line crew would take out, and they would work all day . . . and come in and eat supper, then they'd go back out and work some more that night and come back in and start again the next morning. It went on for [six weeks]."[45]

It also meant accepting that one's own power might remain out, even as one worked to restore power to others. Virgil Leaphart, a lineman for fifty-two years with Mid-Carolina, remembered working during Hurricane Hugo. "I came home five nights in a row, and I didn't have any power, and I had been working all night. Right at that time, I wasn't that happy, but we dealt with it. I think we had about three or four poles down going to my house, and that's the reason it got put off until last. Those poles, you can't get to all of them. Some of those trucks just wouldn't go there."[46]

Ice storms also wreaked havoc when they hit South Carolina. The worst ice storm anyone can recall came in 2014, recalled LaVern Polk, board chair of Coastal Electric Cooperative. "[Power was out] probably about seven days, and we had the majority of them back on by four or five days," Polk recalled. "At the beginning of it, we went totally down for a short time—whole system—then started to bring it back up. . . . Considering the damage we had, we were back on in what I think was record time. We had a lot of assistance from outside crews. . . . We had a couple hundred people that came in from within the state and outside the state."[47] Walter "Sonny" Sanders, a board member from Santee Electric Cooperative, remembered that 2014 ice storm as particularly crushing. "We have over 5,500 miles of line. We had over 600 poles that were broken. The ice was just devastating in the area, so we had a lot of people that were without [electricity]. And the terrain was very difficult in some areas because we have a lot of swampy land. We had amphibian-type vehicles to take line and put poles up, so it took quite a while."[48]

Damages and the outages resulting from such major storms marked significant periods of hardship and sacrifice for customers as well as employees of South Carolina's electric cooperatives. But these widespread outages also highlighted, in ironic ways, exactly how reliable and critical the delivery of electricity had become. People expected to have electric power at any and all times they needed it—and that any outage should be brief. Typically, the cooperatives met that expectation. Major storms produced the exceptions that reminded people of the rule. The men and women who worked the lines played a large and crucial role in making such success possible.

Working the lines has always been challenging, especially in times of crisis, and it has always carried a measure of risk, required a measure of self-sacrifice, and a strong work ethic. The work's rewards have included not only earning a livelihood but the forging of bonds with coworkers that strengthened not only the cooperative's workforce but also the fabric of the communities in which they lived and served. Perhaps Peggy Dantzler summed up the mindset of line workers best when she observed, "People who have never done line work can't possibly understand the brotherhood that develops [among line workers] . . . At any time, day or night, they spend more time with their co-workers than they do with their families. . . ."

4

Electricity and the Rural Home

RURAL FAMILIES "LIVE MODERN"

The arrival of electricity for many cooperative members from 1938 through 1952 almost instantly transformed their lives. This transformation was well captured in the diary entries of Gladys Meetze, who saw her house wired as an adult in 1941. Her sentiments present a fairly typical experience for a rural family in the wake of electrification: "Start to wire the house February the 19th, 1941. Wiring was done by Ira Jeffery. Finished wiring house February 25th, 1941. Lights turn on June the 2nd, 1941, at 20 minutes 'til 6 p.m. Bought iron July the 8th, 1941. Bought refrigerator July the 11th, 1941, from Taylor's Hardware."[1]

The electrification of rural South Carolina, a transformation driven by the electric cooperatives, helped the state enjoy the greatest economic development success in its modern history. The progress of industrialization, diversification, and rural electrification triggered a jump in per capita income in South Carolina from 50 percent of the national average to 80 percent of the national average between 1940 and 1980. Even more strikingly, per capita income in the Palmetto State converged toward the national average during a period in which per capita income in the United States was increasing dramatically, making the South Carolina economic performance during these years even more impressive. To be sure, the Palmetto State rode the crest of a national postwar economic boom that ran from 1948 to 1973, a boom initiated by the return to a peacetime economy after World War II and continued federal spending at near-record levels, but its economy grew enough for the state to converge on the national average for the first time since before the Civil War.[2]

Moreover, the nature of the state's population changed significantly between 1940 and 1980. On the eve of the Japanese attack on Pearl Harbor, the population of South Carolina totaled nearly 1,900,000, with roughly

75 percent of those residents living in rural areas. But beginning with the war years, and continuing through the postwar boom, South Carolina's population both grew rapidly and became dramatically more urban. In 1980, the Palmetto State's total population exceeded 3,120,000, an increase of nearly 80 percent, and by 1980 the state had also urbanized rapidly, with some 54 percent of all residents living in towns or cities, more than twice the percentage of those living in urban areas forty years earlier (less than 25 percent). Yet even as South Carolina's rural population shrank as a percentage of the whole during this forty-year period, the actual size of the state's rural population increased modestly from 1,434,000 in 1940 to 1,689,000 in 1980, an increase of just under 20 percent. So, even as South Carolinians left rural areas for cities and suburbs, rural areas were growing in population and generating increased demand for electricity. Additionally, some of the newly incorporated suburbs developed within existing cooperative service territory and presented new service opportunities and challenges for the state's electric cooperatives.[3]

During this spectacular postwar population boom, and for the first and only time in its modern history, South Carolina's per capita income enjoyed sustained growth at a rate faster than that of the nation. This dramatic economic growth spurred equally dramatic improvements in the quality of life in many South Carolina households, including the rise of reliance on modern conveniences and a much stronger consumer orientation among the state's rural population, as rural incomes increased and national production of consumer goods surged.

South Carolina's electric cooperatives and their members stood at the leading edge of this transformation. From the awe and amazement of the era when the lights first came on through the dramatic postwar economic boom and rise of a modern consumer society in virtually all parts of South Carolina, the availability of affordable electricity remained a driving force of rural economic progress in South Carolina. In fact, the ongoing work of the South Carolina electric cooperatives did much to ensure that rural residents had access to modern opportunities and accompanying conveniences. The mission of the cooperatives was not merely to bring electricity to unserved and underserved rural areas but to raise standards of living and improve the quality of life in the areas they served. In practical terms this meant closing the gap between those living in rural communities and those South Carolinians living in towns, cities, and increasingly in fast growing suburbs. In many instances, the availability of electricity stood as a necessary precondition of rural improvement, but available electricity often only provided a starting point for the modernization of the countryside. Once they had access to electricity, rural South

Carolinians needed information about modern conveniences and comforts and how they might acquire and use them. Information and awareness concerning cost and efficiency were crucial to rural improvement efforts, and the state's electric cooperatives played a key role in meeting those needs.

While important improvements began in the 1950s, the full-fledged modernization of rural South Carolina hit full stride during the 1960s. During the early 1960s, the South Carolina electric cooperatives touted the modernization of the countryside that rural electrification had initiated. Such dramatic improvement led to claims that "the rural level of living has risen as electric power became available until today our rural people also 'live modern.'"[4] To illustrate the point, the cooperatives pointed out that customers who had made the jump to electrification enjoyed new advantages after many years of working without electricity. Eighty-four-year-old Annie B. Coleman, a Feasterville resident whose home had been illuminated for over one hundred years by candles and kerosene, saw immediate benefits from electrification. A pump provided running water to her home from her well, and a refrigerator and television were already in place. As her son explained, "We'd never have got lights way out here in this lonesome spot if it wasn't for our co-op."[5]

The cooperatives informed their members about opportunities to modernize their homes, typically through publications designed to inform member-consumers of the options available now that their homes were electrified. Many such pieces highlighted price drops or underscored the time-saving advantages of certain appliances. One theme that emerged from these articles was the concept that such household products "have helped improve the American level of living."[6] In some instances, articles highlighted the old ways of doing things as a way of both nudging late adopters to make a change and giving early adopters a sense of reward for having left the past behind. The two-hour ordeal of washing clothes in the backyard with fire and a kettle of water clearly illustrated the difficulty of life prior to electrification, a difficulty alleviated when the cooperatives brought electricity to rural areas and increased comfort and convenience to the countryside.[7] Many homes converted to electric heat, using air-to-air heat pumps, which kept the houses cool in summer and warm in winter, but also for alleviating the problem of running out of fuel during the winter.[8]

Other home innovations designed to make life easier were touted to rural South Carolinians through cooperative publications. Some innovations appeared but did not gain widespread acceptance. General Electric's "Portable Intercom" was billed as "watch[ing] baby while you work or visit" and "stand[ing] guard in the sick room day and night." In an article entitled, "The Inter-com Goes Rural," the *South Carolina Electric Co-Op News* reported that the intercom would "shorten the distance around the rural home, industry, and farm."[9] Another intriguing product that flourished for a while before waning in popularity was the "Electro-Warmth," a heating pad designed to sit on top of the mattress rather than function as an electric blanket. With promises that the pad would "relieve restless sleep and quiet your nerves" while not interfering with radio or television, the "Electro-Warmth" remained an item of interest for cooperative customers through the early 1970s.[10]

If intercoms never quite lived up to expectations, improvements in refrigeration units did. Refrigerators, like the new Frigidaire model from the early 1960s, seemed especially useful "for farm families," with frost-free improvements coupled with larger interior space and yet the "slimmest, trimmest, smartest look your kitchen has seen in ages! And you can afford it!"[11] By 1962, Frigidaire was taking out half-page advertisements emphasizing its full line of freezers, including a nearly twenty cubic foot freezer capable of holding 684 pounds of food.[12]

The electric cooperatives also collected and circulated real-life stories of improvements made in customers' lives through the wonders of rural electrification. Writing from Pendleton in October 1961, Winifred R. Mullikin contrasted the onerous requirements of the private utilities with the assistance offered by the cooperatives. "We tried [Duke] several times for power, but they required each family to buy a stove and refrigerator from them before we could have power," Mullikin declared, but with the local electric cooperative involved "after a year, the dark houses in the upper end of Anderson County were bright and families happy. Year by year improvements came into these homes—out went the lamp, ice man's bell, wood box in kitchen, . . . [and] Saturday night tub."[13] The *South Carolina Electric Co-Op News* frequently carried member letters under the column "When the Lights Came On" through the 1960s. Two decades later, as political tensions between the investor-owned power companies and the electric cooperatives reemerged, *Living in South Carolina* magazine returned to member testimonials about how the cooperatives transformed rural members' lives through modernization when the investor-owned utilities refused to provide them with service.[14]

Some of these letters were quite specific about the improvements rural electrification brought to the homes of farmers. Caldon King, writing in August 1962, highlighted his wife's joy at cooking on an electric stove for the first time since they were married forty-seven years earlier, noting, "She said she would not trade her electric stove for a hundred old oil and wood stoves."[15] Other customers offered similar tales. Writing in May 1962, Mrs. H. D. Crook of Woodruff, South Carolina explained:

> No longer did I have to carry in wood for the wood cook stove. We put in a new electric stove. How wonderful it is: turn a button and start cooking! The old hand pump that was so hard to pump water was replaced by an electric pump. No longer did I have to pump and carry it up to the house. Out went our oil hot water heater that smoked up the walls. In its place is an electric hot water heater. We no longer had to haul our ice five miles away for the old ice box, for now we have an electric refrigerator. The old kerosene lamp is tucked away, along with the old flat irons. We even tucked away the old battery radio for a keepsake.[16]

Over time, of course, appliance upgrades also appeared. By early 1963, two-piece, built-in electric ranges in which ovens (either single or double) were installed separate from the surface cooktop became available, and for those unable to afford such luxuries, new "compact, one-piece" ranges appeared, with either option offering a "streamlined design," convenience, efficiency, and the ability to avoid being "tied to a range by your apron strings."[17] Additionally, the cooperatives promoted the safety, affordability, and modernity of electric heat over "fuel fired systems."[18] Clearly, the widespread use of modern electrical appliances loomed as a key element in the modernization of rural homes and a dramatic improvement in the quality of life for areas served by South Carolina's electric cooperatives.

In a sense, the modernization of the rural home created its own dynamic for the electric cooperatives. The availability of electric power and its attendant conveniences and labor-saving devices made the modernization of the home possible in rural areas, and the evolving increase in the number and character of modern homes brought even more demand for cooperative services, certainly including, but hardly limited to, electricity itself. As one cooperative publication put it: "Rural Electrification can never be complete so long as you keep adding water heaters, ranges, freezers, second TV sets, hair dryers, dishwashers, automatic washers, electric shoeshine kits, etc."[19]

Some features linked the addition of new appliances to better physical health. The idea that good electric light promoted better eyesight emerged as a recurring theme during the 1960s. A September 1962 issue of *South Carolina Electric Co-Op News* offered personalized service with addressing lighting concerns in the home. "The folks at your Co-Op will be happy to discuss proper lighting with you. Ask the manager or the power use

personnel about proper lighting for your home."[20] One 1961 feature entitled "Light for Living: Recipes for Better Living Through Better Lighting"
included tips on types of light bulbs and their various uses, wattage recommendations for various locations in the home, how to position lamps
for the best and healthiest lighting, and how to select a lampshade. Related
columns addressed how to light the kitchen and the "home study center"
properly, while a sidebar offered details on proper wiring. Throughout this
feature spread, the low cost of electric lights was highlighted: "Good lighting gives so much for so little. A 100-watt bulb will burn ten hours and use
one Kilowatt of electricity."[21] Other articles simply cautioned rural consumers, "Don't be a visual delinquent."[22]

South Carolina's electric cooperatives also emphasized home safety,
suggesting that the use of new electric lighting made homes safer. Touting
"Good Lighting for A SAFER Home," Jan Reynolds, a residential lighting
consultant for Sylvania, emphasized that more accidents happen at home
than away from home, suggesting that "Home Sweet Home may be a nos-
talgic phrase, but Home Safe Home is certainly a practical one." Reynolds
went on to detail exterior, interior, and working lighting that could help
families avoid dangerous falls plus cuts, bruises, or burned hands in the
kitchen.[23] Similarly, articles on dishwashers cited "scientific studies" to
tout their ability to "reduce the spread of bacteria-caused illness from one
family member to another."[24]

In keeping with the cooperatives' focus on the affordability and practi-
cality of electricity, they often raised questions about emerging alternative
energy options, such as natural gas. Highlighting the safety risk from carbon monoxide poisoning, one cooperative editorial criticized the natural
gas industry's claim that it could offer an all-gas kitchen ("Since there is no
such thing, this will take smooth talking") and that gas refrigerators could
operate more cheaply than the standard cost of operating an electric refrigerator.[25] Accompanying such jousting with competing energy providers,
the electric cooperatives debunked fears that consumers had about new
appliance innovations. The cooperatives touted the benefits of electric
air conditioning, noting that fears about colds, rheumatism, and allergies
were unfounded, since "medical proof contradicts these misconceptions."
To allay fears about cost, the same article insisted that the average air conditioner required "one kilowatt hour of electricity per horsepower for each
hour of operation"—a calculation that suggested a unit for 500 square feet
of space would cost only twenty-four cents per day (twelve hours) to operate, or a little less than eight dollars per month (still a significant amount
for many cooperative members).[26]

During the 1960s, stories in the cooperatives' publications suggested that electrified homes promoted happiness, largely because they supported labor and time-saving conveniences. Explaining that "teenagers find it's 'hip' to help with housework if the kitchen's equipped with modern electric appliances," one article argued that teenagers have more free time from chores as a result of this convenience, while even younger kids could help, since all they had to do was "carry their own dishes to the kitchen, scrape off the food, and place them in the dishwasher." Other time-saving conveniences, such as the automatic oven timing clock, allowed customers to "spend your time . . . any way you wish" while still putting meals on the table in a timely fashion.[27] In some cases, local cooperative publications carried columns, such as the "Home Owner's Question Box," designed to allow members to ask for advice on how to make improvements, and thus improve life for all at home.[28] All of these improvements came through the availability and use of electricity.

Throughout the Cold War era, and especially when fears heightened following the Cuban Missile Crisis of 1962, the cooperatives disseminated much information about civil defense improvements for the home. One story profiled Dickie and Jerry Meetze, two teens who had built and equipped a five-person fallout shelter on their property as a 4-H project, which they hoped would be "a model for friends and neighbors." Their father, a cooperative member, urged readers to pick up plans from the South Carolina Civil Defense Agency in Columbia.[29] Other notices encouraged rural residents to install an outdoor, automated light pole to "protect your loved ones, safeguard your property—for only pennies a day."[30] The automated lighting initiative proved especially popular with members and contributed significantly to a partial lighting of the nightscape in rural South Carolina.

Ultimately, the cooperatives began to incentivize electrification and conversion to electric appliances through their Gold Medallion program, an honor reserved for "member-consumers who have electric heat and the other advantages of modern living in their own homes." One such family, the Marvin T. Gaffney family, was profiled in November 1963: "Of course, the Gaffneys have gone all-out in modern living to qualify for the Gold Medallion. They use baseboard heat in their home, a completely modern kitchen with all the electric appliances to help out on cooking chores. Special lighting effects highlight the planter-room divider separating the living room from the formal dining area. A beautiful crystal chandelier over the dining table is enhanced using a dimmer switch to control the light level at table."[31]

Beyond the modern appliances and electrical upgrades, the cooperatives shared information about fully modern homes, creating momentum across rural South Carolina to abandon or abolish older, out-of-date homes and build a new home on the same property. Popular alternatives to aging homes for those in rural communities with lower incomes but considerable trade and craft skill were shell homes of various kinds and mobile homes. Shell Homes, Inc., for example, offered an entire house including all finish material, wiring, fixtures, and floor coverings, for only a $5.00 down payment, provided the buyer had a lot already in hand.[32] Such finishing details were actually unusual for the shell home model, which typically included just the foundation, framing, siding, roof, and windows and doors; owners of shell homes were expected to do the rest on their own. Nevertheless, shell home plans, such as those sold by Stylecraft Homes, promised luxury design "priced for immediate ownership." The appeal, presumably, was that the rural resident could finish and furnish the home as time and funds permitted.[33] In many cases, the featured models carried names that would have been familiar to South Carolina readers, such as "The Spartanburg" and "The York" from Shell Homes Inc. and "The Charleston" from Wise Homes.[34]

There were pitfalls, of course, to shell home arrangements, and one was the tendency of shell home contractors to employ prefabricated elements, which often encountered a public perception that prefabrication meant low-quality construction. To combat that association, some shell home contractors stopped using the term, instead advertising "custom-constructed" (not prefabricated) economy homes that would include flooring and room framing (basically a shell home), with the option of installing "optional inside materials and fixtures you select . . . for just a few more dollars added to your low monthly payment."[35] Still other advertisements were more direct, insisting that the company in question could actually modernize an existing home through extensive remodeling. J. L. Nipper Construction Company of Columbia, for example, offered a full-service approach, including room additions, kitchens, recreation rooms, screen porches, garages, carports, roofing, siding, plumbing, and redecorating, as well as the necessary planning and bank financing to make such work possible.[36] Modern Homes of Columbia took financing a step further, offering an insured mortgage payment plan that would cover monthly payments if the owner were to become sick or hurt.[37]

During the 1970s, the simplistic shell homes of the 1960s competed for attention with more sophisticated home construction approaches. American Family Homes, for example, offered brick homes of three, four, or five bedrooms that could be erected for lot owners, with the understanding that outside utilities, landscaping, and fuel tanks were the responsibility of the owner. Carpet was listed as optional, implying something more substantial than the shell homes that typically came with interior walls still naked to the studs.[38] Still, the shell home option remained available through Jim Walter Homes and Southern Homes, the latter of which offered substantially upgraded components to the standard shell home model: "We give you what others don't. Plywood corner braces, solid block foundation and poured concrete footers, concrete brick steps, ½-inch plywood roof sheathing, 240# self-seal shingles, 18-inch overhang front and back, roofline soffit ventilation system for a cooler attic, a truss roof for stability and strength, beaded siding for better looks and weather resistance, solid front door with window sidelights for safety, security and beauty, complete 100-amp copper wiring and smoke and fire detectors, 4-inch insulation in floor and sidewalls, 8¾-inch blown ceiling insulation and thermally-insulated windows."[39]

On the other end of the spectrum, a new entrant—Miles Homes— asked "only that you're handy, ambitious, and willing to invest your spare time to make the home you've been dreaming about a reality." In other words, the Miles Homes approach, billed as "The Do-It-Yourselfer's Friend," came with "all necessary blueprints, easy-to-follow, step-by-step instructions, carefully pre-cut materials, and even some foundations supplies," so that the buyer could build his own home from the ground up.[40] Carolina Model Home Corporation, meanwhile, offered their own variety of eighteen floor plans, any one of which could be "completely finished with screen doors, windows, all hardware, and two coats of fresh quality paint." Customers had "options for completing the interior that range from basic home to fully finished home."[41] By 1981, log homes, "once a symbol of America," were also making their way back through the cooperative publications, with specialized weatherproofing of the timbers and modern conveniences never available in the log homes of yore.[42] By the 1990s, advertisements for log homes were as ubiquitous as shell home advertisements had once been in the 1960s.

The 1970s also saw the growing popularity of a comparatively new, inexpensive type of rural housing: the mobile home, which required only a lot and could be transferred relatively easily if it became necessary to move. As mobile homes became more popular in the 1980s, both articles and advertisements appeared with recommendations for weatherproofing the mobile home, thus reducing energy costs.[43] By the 1990s, ads for mobile home improvements had expanded to include carports, awnings, roofovers, and screen rooms, with an offer for a free pressure-treated deck with each roofover purchase, thus reflecting the growing ubiquity of the mobile home on the landscape of rural South Carolina.[44]

The various levels of "shell" or "pre-fabricated" homes plus mobile homes marketed to cooperative members generally represented improved housing for most of the rural residents who purchased them. Though they were not the comfortable single-family homes, often full or partially brick, popular in the more affluent and rapidly growing suburbs in South Carolina (including some in cooperative service areas), these prefabricated and mobile homes generally represented a step up the socioeconomic and comfort ladder for those who purchased them.

During the 1970s, improvements in the yards and areas around rural homes as a way of modernizing the home emerged as an additional emphasis of cooperative communications. The latest innovations for the area around the home included above-ground, in-ground, and recessed swimming pools, an element of luxury generally not available to cooperative consumers just ten years earlier.[45] Utility buildings also emerged as a common home area addition. These all-purpose buildings appealed to a variety of consumers, including outdoor enthusiasts and farmers who needed a place to store their equipment and machinery. Utility buildings capable of holding a large motorhome, a pick-up truck, a motorcycle, a tractor, a boat on a trailer, a truck to pull said trailer, and a large workbench space grew popular and quickly became a common sight across the Palmetto State's countryside.[46]

Still another example of home and yard improvements was Royal Paulownia, a Chinese ornamental tree renowned (and later infamous) for its remarkable growth rate. Later listed as an invasive species in numerous states, the tree was marketed as the solution to shade for the home, an archway around the driveway to the home, and a resource for hanging a hammock in the shade of two such trees.[47] Flowering walnut trees—which offered not only shade and the other aforementioned advantages but also the chance to harvest up to five bushels of walnuts per season—later displaced the Royal Paulownia in popularity.[48] By the 1990s, the annual plant of choice was the "Hardy Hummingbird Vine" (Campsis radicans), another invasive species, prompting one reader to write to Living in South Carolina, complaining about the plant.[49]

Even during the prosperous 1960s, with overall energy prices low, energy conservation emerged as an important element of the cooperatives' overall energy strategy. The cooperatives focused on encouraging members to save on energy costs even as they modernized the rural home. One 1962 article emphasized the benefits of employing white or light-color roofing instead of traditional black roofing material, noting that studies determined that "homes roofed with [lighter colored] asphalt shingles were 8 degrees cooler at 8 P.M. on a summer's day than similar houses with black roofs."[50] This meant spending less electricity on cooling the home with one of the new air conditioners that were growing in popularity, affordability and use during South Carolina's often-stifling summer heat waves. The cooperatives also touted the benefits of "matchless," electric heat over systems relying on "conventional flame fuels," highlighting the cost-saving benefits of "individual room controlled electric heat" over fuel-based systems that relied on a centralized thermostat, as well as the absence of maintenance and air filter expenses.[51] In some cases, articles in cooperative publications provided direct comparisons of costs between electric heating and flame fuel heating, emphasizing savings on installation as well as the cleaning, and maintenance costs of a fuel-based system.[52] The cooperatives continued to emphasize cost-savings resulting from modest cash outlays, such as encouraging dishwasher installation and home insulation.[53] Indirect cost savings from electrification were also celebrated in a national advertisement in September 1962, emphasizing that electrification of rural chicken farms had caused the price of chicken to drop dramatically, transforming chicken from "a Sunday Treat" into something "most families can afford every day."[54]

The long postwar economic boom flourished until the Organization of the Petroleum Exporting Countries (OPEC) monopoly drove petroleum product prices through the roof during the Arab–Israeli conflict of 1973–74. With the embargo, the general nature of public discourse over energy in the United States took a dramatic turn as it triggered a nearly decade-long energy crisis that shocked all Western economies, including the American economy. In addition to many practical inconveniences (such as long lines at the gas pumps and gasoline rationing), the embargo revealed the nation's dependency on reasonably inexpensive foreign oil as a primary driver of its economic progress. In 1974, OPEC, a modern cartel of oil producers dominated by the Arab states, declared a 400 percent increase in per barrel oil prices, largely in response to American support for Israel in the second Arab–Israeli War. The higher energy prices drove inflation (already rising) to an annual rate of 11 percent in the United States, and unemployment rates spiked, triggering a recession that doomed the presidency of Republican Gerald Ford. Later, the crisis prompted President Jimmy Carter, a Democrat, to deem it the major cause of a "crisis of confidence" among the American people, which, in the end, doomed Carter's presidency as well.[55]

With the impact of high energy prices felt on all sides, Americans quickly shifted their emphasis from energy consumption to energy conservation, and they gave new and serious consideration to the opportunities offered by new energy technologies and new energy sources. South Carolina's electric cooperatives proved no exception to these trends. As the energy crisis of the 1970s took hold, the cooperatives advised their customers on new ways to conserve energy in the home. An interview with Clemson University Extension family life specialist Tom Mounter urged families to mount their own campaign against high energy prices by forming a family council to make collective decisions about energy use and conservation. In particular, he called on families to avoid long vacations in the car, turn out the lights when leaving a room, and avoid driving around mall parking lots looking for a space close to the entrance.[56] Other cooperative efforts offered instructions on behavior in the home that could help conservation, including recommendations that the air conditioner not be turned on "until you just have to," and even then, that the thermostat be set at 78 or 80 degrees.[57] Sometimes such advice was accompanied by devices facilitating energy savings for the home, such as the water flow restrictor offered by Santee Cooper in conjunction with thirteen electric cooperatives in South Carolina. A small, dime-sized device that fit into shower heads, the water flow restrictor was estimated to cut shower water use in half, thus cutting the cost of heating water in electric water heaters. The average yearly savings was projected at $56.[58] Still, recommendations of austerity fell on the ears of reluctant hearers. High energy prices, rather than the spirit of sacrifice, promoted energy conservation.

New, innovative products also emerged to combat high energy prices. One such product was the Intertherm hot water electric baseboard heating system, which claimed to be "revolutionary" and offer all the "advantages of hot water heat without plumbing!" Pitched as a suitable and affordable replacement for central heating systems, the Intertherm was also described as the antidote to one of the great threats to household budgets during the late 1970s: "oil and gas shortages and skyrocketing prices!"[59] Cooperative members also received occasional tips on how to save money on their electric bill, beginning with innovations such as storm windows and doors with thermal glass, and weather stripping. Moreover, during the oil and gas crisis of the 1970s, the electric cooperatives offered detailed information on the benefits of installing new innovations such as electric heat pumps, which were described as "the most efficient method of electric heating presently available."[60] Beginning in 1977, with the energy crisis looming large, the Farmers' Home Administration began offering loans through the cooperatives to assist homeowners with weatherizing improvements.[61] As the energy crisis again worsened in the late 1970s and into the early 1980s, with gasoline prices at the pump exceeding a dollar a gallon for the first time, the South Carolina Governor's Division of Energy Resources went so far as to take out a three-page advertisement in *Living in South Carolina* to highlight eleven proactive measures consumers could take to cut their energy consumption.[62]

The 1980s brought even more innovations to improve energy efficiency in South Carolina homes, most notably the availability of aluminum and vinyl siding, insulating windows, shutters, trim, railings, gutters, and downspouts.[63] Perhaps the most intriguing, and longest lasting, of the innovations highlighted by the cooperatives during the 1970s involved the growing interest in the potential of solar power. An early solar home, described as an "experimental, low-cost, low-energy-use house" built into a hillside emerged as a joint initiative of the Rural Housing Research Unit of the United States Department of Agriculture (USDA) and Clemson University. Solar energy was collected as hot air from the south side of the house, then used to heat water in large metal tanks. At times when the air was not sufficiently warm to heat the water, the air was instead transferred to a rock bed buffer below ground to help cut heat loss. While not commercially available, the solar house pointed to cost saving measures viewed as the foundation for future innovations.[64]

Less than a year later, in 1978, *Living in South Carolina* featured the future use of solar energy homes in a manner that would soon be accessible, affordable, and practical for most cooperative customers. While "solar units" were dismissed as being too expensive for most customers—$3,000 for the average home—solar assisted heating was presented as an idea that "may become practical in the near future."[65] The following year, another article on solar power promoted a Clemson professor's invention of a new kind of solar cell that "could make solar-generated electricity cheaper, easier to store, and use" was covered by the publication.[66] These early explorations with solar energy inevitably proved enticing regarding prospects but they offered too little, too early to have an impact in the short run. The expense of solar panels and the technological challenges of finding batteries that could efficiently and safely "store" solar power remain thorny issues even in the third decade of the twenty-first century, but the idea of harnessing energy from the sun to help meet Earth's power needs has remained a matter of interest and research since the energy crisis of the 1970s and promising results appear on the energy horizon.

With most of rural South Carolina enjoying the benefits of electrification by the late 1970s, largely through the efforts of the state's electric cooperatives, the cooperatives themselves turned their attention to other challenges: meeting the new energy price crisis, serving a growing number of members flowing into their service areas, especially in suburban communities, the need for local industry to sustain economic growth and development and to balance the load-factor (the ratio of maximum load to average load), and also to modulate between energy consumption and energy conservation. National Rural Electric Cooperative Association (NRECA) president Robert Partridge addressed the evolving role of South Carolina's electric cooperatives in the face of the new and prolonged energy crisis as early as 1977. "Modernizing a whole way of life does not end the rural electric story, by any means," Partridge observed. He insisted that rural electric cooperatives "must keep pace with the growing needs of their consumer-members. And because they are consumer-owned, they are consumer-oriented. Rural electric cooperatives have been in the forefront in alerting the nation to the seriousness of the energy-supply problem and working for national policies in the consumer interest. Their local, regional, and national meetings provide open forums through which consumer-members discuss various ideas and concepts and participate in the formulation of policies their cooperative entities lay down."[67]

As the convenience and even luxury of "modern" home living became available across rural South Carolina and with residents now enjoying the full benefits of electrification, the cooperatives confronted new challenges. "The challenge of today is enormous for the rural electric systems," one editorial in December 1981 stated: "More and more people are pouring into those areas that were made desirable for living because cooperatives electrified them," and "as a result of this continuing growth, the [cooperative] systems must invest heavily, not only in new line extensions, but in beefing up existing lines to handle the ever-increasing demand made by the convenience of electricity."[68] The cooperative publications repeated this message often as the 1980s progressed, reminding consumers, "You can't just run a wire out to rural America and call it quits. The job of rural electrification is never finished."

The cooperatives had formed an enduring partnership with their members. The mere presence of electric service in their area remained foundational, but the work of the electric cooperatives evolved, and the need for their services persisted. By the end of 1984, rural electric cooperatives supplied "nearly half the nation's poles and power lines" while serving "only 10 percent of the population."[69] By 1990 in South Carolina, the electric cooperatives were responsible for 52.7 percent of the line mileage within the state and serviced 26.4 percent of the state's electricity customers.[70] In short, the South Carolina electric cooperatives were not going anywhere; they were here to stay and to serve South Carolina.

Easy Cooking, Easy Cleaning Built Into New Electric Range

SOIL-RESISTANT and easy to clean, today's electric ranges are equipped with such features as lift-up tops, removable doors, storage drawers, and lift-out reflector pans to cut after-cooking clean-up time.

Lampblacking the old coal stove was a cinch compared to trying to clean some of the so-called "modern" ranges that came along in the 'twenties and 'thirties. Cracks and crevices, gratings and grillwork caught and held spillovers, ovens were inaccessible, and the whole stove had to be moved to get at dust underneath.

Electrical appliance manufacturers today have listened to the cries of busy housewives and now make ranges that not only help her cook well and efficiently, but are designed for convenience of cleaning, inside and out.

Among the features that make the new electric ranges easy to clean are hinged lift-up tops, ovens that pull all the way out, removable oven doors, throw-away oven liners, storage drawers that come out for cleaning under the range, recessed cooking tops that prevent spillovers, and removable reflector pans under the elements.

For cooking convenience, new electric ranges may be equipped with double ovens, automatic removable rotisseries, extra-fast cooking elements, thermostatically controlled top elements, meat thermometers, automatic oven timers, broilers that heat instantly, and heat controls for selecting a variety of uniform heats.

Cooking and cleaning convenience, added to the cleanliness and safety of cooking with electricity, make today's electric ranges and wall ovens among the most prized possessions in the modern home.

HOUSEHOLD HINT
How much spaghetti, macaroni or noodles to cook can sometimes be a puzzle. No need to worry, though, if these simple rules are followed. Macaroni and spaghetti practically double in

ABOVE: Marion County's Rural Fire Department demonstrates their services for members of the Cash community in 1972. Pee Dee Electric's rural development committee led an effort that helped establish a similar fire department for the Chesterfield County community.

Advertisements—like this one from a 1961 issue of *South Carolina Electric Co-Op News*—encouraged co-op members to improve their quality of life by purchasing electric appliances for their homes.

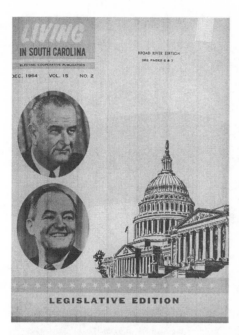

LIVING
IN SOUTH CAROLINA

ELECTRIC COOPERATIVE PUBLICATION

BROAD RIVER EDITION
SEE PAGES 6 & 7

DEC. 1964   VOL. 15   NO. 2

LEGISLATIVE EDITION

Born in politics, electric co-ops have continued to serve as advocates for their member-owners through grassroots efforts in their communities and an ongoing presence at the South Carolina State House in Columbia and in Washington, DC.

BELOW: In 1965, *Living in South Carolina* magazine gave South Carolina Electric Cooperative Association (SCECA) manager R. D. Bennett a bully pulpit from which to battle investor-owned utilities' attempts to take over local electric co-ops.

Burning automobiles (sell out to insurance companies) when owners were unable to keep up payments was not uncommon in sections of the state in the early and mid 1930's.

An acquaintance of mine, who in addition to his regular work, would burn automobiles for a small fee. This fellow used to tell about the time he was burning a car for a friend. Having driven the car out into the country and soaking it good with gasoline, he ignited it. (To be sure the car would continue to burn he always carried with him a small fire extinguisher filled with gasoline). Shortly after he got the car burning, a traveling salesman drove up, hopped out of his car with a fire extinguisher filled with foam and started putting the fire out in the burning car. My acquaintance, in telling this story, remarked, "You know, it was all I could do to keep that darned car burning with the salesman on one side shooting foam on it from his fire extinguisher and me on the other side shooting gas from my extinguisher."

STAND TALL

FOR S. C. ELECTRIC COOPERATIVES

Also in the early 1930's rural South Carolinians had a burning desire to have electric service just like their city cousins but were denied this opportunity when existing power suppliers refused them service. Not until the electric cooperatives came into being in 1939 did rural South Carolina get electrified.

Today the same power suppliers who refused to serve rural areas with electricity, are trying to destroy the electric cooperative flame. They propose to do their dirty work by controlling all sources of wholesale power, turning public opinion against consumer owners, buying out consumer owned electric suppliers, and their latest move is to trick the General Assembly into imposing a heavy unrealistic tax burden on cooperatives, causing them to increase their electric rates to consumers.

You electric cooperative consumer-owners had better arm yourselves with the facts and be prepared to fight for your rights! These power companies who picture themselves as a true symbol of the American Free Enterprise system, are actually monopolies serving generally in heavily populated areas with no competition. They are guaranteed a rate to give them a high return from their investment. These out-of-state controlled monopolies have an average income of $7,000 per mile of line. The cooperatives have an average annual income of only $460 per mile of line.

Yet, the bigwigs in the power companies say the cooperatives should pay the same taxes as they do. This makes about as much sense as a one-horse farmer paying the same annual tax as a large plantation land owner.

Be prepared to defend your rights to own and operate your electric cooperative business. These monopolies, dressed in sheep clothing, are after your business.

South Carolina is a great State. There is plenty of room for all power suppliers, both consumer owned and commercially owned. Should either of these organizations be put out of business the people in the State of South Carolina would be the great losers. A check and balance is good in all business.

By R. D. Bennett
MANAGER

SOUTH CAROLINA
ELECTRIC COOPERATIVE
ASSOCIATION, INC.

Governor John West visits a rural Richland County home in 1972 to help dedicate a new "snap-on" bathroom. West partnered with the SCECA's Stand Tall Commission on his Privy Project (aka "John's Johns"), modernizing hundreds of rural homes by adding low-cost indoor plumbing.

BELOW: In the 1960s and '70s, Tri-County Electric in St. Matthews and other co-ops offered local women an opportunity to work outside the home.

Early co-op linemen performed often dangerous jobs without the hard hats and other personal protective equipment that have made modern electrical line work safer.

Since South Carolina co-ops began participating in 1968, high school students on the co-ops' Washington Youth Tour have met with members of the state's congressional delegation. Here, '70s-era students pose with late US Senator Strom Thurmond, *right*.

5

South Carolina's Electric Cooperatives and the Changing Role of Women, 1950s–1980s

The broad availability of electricity in rural South Carolina, an availability made possible largely through the efforts of the state's electric cooperatives, changed the nature and quality of life for women in those areas dramatically for the better. As we saw earlier in Chapter 1, life before rural electrification for hundreds of thousands of people in rural South Carolina consisted mainly of difficult domestic labor, hard farm work, limited alternatives, and long periods of darkness. With the beginning of rural electrification in the state, starting with the founding of Aiken Electric Cooperative in 1938, rural populations throughout the state began a transition to a way of life already well established in South Carolina's towns and cities. The bulk of that transition would be completed within twenty-five years, although, for a variety of reasons, some rural residents would not get their first electricity connection until well into the 1980s. In many respects, the arrival of electricity revolutionized the lives, the households, and the farms of rural South Carolinians. We have already seen that no group experienced a more remarkable transformation "when the lights came on" than women, who not only saw their domestic lives change but also saw their place in the world change, in part because of the forward-looking, "modernizing" initiatives of the electric cooperatives.

The initial arrival of electricity unquestionably lightened the burden of domestic labor for women. William F. Robinson, who grew up in the Lynches River Electric Cooperative area, remembered the conversion from an old wood stove to an electric range as transformative for his mother. "Oh, absolutely, it took a load off of her," he said. "If she wanted to make biscuits, she could turn the knob on the oven. The stove, you had to get the stove hot, but if you got it too hot, the biscuits would burn, and if it was not hot enough, the biscuits wouldn't bake . . . If they burned, my dad would say, 'I don't want that biscuit; it's burned on the bottom and not brown on the top.' But the electric stove did it just right."[1] A few, like Walter Baker from the Lynches River Electric Cooperative area, remembered their mothers resisting the switch to modern appliances, largely because they were "just used to [their] old way of doing things." But many earlier cooperative members recalled their mothers embracing the new technology wholesale. Kirk Roberts, who grew up in the Fairfield Electric Cooperative service area, remembered electrification as a "godsend" for his mother. "She loved it . . . It was just so much better to have electricity than what we were used to . . . My mother didn't care anything about anything old," he reported, "She loved modern equipment, and it wasn't any trouble for her to get used to an electric stove, or a refrigerator, or an electric iron. She was happy to have it."[2]

The excitement and drama of the early days with electricity may have dulled a little over time, but even in the 1960s, the transformative influence of electric power on women's lives and the attachment of those women to the local electric cooperatives remained evident. By the 1960s, the official publication of the cooperatives included a regular column, "When the Lights Came On," that included letters from many women extolling the benefits of electrification. These letters often highlighted improvements in domestic convenience. Writing in December 1961, Mrs. N. D. Clayton of Fountain Inn in the Upstate insisted, "We thought it was the grandest thing [that] had ever happened in our home when the electric lights were cut on . . . I could even read fine print without my glasses and then the old wood stove was put out of the kitchen and the water brought in by electric [service] then the refrigerator instead of carrying our milk to a spring." Later, she remembered, her family acquired a "freezer to keep our food and also the washing machine." The positive contribution of electrification was contrasted with the shortcomings of the investor-owned power companies which had failed to provide service to many rural areas. "We tried to get electric from Duke." Clayton recalled, referring to the major provider of electricity to the towns and cities of the Upstate, "but failed."[3]

Evidence of the change electrification brought to rural women's lives was palpable in the publications of the electric cooperatives. Indeed, much of the content of these publications specifically focused on female members of cooperative families. Following the pattern of most newspapers of the time, the monthly cooperative publication included a page edited by Virginia Ruth called "For the Ladies." Typically, this page offered a variety of the usual fare for such columns: tips for cooking, recipes, decorations, and suggestions for dress patterns.[4] Additionally, as rural incomes rose rapidly during this era, the acquisition of modern electrical conveniences became common in rural homes. Advertising in cooperative publications often focused on persuading women of the value of modern conveniences, especially kitchen appliances. One advertisement, typical of the period, for the "Fabulous 'No-Frost' Foodarama by Kelvinator" included a drawing of this side-by-side refrigerator/freezer with a smiling housewife in her party dress and apron searching for room in the fully stocked appliance.[5] This advertisement suggested the rising standard of living in rural areas and the continued rural residence of families who had left farming for jobs nearby. Still another feature on washing machines framed the discussion by referring sarcastically to the "good ole days" of using "the ole iron washpot, zinc-tub, and rub-board" as a contrast to the convenience automatic machines could offer. A photograph of an elderly woman, Mrs. Stanley Williams of Galivant's Ferry, shown "demonstrating the 'good ole way' of washing clothes," only underscored the point that a smart homemaker would insist on one of the modern machines. The article then offered tips on how to use the automatic washers before adding, "Automatic electric clothes dryers are the greatest beauty aid to reach Mrs. Homemaker since the invention of the wringer and automatic washer."

Modern electric conveniences, of course, encouraged use of electricity, increased the demand, and lowered the unit cost of producing electricity, allowing the cooperatives to serve their sprawling territories more efficiently and charge lower rates. Seeking to encourage the purchase of modern conveniences, local cooperatives frequently brought in brand-name appliance vendors to conduct cooking schools and laundry demonstrations for "the ladies" of the local cooperative.[6] In other cases, cooperative articles appealed to the tight budgets of young married women, suggesting economy-minded solutions to their cooking needs. For example, "The bride is in a quandary," one such article began. "She wants a certain kitchen range—but its price would strain her budget." The solution? "Portable electric cooking appliances may . . . [allow the bride] to get along quite well without a range until she can afford to buy the one she wants." The article then compared the price of a frying pan, two saucepans, and a portable oven—all electric and priced at $116—with the cost of the same set of non-electric utensils plus an electric range at as much as $275.[7]

As these examples suggest, articles and advertisements in cooperative publications during the early 1960s tended to emphasize the traditional domestic role of women as homemakers. Many articles highlighted the health benefits of modern conveniences over traditional methods of domestic labor. In one article, for example, the traditional method of washing dishes rendered it "extremely difficult for a housewife washing dishes by hand to get them as sanitary as an automatic electric dishwasher... The housewife knows the dishes she's removing from her new automatic electric dishwasher will be cleaner and safer for her family than if the dishes had been hand-washed."[8] Other articles promoted the culinary benefits of electrically baked cakes. Readers learned that "a beautiful home-made cake—tender, moist, and tasty—is the source of pride and pleasure for the woman who has created it." Electric ovens eliminated the guesswork of baking "since accurately controlled heat that's evenly distributed throughout the oven is a vital part of perfect cake making, any woman—or her teenage daughter—who will follow directions carefully can bake perfect cakes consistently if she uses a new electric range." The article concluded that such ranges "help every woman, whether amateur or expert, to be a proud cake-maker, and a better, all-around cook."[9] In sum, electric ranges were shortcuts to cooking success.

Similarly, cooperative publications often carried articles giving exhaustive instructions on how to freeze a wide variety of foods.[10] Eventually, reader interest led to a recurring column known as "Cook's Corner," in which cooperative customers—nearly always women—would write in with their favorite recipes, for which contributors were paid $2 if the recipe was printed.[11] "Cook's Corner" was still a regular feature in the 1970s, and by that time, Living in South Carolina was also advertising dress patterns and needlecraft patterns as "Fashions for the Ladies."[12]

Articles in the cooperative publications also hailed the advantages of other new appliances with specific appeals to women. A February 1961 article on electric water heaters insisted, "Today's homemaker wants her new home equipped with all the appliances that will add a spot of attractiveness as well as provide her with efficient service." The article then went on to discuss the merits of an electric water heater, insisting that "no new home is completely modern" without one.[13] Other advertisements were even more direct in their appeals to women. One advertisement for Frigidaire's 1961 range with a divided top and a pull and clean oven was pitched as being specifically "designed for rural families... to handle 'family reunion' meals." Featuring a homemaker wearing her apron over her party dress, the ad promised that the buyer would "feel like a Queen with this Frigidaire farm family favorite."[14] But these articles suggest far more than simply the effort to sell ever more modern conveniences to rural women; they also suggested that the roles and concerns of rural women were changing, growing more wide-ranging, however gradually. They indirectly highlighted the fact that rural women no longer had to labor over a hot wood stove for hours to prepare daily meals or to have family or company over for a meal on special occasions. Such work could be done in less time, and often partially in advance. When time to entertain arrived, women could dress nicely, just tying on an apron to serve the food, and enjoy the occasion as much as anyone. The deeper impact of the availability of modern electric conveniences was implied by the phrase "feel like a Queen" in the Frigidaire advertisement, suggesting that rural women no longer had to feel more put upon than town or city women and that nothing about rural life needed to be second class any longer.

Nonetheless, the temper of the times still valued primarily the traditional roles of women, and cooperative meetings of the era reinforced such attitudes. Highlighting the 1961 annual business meeting of Aiken Electric Cooperative was "the three Jones sisters of Route 2, Batesburg." One of them, Maggie Jones, the reigning "Miss Aiken Electric Cooperative," crowned her sixteen-year-old sister, Dorothy Lois Jones, in the 1961 beauty contest. Their sister Carolyn finished in third place. Prizes included $50 in cash, a trophy, an 18" × 20" oil painting, and an all-expense paid trip to Columbia to compete in the statewide contest. At the statewide contest, competition included evening dresses, bathing suits, and a talent show (closely paralleling the Miss America pageant popular during this era).[15] Two months later, coverage of the upcoming statewide cooperative meeting announced that "Beauties, Business, and Talent Highlight State Co-Op Session." The "business side" of the meeting consisted entirely of men, most of them executives and cooperative committee heads. The "entertainment program," which kicked off the statewide meeting, was made up almost entirely of female beauty and talent contestants divided into those two categories.[16] Dorothy Lois Jones emerged as the winner of the statewide contest and appeared frequently in magazine features on the Miss South Carolina Electric Co-Op.[17]

Other contests underscored women's role in the kitchen. In October 1962, for example, *South Carolina Electric Co-Op News* carried two letters to the editor highlighting the State Chicken Cooking Contest at Farm and Home Week, a cooperative sponsored event at Clemson College. Maudene P. Leschinsky, the contest winner, wrote in to announce that she had donated her prize (a new oven range) to "a small Baptist Mission Church," while Myrtis W. Sowell, the third place finisher, wrote not only to thank the cooperative for her prize (an electric fry pan) but also to ask for an instruction book on how to clean and care for the pan.[18] These letters to the editor only served to underscore a broader assumption about domestic duties clearly on display in a November 1962 article that included recipes for holiday turkey dishes with an implied pitch for the economic uplift encouraged by rural electrification. "Thanks to modern food processing and poultry growing methods, millions of housewives across the country will be turning out Thanksgiving and Christmas banquets fit for kings— and they'll be able to enjoy the fruits of their labor as much as anyone."[19] The phrase "fit for kings" suggested that rural electrification had played a large role in diminishing a feeling of second-class citizenships among rural citizens, even if the suggestion of rural royalty remained chiefly humorous hyperbole.

Perhaps the most overt appeals to women during the 1960s and into 1970s came in the annual May issue, when the cooperative publications extolled the virtues of motherhood to coincide with Mother's Day. Often, the cover was devoted to the topic, and occasionally other content would also celebrate motherhood.[20] In many cases, this content seemed to offer examples of model mothers who went beyond the normal call of duty. One Mother's Day article, for example, hailed as the cooperatives' "Modern Madonna" and exemplar of "American Motherhood . . . Mrs. Bobby Richardson of Sumter, a progressive young mother, wife of a famous baseball star, mother of three beautiful youngsters . . . a Christian mother dedicated to her home and God." Mrs. Richardson, the article explained, was particularly deserving of the honor because of the "problems involved to keeping two homes—one for baseball season and one for off-season— and the greater problem of rearing unaffected, happy youngsters so near the bright glare of publicity attending Bobby's baseball success."[21]

Another way the South Carolina cooperatives appealed to rural women was by showcasing particular individuals who were judged to possess unusually remarkable degrees of character and social concern. One such case was Lois Myrick, an Allendale "homemaker and mother" who was renowned in her community as a "modern-day Florence Nightingale . . . through her nursing and good-neighborliness." In selecting Myrick as the Palmetto Personality for February 1961, the editors of the *South Carolina Electric Co-Op News* declared, "In naming her, we feel that we are also honoring those thousands of other rural South Carolina ladies who walk the same path with Mrs. Myrick in Christian service to home and community."[22] It was doubtless difficult for the typical rural farm wife of the 1960s to find time for caregiving and community-building in addition to the regular work load on farm and in home, but many women made prodigious efforts to do so.

Throughout the 1960s, advertisements in cooperative publications continued their appeals to women looking to reduce the burdens of housework. One advertisement from the National Rural Electric Cooperative Association (NRECA) that appeared in October 1962 featured the Association's new slogan: "Electricity—the heart of modern living," with NRECA's mascot, Willie Wiredhand, grasping onto a heart shape drawn around the word "heart." The ad included a photograph of a heaping pile of laundry with the headline "Ever feel like screaming on Monday?" The body of the advertisement, proclaimed, "Let's face it! You're the one who does the family wash. You can keep on doing it the hard way or you can do it the easy electric way," thus freeing up time to "catch up on other chores, or just relax."[23]

Yet gradually cooperative publications began to develop more well-rounded portrayals of women cooperative members. They began to showcase young women who displayed a knack for independence and industriousness, and at times invited impressive young women to address their institutional meetings, and then published features on those women. Jonnie Flyn McCormac of Dillon County, for example, was highlighted in 1961 as the choice to speak at the NRECA's annual meeting in Dallas, Texas. The nineteen-year-old college student and "national 4-H electric project winner" was slated to speak after presenting her talk on "Americanism" to meetings in Chicago, Louisville, and Columbia, South Carolina. McCormac, in turn, thanked Marlboro Electric Cooperative electrification advisor Estelle Chamness, noting that her success was owed in part to Chamness's counsel.[24] Other young women, such as twenty-year-old Ruth Rapin of Switzerland, arrived in South Carolina through their participation in the International Farm Youth Exchange program, which paired experienced young people from abroad with farm families in South Carolina for two weeks at a time.[25] Another participant in the Youth Exchange program, Irmgard Schafer, a "21-year-old German farm girl," visited South Carolina in 1962. During her stay, she lived with and learned from three different South Carolina farm families before moving on to South Dakota and Minnesota for similar experiences.[26]

Indeed, the question of the capacity of young women as workers took on new prominence as the 1960s progressed. One 1963 article focused on the question of whether "girls make better school bus drivers," noting that such an idea might "get male drivers 'steamed up.'" The article reported a spike in the number of women applying for school bus training courses, with the revelation that school officials preferred "girl drivers" because "the girls seem to do a better all-around job of driving." One school official explained, "Girls are more mature, demand greater respect, are less tolerant of misconduct, do not try to 'show off,' observe safety rules more strictly, [and] keep buses cleaner and safer than do the boys."[27]

Moreover, the cooperatives were surprisingly innovative and forward thinking for the era in highlighting the emerging role of nontraditional positions for women outside the home. Elizabeth W. Potter, a married woman, was listed in a February 1961 article as the "Clemson extension home management specialist," then quoted at length about her insights on which appliances might prove most beneficial to saving time and labor in the home.[28] Other features sometimes illustrated the availability of jobs for married women, such as the inclusion of a photograph of the Horry Electric Cooperative's director, H. G. McNeill, receiving a demonstration of an addressograph machine from Mrs. Margaret Baiden, Horry Electric Cooperative's ledger clerk.[29]

Women who were employed by the cooperatives during this era tended to look back fondly on the annual meetings as a source of entertainment, enjoyment, and opportunity for women to display some of their talents, whether in the kitchen or on the stage. One anonymous worker for the Berkeley Electric Cooperative who started in 1966 loved the original model for the annual meetings:

> I liked the beginning annual meeting. They had the best pre-
> serves put up. . . . All of the women on the lines would enter their
> preserves and their green beans and their potatoes and whatever,
> smoked ham. And then they were judged. And then they had the
> best pig and the best horse and cow. That was judged. Then they
> had the beauty contest. We were under this enormous tent taking
> the annual meeting, and to me, the annual meetings at the very
> beginning when I first started at the co-op, I liked the best. . . . They
> were wonderful: the beauty contests. And we were right there. We
> could see all of this happening and the judging and all that. The
> quilt-work . . . it was beautiful. I don't know [why they got away
> from that]. It was fun. And it was always interesting to go around
> and see all of that stuff. . . . So, I don't know. It's just times have
> changed. Maybe they ought to have the best computer. I don't
> know. You worked, but it was fun . . . and you got to see people,
> and it was just a slower time, I guess.[30]

While popular among many cooperative women, the annual meetings did emphasize traditional roles of women as homemakers, housewives, mothers, and yes, beauty queens. The cooperatives sought to provide a sense of community among their members, and their annual meetings appeared to achieve just that. Theresa Hicks, who won the Miss Lynches River beauty contest in 1964, used her participation in the contest as a gateway to employment. "They needed summertime help, and they asked me if I would help out that summer. And I did, and I helped out the next summer. And then they called and asked if I wanted a permanent job. So, that was in 1964. And I retired in 2001."[31]

Cooperative publications during the 1960s also carried prominent columns provided by the women of the Garden Club of South Carolina on topics important to rural farm women, such as Mrs. W. E. Dargan's article on the importance of getting conservation taught in rural schools.[32] Passing references in the cooperative publications suggested a variety of cooperative jobs with specific appeals to prospective female employees, usually for jobs traditionally perceived as particularly well suited for women, such as Claire Stoller's role as the home economist at Edisto Electric Cooperative in Bamberg, or any number of office positions, though generally not management positions in the 1960s.[33] One 1961 feature article emphasized the numerous job opportunities "open to both men and women" in a variety of cooperative organizations in the state. Curiously, this feature was the prizewinning essay of a 1960 contest among various South Carolina cooperatives, and its author was a sixteen-year-old girl, suggesting a future of young women seeking broader opportunities within the cooperatives.[34]

Moreover, the cooperatives called on women to play a part in the political struggles the cooperatives faced during the 1960s, marking a new turn toward harnessing women's political power. Specifically, Erma Angevine, the Coordinator of Women's Activities for the NRECA, the national organization of the cooperatives, suggested a number of ways women could support the aims of cooperatives. Angevine encouraged women to hold coffee parties focused on the story of rural electrification, write letters to their elected officials, participate in 4-H Club work and use the opportunity to tell the story of rural electrification, get involved in essay contests and other public relations initiatives, attend cooperative meetings at all levels, attend legislative meetings covering the cooperatives, create organizations consisting of the wives of cooperative directors and employees, sign and circulate petitions, and serve as boosters of "all-electric living at every opportunity." Interestingly, the one missing recommendation was the suggestion that women use their vote in statewide and federal elections to support candidates sympathetic to rural electrification initiatives. This omission was especially curious since by 1963 large numbers of white women in South Carolina and the nation had routinely voted for decades.[35]

At the national level, NRECA also recognized the importance of recruiting female cooperative customers into the political fight for the survival of rural electrification. In 1963, for example, NRECA regional meetings incorporated a panel discussion, "Women Want to Know," where women could learn about "the relationships of members, local systems, state association, NRECA, and the Rural Electrification Administration," then ask questions. The session was a direct result of women complaining about the usual fare at NRECA events. "Women . . . asked for more 'meaty' programs," *Living in South Carolina* reported. "They said they were tired of luncheons, style shows, and entertainment. They wanted something they could get their teeth in. They wanted more information, so they could speak up when their Co-Ops were attacked." As a result of the request, the NRECA Board of Directors established a Women's Activities Committee to replace the former Hostess Committee, with members of the new national committee selected by women at regional meetings.[36] Locally, cooperative publications touted the efforts of women who had taken on the investor-owned power companies, such as Mrs. J. W. Murray, a member of Pee Dee Electric Cooperative, who refused to give Carolina Power & Light Company (CP&L) a right of way across her land when a new subdivision started to spring up nearby, noting that CP&L would be crossing territory controlled by the local cooperative.[37]

During the 1970s, as women's rights issues gained more prominence nationally, attitudes toward women in South Carolina evolved slowly, but they did evolve. By the late 1970s, cooperative publications no longer published the height and weight information on beauty pageant participants. When NRECA's 1976 Miss Rural Electrification, twenty-one-year-old Paula Wuertemberger from Richmond, Indiana, appeared at Berkeley County's Annual Hell Hole Swamp Festival, coverage of her appearance took pains to detail her numerous scholastic and volunteer accomplishments in life rather than merely praising her appearance.[38] Coverage of the beauty contests in *Living in South Carolina* waned dramatically by the end of the decade.[39]

Even in the 1970s, though, there existed a presumption by the leadership of the cooperatives that women were not well suited for leadership or management roles in the cooperatives. Writing in May 1978, R. D. Bennett, the executive vice president of the South Carolina Electric Cooperative Association, urged members to attend their annual meetings and vote for trustees for the Cooperative Board: "Your vote should go for the men of finest character and with the best record of unselfish community service."[40] At the same time, however, the cooperatives' publications more widely recognized opportunities for young women to showcase their leadership skills. One such example was the NRECA's Youth Consulting

Board, established in 1976. The group consisted of ten young people selected from membership regions of the NRECA, at least three of whom
were young women aged sixteen and seventeen.[41]

In some cases, cooperative publication articles showcased the accomplishments of adult women. A 1978 piece focused on Horace W. "Bud"
Hennecy, a district supervisor for the Pee Dee Electric Cooperative who
was the first winner of an award named the Hettie Rickett Community
Development Award. Established by the South Carolina Community
Development Association, the award was named for a deceased Kershaw
County resident who "was a fireball when it came to activities designed
to upgrade the quality of life in her community" and given annually to an
individual who "best exemplifies the ideals of Miss Hettie."[42] A particularly compelling article was another 1978 piece focused on Luemer and
Della Plumley, sisters from Glassy Mountain in Greenville County who
had been fighting for decades for rural electric service to be extended to
their ancestral family cabin. Blue Ridge Electric Cooperative of Pickens
finally extended this service that year, illustrating that the cooperatives
were still bringing electricity for the first time to residences in remote
parts of the state as late as the 1970s.[43]

By the 1980s, articles on traditional domestic roles shifted to matters
that ventured outside the home but still carried strong gender connota-
tions. One such topic was couponing to save money at the grocery store,
highlighting the efforts of Cheryl Pevehouse of Columbia, who had already so mastered the art of couponing that she typically paid nothing for
her groceries and often received a refund from the store once the coupon
values had been applied. As a result of this approach, her grocery trips
"[were] always exciting." To assist others, Pevehouse started a publication known as *Cash from Trash*, which offered "a long list of free offers
and addresses shoppers can write for free or money-saving coupons."[44]
Also in the 1980s, an ad for Trimline "Instant Slimmers"—essentially a
modern-day corset—pitched the product as "an alternative to the diet
that takes weeks" by offering the wearer "a lightweight, effective way to a
slender, athletic figure."[45] For the most part, though, gender-based article
content and advertisements had gradually disappeared from cooperative
publications, reflecting the progressive shift from traditional gender roles
already afoot in American culture. By the early 1990s, *Living in South Carolina*'s only remaining domestic-themed content for women was "Cook's
Corner" and "Fashions for the Ladies." For other features, the magazine
occasionally ran features directed explicitly at women without any role-as-
signing baggage attached, such as a March 1992 column on Social Security
issues that were unique to women.[46]

Cooperative publications also occasionally focused on female leaders and their accomplishments, featuring women such as Jean Hoefer Toal, the first woman to serve on the South Carolina Supreme Court.[47] By the 1980s, some stories even focused on women working on behalf of the cooperatives themselves. A January 1984 piece, for example, highlighted a resolution from the Coastal Electric Cooperative Board of Directors honoring Joan P. Bruce, president of Women Involved in Rural Electrification (WIRE), for her work on behalf of the cooperative. Nonetheless, WIRE's overall objectives appear to have mimicked to some degree the tasks of the Women's Activities Committee of the 1960s: key initiatives included awarding scholarships to youth, community involvement training, sending out a quarterly newsletter to WIRE members, assisting with letter-writing on legislative issues, providing financial assistance to the poor and victims of natural disasters, and selling copies of *The Best of Cook's Corner*, the recipe column from *Living in South Carolina*. Membership in WIRE, which was established in December 1981, was restricted to female consumer-members, wives of consumer-members, female employees of the cooperatives, and wives of employees of the cooperatives, thus suggesting that the leadership structure of the cooperatives remained largely segregated along gender lines even as late as the mid-1980s.[48] Also, as late as 1987, one of WIRE's principal fundraising mechanisms remained asking women from cooperatives throughout the state to donate crafts and baked goods, which were then sold at the statewide annual meeting.[49] In 1988, the National Rural Electric Women's Association awarded the South Carolina WIRE with one of eight Promoting Excellence in Rural Life awards for their fundraising activities.[50]

As political tensions between the cooperatives and South Carolina Electric & Gas Company (SCE&G) heated up in the late 1980s, female cooperative members spoke out. The April 1989 issue of *Living in South Carolina*, for example, featured a full-page letter from Ilene C. Harral of Aiken describing her advocacy on behalf of the cooperatives for passage of South Carolina House Bill 3398, which was intended to protect the cooperatives from a "hostile takeover" by SCE&G.[51] It was a period of transition in which appeals to traditional gender roles existed alongside efforts to mobilize women politically and expand gender roles within the cooperatives.

By the mid-1980s, young women were also being recognized equally with their peers by the cooperatives through initiatives like the Co-op Youth Tour to Washington, sponsored annually by NRECA and thirteen of the South Carolina cooperatives. The program, which required applicants to submit an essay, oratory, or oral exam on the history and business model of the cooperatives to qualify, appeared to be about evenly split among young men and women in 1984.[52] By 1992, even as the ranks of the trustees and officers of the cooperatives remained dominated with men, the Co-op Youth Tour class was becoming progressively more lopsided toward female participants, with sixteen young women and only seven young men going to Washington that year in recognition of their "potential for leadership."[53]

Women employed by the cooperatives also made some progress toward entering more senior positions within the cooperatives. One employee, Myrtle Faile, started at Lynches River Electric Cooperative as a home service provider in 1967. Her initial position required her to provide demonstration programs on "the wise use of electricity, canning all kinds of food preparation," and other topics to churches, schools, and clubs, but after three years she transitioned to member services. Her final position with the cooperative was as member services director when she retired in 2000.[54] One article in the March 1984 issue of *Living in South Carolina* included a photograph of Faile, then member services director, presenting a talk on energy conservation with landscaping to the Jefferson Garden Club.[55] A 1988 article included an image of Judy Reeves, president of Coastal Electric Cooperative.[56] By that same year, women were beginning to make in-roads as trustees, too, as evinced by a photograph in *Living in South Carolina* showing Dorothy Scarborough, trustee of Pee Dee Electric Cooperative, receiving a management certificate.[57]

Eunice Spilliards, who joined the board of trustees of Palmetto Electric Cooperative in the early 1990s, highlighted the concerns of women seeking leadership positions within the cooperatives at that time:

> I was the first woman to go on our board many, many years ago, and it's been a wonderful experience. I was reluctant because I had heard that the man, I took his place; he retired, and he recommended someone else for his place on the board. And I sent word through these men that I would run [against] anybody that took his place on the board. And so I actually *ran* for the board and won it with 32 votes. How 'bout that? And so I was scared to death and very reluctant because I just thought the men were going to treat me horribly. From the day I walked into the first board room, they have treated me just like one of the board members. And I have had a wonderful experience. No problem whatsoever. I think they were ready.[58]

Nevertheless, while WIRE remained a powerful women's organization for the cooperatives into the early 1990s, the presence of women in leadership positions—as trustees and officers of regional cooperatives—remained small compared to that of men.

In spite of this ongoing gender imbalance within the cooperatives, women employees were making names for themselves and finding that hard work was rewarded with a general sense of equality by the men working for the cooperatives. Peggy Dantzler, who started out as a meter reader in 1990, took a position as a line worker in 1993—a position traditionally held by men. To her surprise, the emphasis for new line workers was squarely on proving that you were capable, regardless of gender:

> There was still a lot of [hazing] around whenever I went out on the line crew. There's always going to be some form of rite of passage for these line workers. People who have never done line work can't possibly understand the brotherhood that develops. And it doesn't matter if you're female or male; it really is a brotherhood. I would say sisterhood, but it's not. It's a brotherhood. And you can still be female and be a part of that because you have linemen that have worked in probably some of the worst conditions. At any time, day or night, they spend more time with their coworkers than they do with their families, in most instances. And they're dealing with something that is so deadly, their focus has to be there all of the time. Because if not, the consequence is dire.[59]

Charlene Haynes, who joined the Little River Electric Cooperative board in 1989, noted that one of the characteristics of the boards is that turnover tended to be low, thus amplifying the imbalance between men and women on the boards and explaining the apparent resistance to gender balancing. "Another good thing about our board," she added, "[is that] we have three women on the board. I joke lots of times that when we have our meetings, and we sit around the table, we have the three women on one side and all the men on the other. We are a very amiable group."[60]

When asked in 2014 about her experience as an employee, one-time beauty contest winner Theresa Hicks, who worked for the cooperatives for thirty-seven years, expressed a sentiment common among cooperative employees, past and present: "It's not your blood family, but it's your family. And everyone was concerned with what goes on in *your* family. So, it's just a family type of environment. And even now, well after I retired, it was still family."

The Politics of
Rural Electrification in
the 1950s and 1960s

SERVING THE NEEDS OF THEIR MEMBERS

E ven though South Carolina's electric cooperatives were established and serving their members by the 1950s, they still found themselves necessarily involved in an era of ongoing social and cultural change. They also found themselves immersed, along with the rest of the nation, in both a national economic boom that was raising living standards and a political climate emotionally and ideologically charged by the emerging Cold War against the Soviet Union and communism more generally. As home to a number of military bases and the Savannah River Site, a newly acquired federal nuclear facility, South Carolina had a large national defense profile during this era.[1]

As a result, during the 1950s, the investor-owned utilities tried to harness the fear of the Cold War era's Red Scare as a rhetorical device to criticize the member-owned electric cooperatives. One of the byproducts that emerged from the anti-communist sentiment fueled by the Cold War was the effort by certain private interests to tar any idea or program that involved government assistance with the brush of socialism. For example, newspaper advertisements run by investor-owned power companies frequently referred to the cooperatives as "socialized electricity." Americans, these advertisements claimed, wanted money spent on defense, not "unnecessary government spending." Ads argued that federally financed transmission lines built by the cooperatives merely duplicated those already being built by "business-managed companies." Far and away, though, the most powerful appeal messages played to public fears about the intrinsic anti-capitalist threat posed by the existence of any type of cooperative in the American economy. "It's socialism!" emerged as a common cry in these advertisements. Advertisements often referred to national polls appearing to show that Americans did not want the federal government owning their utilities as part of a case against electric cooperatives even though cooperatives were owned by their members.[2]

Attacks on cooperatives as socialism gained enough traction during the height of the Cold War between the United States and the Soviet Union to sustain the power company strategy of hitting the cooperatives hard in the press whenever they could. Sometimes this came in the form of editorials by newspaper staff aligned with the power companies. For instance, in the *Aiken Standard* on August 12, 1953, the cooperatives were never mentioned directly, even as the editorial applauded the recent congressional decision to fund $400 million in hydroelectric development of the Niagara River by "five taxpaying, publicly-regulated electric companies." Instead, the editorial warned readers against "the 'creeping socialism' of which President Eisenhower recently spoke." The newspaper immediately followed with another editorial rehashing details of a recent *Saturday Evening Post* editorial decrying the horrors of "socialized electricity." Noting that private utilities paid $1.25 billion in federal and local taxes compared to $5 million paid by the cooperatives to state and local government in lieu of taxes, the editorial declared, "The price of socialism certainly comes high."[3] Other attacks were more direct, coming in the form of large newspaper advertisements that posed accusatory questions for the reader, such as, "Who asked you for permission to keep on building expensive socialistic power systems when every tax dollar and every pound of critical materials is needed for defense?" The answer provided by the advertisement text was a resounding: "Nobody!"[4]

Tensions between the investor-owned power companies and the cooperatives during the 1950s rose so high that the two sides even became embroiled in a protracted lawsuit over their respective advertising mascots. Created in 1926 by Alabama Power Company executive Ashton Collins, Reddy Kilowatt was a lighthearted figure with lightning bolts for limbs and torso and a light bulb for a nose. By the early 1950s, Reddy had been adopted as the spokes-character of nearly 200 power companies throughout the United States. When the National Rural Electric Cooperative Association (NRECA) came calling, seeking to license Reddy for use by the cooperatives, Collins declined, citing the "socialism" of the cooperatives and warning that he would pursue legal action if his trademark were infringed.[5] Not to be deterred, NRECA hired freelance artist Andrew McLay to come up with its own spokes-character in 1950—a grinning and waving character named Willie Wiredhand, that featured a light socket for a head, a wire for his torso, and an electrical plug for his pelvis and legs.

He appeared publicly for the first time in February 1951 in a contest to select the new spokes-character for the cooperatives and he was an immediate hit with customers. By the 1960s, Willie's popularity had soared sufficiently that NRECA upped their game, giving Willie Wiredhand his own line of comic books for the kids, allowing the cooperatives to educate families about the benefits of rural electrification as well as the evils of doing business with the investor-owned utilities.[6]

Collins and the commercial utilities were not amused by Willie's emergence in 1951. After a series of efforts by Collins to block Willie's appearance in cooperative publications, arguing not that Willie resembled Reddy but rather that merely using a cartoon figure to market electricity was a trademark infringement, Collins and several allied power companies created Reddy Kilowatt, Inc., to establish legal standing to sue. Reddy Kilowatt, Inc., filed suit in June 1953. What might be most surprising, though, is that even within the confines of this argument over advertising characters as a trademark infringement, Collins and utility companies grounded their legal argument in the concept of the direct competition for customers between the cooperatives and the investor-owned companies, in large part because of the "existing difference of opinion regarding public versus private power and private enterprise versus 'socialism.'"[7]

The case—*Reddy Kilowatt, Inc. v. Mid-Carolina Electric Cooperative, Inc., and National Rural Electric Cooperative Association*—appeared before the US District Court for South Carolina in June 1956. The district court found no trademark infringement through the cooperatives' use of Willie Wiredhand, and "no merit" in the contention that direct competition existed between the utility models because of the argument over whether the rural electrification model was a version of socialism.[8] Reddy Kilowatt, Inc., appealed to the US Court of Appeals Fourth Circuit, but a three-judge panel unanimously affirmed the lower court's ruling in January 1957.[9]

By the early 1960s, the cooperatives attempted to counter the politically freighted charge of socialism with advertisements of their own that highlighted the motivations of the investor-owned utilities. Advertising in *Living in South Carolina* in January 1963, NRECA touted its accomplishments in bringing electricity to "rural people [who had been] by-passed by stockholder power companies as too small or too unprofitable to serve" since the 1930s. Moreover, this same advertisement portrayed rural electrification as patriotic, highlighting increased farm production, improved rural living standards, and the creation of new jobs and opportunities as a "bonus for all Americans."[10] Cooperative editorials were even more damning, in one case critiquing a Duke Power Company advertisement during a Clemson football game that referred to Duke Power as "your local power

company." The editorial pointed out the absurdity of this claim by repro-
ducing the notice of a Duke Power stockholder meeting scheduled to take
place in Flemington, New Jersey, its corporate home.[11]

Other editorials from the cooperatives derided the power companies
for trying to establish monopolistic control over "the atomic electric development" in violation of the patent clause of the Atomic Energy Act.
Complaints about the power companies also included criticisms of the
hyper-capitalist model that are familiar today: high salaries for executives,
high advertising costs and loan interest (the costs of which were incorporated into rate levels for individual customers), monopolistic practices
that created "captive customers," and little risk of capital or loss of profits
because they enjoyed monopolistic control and regulatory protection.
Specific complaints focused on 15 percent profit levels, with 11 percent
of all utility revenue going to stockholders.[12] Beyond these immediate
concerns for the consumer, the cooperatives also frequently highlighted
aggressive and questionable behavior by the corporate utilities. In one
such instance in 1962, the *South Carolina Electric Co-Op News* reported on
South Carolina Electric & Gas Company (SCE&G) attempting to rewrite
its twenty-year contract with the City of Aiken, effectively doubling the
monthly price paid for powering the city's streetlights—all without ever
bothering to tell City of Aiken officials. Allen Mustard, the president of
SCE&G, reportedly dismissed the situation as "a mistake."[13]

Much of the rhetoric from the cooperatives focused on the ownership
of South Carolina's corporate utilities and the fact that the end-of-year
margins were sent "to New York and Boston investors" as profit, rather
than returned to the South Carolina customers of those utilities. Indeed,
many of the editorials in the cooperative publications contrasted the cooperatives with the corporate utilities by emphasizing the direct say that
cooperative customers had in "meeting in direct assembly . . . to personally cast a vote for members of their governing Board of Directors [and]
approve policies of the business, insuring local control, and freedom
from domination by small groups, special interests, or one-man dictator-
ship." Indeed, these same editorials even attempted to turn the common
refrain of the investor-owned utility message of the 1950s on its head,
claiming that "the widespread ownership of corporate and cooperative
private enterprises are . . . bulwarks against rampant socialism and dictato-
rial communism. As an electric Co-Op member, you can be most proud
of the fact that no other business in the U.S. is owned by so many individuals."[14]

By taking on the charge that cooperatives were socialistic directly, the
cooperatives hoped to blunt the long-running attempts of the investor-

owned companies to equate the cooperative model with socialist collectivism. In late 1960 and early 1961, *South Carolina Electric Co-Op News* even ran a series of articles by frequent cooperative columnist Kirby Able on "How to Defeat Communism," highlighting the evils of collectivism and the disappearance of private ownership "with the advent of statism."[15] One installment crystallized the tension between the cooperatives and the corporate utilities in the context of socialism, noting:

> It is hardly a secret that there has long been a well-financed campaign designed to associate Cooperatives with programs undesirable to our American way of life. The campaign over the years has been, in a general way, one that paints "free enterprise" as Christian and American and at the same time leaves the impression that Cooperatives are NOT free enterprise. That, of course, would suggest that Cooperatives are un-American and un-Christian, even though only making the insinuation rather than a bare statement. Those Americans identified with Cooperatives have always urged that the public accept Cooperatives as true free enterprise. Which, of course, they are.

Able concluded by pointing out that cooperatives "are the middle road approach" to closing the "ever-widening and more dangerous" gap between business and government. The cooperatives, this argument suggested, were better examples of and models for free enterprise than corporations themselves.[16]

Kirby Able's views were just another variation of a theme being expressed throughout the country about the role of the electric cooperatives. Speaking at the NRECA Annual Meeting in Dallas in 1961, Dr. Raymond W. Mack of Northwestern University enumerated effective approaches to communication with the public about the benefits of cooperatives. "Stress shared values," Mack said, such as competitiveness and progressivism. Most importantly, Mack insisted, "Cooperatives offer a free man's alternative to 'the Welfare State.' They are a potent weapon against monopoly; they are a bulwark against the polar evils of Fascism and Totalitarian Socialism."[17] As this argument continued to evolve into the mid-1960s, the cooperatives drew the distinction more often between "private enterprise" and "free enterprise," arguing that private enterprise was about private gain while free enterprise was democratic and committed to the public good. "There is nothing private about cooperatives," W. V. Thomas wrote in *Living in South Carolina* in July 1963. "Neither is there anything private about the type of enterprise that has made America great. The prize feather in our national cap is not *private* enterprise—it is *free* enterprise, and these are essentially different."[18]

Because the cooperatives most often served farmers and rural areas, cooperative publications frequently ran editorials highlighting the frustrations of farmers or encouraging behaviors that were beneficial to sustaining farm practices. One example was a December 1961 editorial deconstructing recent complaints in the media about a forthcoming rise in the cost of bread and the assumption that federal support prices on wheat played a role in the increase. Calling it "an old story with the food industry— passing the buck to the farmer," the editorial explained that farmers actually received "12 percent less for the USDA's typical 'market basket' today than [they] did in the 1947–49 period," while consumers paid more, in large part because of the 35 percent increase in marketing costs over that period.[19] Other articles highlighted the benefits of conservation and the role of local garden clubs in promoting this activity.[20] And the cooperatives proudly took credit not only for the success of America's farms but also for the nation's standing as a world leader in agriculture, noting, "Largely as a result of the REA victory, American agriculture has become the envy of the world, and it is our country's most potent weapon in the defense of democratic government."[21]

Similarly, the cooperatives advocated major national initiatives to prevent rural decline. One such proposal was the 1961 Area Redevelopment Bill in the US Senate, a piece of legislation intended to provide low-interest loans to stimulate new industry and redevelopment, offer federal funds to support the rural infrastructure needed for industrial growth, provide funding for technical training to residents, and offer technical assistance to communities to identify the needs and options for redevelopment of rural neighborhoods.[22] The cooperatives also reminded their customers that the work of the cooperatives was still not done, given that over a million Americans still did not have electricity in their homes as of February 1963, and that this was work that only the cooperatives would take on. More importantly, while 97 percent of homes in America had electricity as of that date, the work of the cooperatives was not complete so long as customers continued to add new appliances to their homes, necessitating additional transmission lines.[23] Still other stories focused on allegations of overcharging by investor-owned power companies—a NRECA argument that "allowed" for "6% as a fair rate of return" for the power companies, then treated the remainder as a "piped off" overcharge that lined the pockets of power company stockholders.[24] As a result of these different approaches to advocacy, the cooperatives made it clear that their interests were aligned with those of their member-customers, promoting loyalty and suggesting the presence of a potent ally when state-level political fights became necessary.

Competition between the cooperatives and the investor-owned utilities was fierce in other respects. One frequent refrain was criticism of the corporate utilities for "pirating" cooperative customers. One example emerged from the case of a Richland-Lexington District 5 public school near Irmo, which for many years had been a customer, along with a nearby church and dozens of rural homes, served by Mid-Carolina Electric Cooperative. After securing permission from the state Public Service Commission, South Carolina Electric & Gas, according to the *South Carolina Electric Co-Op News*, "built some 3½ miles of line from Irmo to serve the school," to the exclusion of the nearby church and homes. This was presented as "evidence of power company tactics in seeking to take away consumers already receiving service from another source."[25]

The tension between the electric cooperatives and the investor-owned utilities focused chiefly on areas that had once been rural and served by the cooperatives but, as cities expanded and suburbs appeared, and population density in these areas increased or if a large consumer (factories or schools) of electricity located in an area, then the investor-owned utilities often tried to wrestle the territory away from cooperatives now that it would be profitable to serve those areas. Concerns over intrusion by the investor-owned utility companies into territory controlled by the cooperatives led to frequent calls for fairness, perhaps most powerfully represented in "Operation Fair Play," a 1962 initiative to secure "protection under the law" for members of the cooperatives.[26] At the heart of this initiative was the recognition of the reality of changing boundaries between traditionally rural and urban landscapes. While backers of the corporate utilities often liked to frame the situation as cooperatives "expanding into suburban, city, and industrial areas," the reality was that urban and industrial centers were growing outward, spreading into territories long served by the cooperatives because the corporate utilities refused to serve them. Writing in February 1962, Terry Gunn, the editor of *Rural Electric Minuteman*, summarized the flaw in the claims advanced by the private sector suppliers:

> The propaganda is designed to lay the groundwork with city people, suburbanites, the general public, and with you so that your co-op territory may be taken away and turned over to a power company to serve. Thus, the commercial utility that was unwilling or unable to electrify the area when it was sparsely populated will now be handed the business when it has become more thickly

populated. After this happens a couple of times, the co-op is left with territory so thin that even cooperative enterprises will be unable to continue to provide service at rates you can afford to pay. The solution to this problem, Gunn argued, was not to have the cooperatives themselves wade into state politics but rather to have the private citizen members of the cooperatives put direct pressure on their legislators.[27]

Toward this end, the cooperatives had long made a point of keeping their customers politically informed. Perhaps the most striking example of this was the decision a year earlier, in March 1961, to publish the entire roster of the South Carolina General Assembly, replete with individual biographies on each member, "as a public service to our readers in order that you might become more familiar with those men and women who serve so well in public office."[28] In conjunction with Gunn's 1962 article, the *South Carolina Electric Co-Op News* even went so far as to urge the members of the Salkehatchie Electric Cooperative to contact Speaker of the House Sol Blatt to "let Mr. Blatt know of their support of the Fair Play bill," since he was the one man with "the power to send the bill to committee ... direct debate on the bill ... choose the timing of its appearance ... to control its destiny."[29]

By all accounts, the fight in the legislature was a brutal one. *South Carolina Electric Co-Op News* devoted the entirety of its March 1962 issue, using the opportunity to highlight the cooperatives' commitment to fair play for all. This included a "Statement of Principle and Purpose," which bluntly laid out the issue at hand: "The Electric Cooperatives of South Carolina do not desire or intend to take any customer or territory from any other power supplier, nor move into any town or city in our state. All we ask is to be allowed to continue to serve the consumers and territory we now serve."[30]

Columnist Kirby Able laid out the hypocrisy of the media outlets backing the corporate utilities more bluntly, noting that the *Columbia Record* was a fierce opponent of the cooperatives, even though it had just recently celebrated its membership in the Associated Press, "the world's oldest and largest news agency [and] a non-profit cooperative," touting the relationship as vital to the readers of the newspaper through "the benefits of a worldwide staff of expert newsmen." Able also pointed out that Duke Power, Carolina Power & Light, Virginia Electric Power, and SCE&G had all recently formed the Virginia-Carolina Nuclear Power Associates—a cooperative organization.[31]

As debate continued, many rural customers were startled to see their local mayors, town councils, and chambers of commerce from their rural communities come out against the Fair Play proposal. By early April 1962, thirty-nine towns had filed letters of opposition to Fair Play. Observers from the cooperatives noted that many of those elected officials fell into two groups: "Chamber of Commerce officials and . . . commercial power company officials." The good news was that none of the other two hundred communities in South Carolina had expressed opposition to Fair Play.[32] Tensions ratcheted up even further when SCE&G advertised in the Farm Bureau newspaper the *South Carolina Farmer* with a blistering attack on the cooperatives in an "effort to drive a wedge between Farm Bureau members and Co-Op members," who had long been close allies. Calling the move "a blatant disregard of a gentlemen's agreement on the type of advertising the Co-Ops and Power Companies" would place in the paper, the *South Carolina Electric Co-Op News* called on the *South Carolina Farmer* to take a strong stand against the power companies.[33] Ultimately, the Fair Play legislation failed during the 1962 session.[34]

Undaunted, the cooperatives were back at it the following year, introducing two Fair Play bills during the 1963 legislative session.[35] This time, the effort picked up important backing from South Carolina's farmers, as evinced by the endorsement of the South Carolina Council of Farmer Cooperatives on March 16.[36] Unfortunately, by the end of the session, little progress was made, and it would not be until six years later, when multiple issues between the cooperatives and the power companies emerged, that compromise on this front was possible.

One frequent rhetorical target of the investor-owned utilities was the system of credits that the cooperatives paid to their customers from revenues generated during the year. Profit-focused generators insisted that the credit system essentially functioned as a tax avoidance mechanism and created a drain on the federal government. Other observers rightly characterized the program by noting that the cooperatives' "so-called tax advantage . . . excluding their refunds from their taxable income . . . is available to every businessman. Any business can enter into a contractual agreement with those it serves to return to them savings resulting from their patronage and free itself from income tax on those amounts."[37] The cooperatives had another rejoinder, noting that the whole reason a Public Service Commission existed and regulated the corporate power companies was "because of abuses of the public welfare and trust by those very same power companies. The Public Service Commission was created to protect the consumer from the greed and poor service provided by those out-of-state-owned power companies."[38]

The cooperatives often distributed publications to their members highlighting the competition-killing tendencies of the investor-owned power companies. Speaking in early 1963, United States Representative Clarence

Cannon of Missouri, the chair of the US House Appropriations Committee, weighed in with an observation that was picked up by the cooperatives in South Carolina: "The power trust is making every effort to destroy REA [Rural Electrification Administration] and TVA [Tennessee Valley Authority]. They are making every effort to take over municipal ownership. They are overlooking no possible means of establishing a complete monopoly under which they would . . . be able to levy tribute on every consumer in America."[39]

While this tension over the so-called tax advantage of the cooperatives continued, other political battles were percolating to the national stage as well. By early 1961, a major political clash was brewing over federal development of the Savannah River Valley for electrification, most notably in the proposal of a new project at Trotters Shoals. Federal plans called for a total of eleven generating sites along the three-hundred-mile length of the Savannah River, capable of generating as much as 742,000 kilowatts. Clarks Hill was already online by that point, and the area behind Hartwell Dam was being filled with water so that it could go online.[40] The cooperatives defended the extensive Savannah River project by noting that public generation projects in 1960 routinely provided more power at a lower cost to the cooperatives than did commercial firms.[41]

Nevertheless, the cooperatives were concerned about the private utilities, particularly Duke Power, buying up all of the power that would be generated by these new dams and generating stations, then selling that power at a profit to its customers.[42] Using a conservationist argument, the cooperatives called for ownership of the river to "remain in the control and ownership of the people of the nation," rather than "only the stockholders in a giant out-of-state corporation."[43] By late 1962, Duke Power was objecting to federal funding for both the Trotters Shoals dam (which would have provided more capacity than Clarks Hill and Hartwell combined) and, somewhat inexplicably, its own proposed diversion dam and steam plant in the same vicinity.[44]

The conflict over Trotters Shoals was a major flashpoint of the 1962 elections in South Carolina. By the spring of 1962, the *South Carolina Electric Co-Op News* was reprinting comments by Olin D. Johnston (running for re-election to the US Senate), Donald Russell (nominated for governor), and Robert E. McNair (nominated for lieutenant governor) that universally expressed support for the rural electric cooperative program. This coverage brought with it a bit of editorial circumspection, though. "Yes, by their words ye shall know them," the paper's editor wrote, "but also by their *works* ye shall know them. We shall observe with interest."[45] By October 1962, the *South Carolina Electric Co-Op News* was carrying public statements from each of the South Carolina candidates for the US Senate and the US House of Representatives, Second District. That the main publication of the electric cooperatives could pull such responses from each candidate exemplifies the significance of the tension between the cooperatives and the corporate utilities for voters throughout the state.[46]

In 1962, popular outgoing governor Ernest Hollings ran for a US Senate seat against incumbent senator Olin D. Johnston, who was a long-term supporter of the state's electric cooperatives, in the Democratic primary. During the campaign, Hollings commented that he remained committed to the "full and comprehensive development of the Savannah River Basin," but added that his commitment "does not include Trotters Shoals, or any further dam construction." Hollings lost to Johnston by a 2-to-1 margin in the Democratic senatorial primary. Hollings' failed challenge to Johnston strengthened the hand of the champions of the Trotter Shoals project. In the fall general election, former University of South Carolina president Donald Russell won the governor's race easily. Senator Olin Johnston comfortably turned back the first serious Republican senatorial candidate of the modern era, journalist William Workman, 57 percent to 43 percent, and an inside analysis of the numbers suggested cooperative member votes went heavily for Johnston. Both the Johnston and Russell victories boded well for the Trotter Shoals project.[47]

Duke Power, however, continued to oppose the dam at Trotter Shoals. An early 1963 editorial in a cooperative publication sharply criticized Duke Power for its efforts to block the Trotters Shoals project along the Savannah River. "It's the same old story of the power interests against the people's rights that those who fought so long and hard for Clarks Hill and Hartwell Dams well remember. The Savannah River belongs to the people and not Duke Power Company."[48]

The Mead Paper Company's long-standing effort to establish a paper mill at nearby Calhoun Falls on the Savannah River also complicated the prospects for the Trotters Shoal project. In March 1963, *Living in South Carolina* (the newly retitled publication of the cooperatives) ran coverage of a new effort to block Mead's plans. Concerns focused on treated pulp mill waste polluting the downstream Clarks Hill reservoir and a lack of regular water flow from upstream Hartwell Dam that would make the paper mill's operations feasible.[49]

By late 1963, prospects for a new dam at Trotters Shoals under public control diminished when both Senator Strom Thurmond and incumbent governor Donald Russell (in a turnaround), took positions favoring Duke Power. In 1946, Thurmond, a decorated World War II veteran, ran for governor as a champion of progressive change and as a sharp critic of the powerful legislative establishment known as the "Barnwell Ring," led by House Speaker Sol Blatt and Senate Finance Chair Edgar Brown, both legislators from Barnwell County. As a war hero and an insurgent candidate, Thurmond stormed into the governorship with broad popular support. By 1963, Thurmond was a US senator who had gained support from many state business leaders. He had also emerged on the national scene as a fierce defender of segregation who used rhetoric that linked civil rights with socialism. The emergence of Thurmond's opposition was soon followed by Governor Russell's surprise opposition to the Trotters Shoals project and announcement of his support for the plans offered by Duke Power.[50] In an effort to prevent investor-owned control of Trotters Shoals, South Carolina's cooperatives published an old statement made by Thurmond seventeen years earlier in 1946. In that year, Thurmond argued vehemently against investor-owned control of projects along the river and in favor of federal management.[51]

Thurmond responded sharply upon learning about the publication of his past remarks. The senator claimed that the column gave the impression that he had written it explicitly for *Living in South Carolina* in 1963. Writing to the magazine two months later, he issued a clarifying statement critiquing the role of the federal government in South Carolina's affairs and signaling his clear opposition to the project at Trotters Shoals: "In 1946, I supported the plan for development of the Savannah River which appeared to offer the most benefits for the people of South Carolina. Today I favor the position which would offer the most benefits for the people of South Carolina. On neither occasion did I favor the building of a power apparatus for the benefit of a few bureaucrats."[52]

In spite of these setbacks, the cooperatives still had allies for the Trotters Shoals project at the national level, most notably from South Carolina senator Olin D. Johnston, often heralded by the cooperatives as not only a friend of rural electrification but also a "champion of the little man."[53] Johnston's influence was pivotal in securing US Senate committee approval for the Trotters Shoals project in mid-July 1963.[54] Although it would take several years before the project finally secured approval, the tide had begun to turn in favor of the cooperatives' argument for federal intervention in full development of the Savannah River. Ultimately, the long fight was finally settled when Congress passed the Flood Control Act of 1966, which authorized a new dam and reservoir at Trotters Shoals. Work would finally begin in 1974, despite lingering protests from environmentalists. The project is known today as the Richard B. Russell Dam and Lake.[55]

Anguished by signs that federal support was beginning to align with the interests of the cooperatives in 1963, the three power companies in

South Carolina attempted a hostile takeover of the cooperatives. During the renewal of arguments about taxing the cooperatives (which, curiously, had been initiated by the cooperatives themselves via a request to the South Carolina Tax Study Commission), Duke Power's John D. Hicks, representing all three commercial utilities operating in South Carolina, appeared before the commission in August 1963 and offered to "solve" the problem of setting taxation rates for the cooperatives. Rather than put the commission through the challenge of coming up with a fair taxation model, Hicks proposed that Duke would simply buy out all of the cooperatives in the state at "net book value," which he estimated at about sixty cents on the dollar of value. Under this plan, existing cooperative consumers would still enjoy "lower power rates," while new applicants—including those in rural areas—would be served at standard rates, setting up the possibility that immediate neighbors might end up paying two wildly different rates. Existing cooperative employees would all be offered jobs, and cooperative board members would be permitted to serve on an "Area Advisory Board." No promises were made, however, about how long these terms would remain in effect.[56]

The cooperatives abruptly declined this "offer" and lambasted it in the media. Responding publicly to the power company proposal, state cooperative association manager Bob Bennett countered, asking the South Carolina Tax Study Commission whether the power companies would consider being bought out at "net book value" (the basis for the offer on the cooperatives), why the power companies overcharge their customers routinely, why there was a significant variance in rates among the three power companies in different parts of the state, and whether the power company offer was made to avoid further scrutiny of their business practices. Bennett also called for an official state investigation into those power company business practices, noting, "Because electric Cooperatives are in effect organizations composed of individual consumers, we feel duty bound to protect the welfare, not only of our own members, but of all electrical consumers in South Carolina."[57] The fight got even nastier when the cooperatives then began publishing details about the ten-largest stockholders in SCE&G, Duke Power, and Carolina Power & Light. All of these stockholders proved to be out-of-state interests, many concentrated in New York. Only two of the thirty largest stockholders among the three companies were in the Carolinas.[58]

Finally, in 1969, in response to continual territorial disputes between cooperatives and investor-owned electric companies, the South Carolina General Assembly passed the Territorial Assignment Act. The legislature designed the Territorial Assignment Act to reduce the cost of electricity for customers through a reduction in duplication in facilities and ensuring certainty when either cooperatives or investor-owned companies built new infrastructure in an area. The legislature believed the act would increase efficiency and keep electricity rates low for customers. The legislature also hoped to eliminate "poaching," which occurred when the power companies were building transmission lines into each other's area surreptitiously to "poach" new loads. Poaching often resulted in expensive and unnecessary infrastructure paid for by the customers. While the cooperatives insisted this was the result of urban areas growing into their territory, the power companies countered that the cooperatives were coming into the markets on the fringes of settled communities to take customers. To address complaints about the taxation plan for the cooperatives, the new law (which had been promoted in the media as "a bill for taxing the state's electric cooperatives") repealed the cooperatives' tax exemptions but also ended the ad valorem tax exemption on commercial lines in rural areas.[59]

The Territorial Assignment Act required the Public Service Commission to designate territorial boundaries determining which electric utility supplier could serve any given area.[60] The Public Service Commission asked the electric utility suppliers to propose boundary lines, a process resulting in approximately five years of mapping and negotiating until finally a territorial map gained approval. The law also created rules to be followed in deciding who would serve customers in disputed areas. If a structure was wholly within an assigned territory, then the provider who was assigned that territory had the exclusive right to serve. The major issue with the Territorial Assignment Act arose when a customer was granted the choice between two providers because their building, structure, facility, or premises extended over two assigned territories. While the law itself specified a three-hundred-foot buffer between the customer's premises and nearby transmission lines, the vagueness of the law regarding what constituted a "premise" led to countless court battles. To help bring an end to litigation emerging from the vagueness of the Territorial Assignment Act, new rules were finally established in 2007 to help clarify which power authority was eligible when customer choice applied.

The two decades following the conclusion of World War II produced significant political controversy between South Carolina's electric cooperatives and the three investor-owned utilities that operated in the state. The latter often portrayed the cooperatives as a government-subsidized experiment designed to bring electricity to large portions of rural America in which population density rendered delivery of electric power unprofitable. Once the expensive infrastructure was built, however, investor-owned utilities proved eager to step in and serve areas already served by the cooperatives, especially in those areas where the population was growing due to new job creation and the development of suburbs. Expansion into these areas promised profits to the investor-owned utilities. The cooperatives collectively prevented the loss of service territory to the investor-owned utilities by appealing to their members to make themselves heard in the legislature and other public forums. The members rallied behind the cooperatives, which had brought them electric power when other entities would not.

Today, South Carolina's electric cooperatives still own nearly three-quarters of service lines in the state but have only one-fourth of the state's residents as members. Those member-consumers represent the strength of the cooperatives, now as well as then, and their involvement keeps the cooperatives laser-focused on their mission: serving the needs of their members.

7

Public Policy and Electric Power in the Late Twentieth Century

The final decades of the twentieth century generated political and policy issues that drew South Carolina's electric cooperatives into public discourse and political arenas on a series of matters that captured public attention. The electric cooperatives articulated their positions clearly to both their members and the larger public, and on occasion, drew them to the forefront of political debate on issues critical to the future of the cooperatives. During the 1970s, renewed controversy emerged over the construction of the Russell Dam (also known as the Trotters Shoals project). Other key issues involved new territorial battles with investor-owned South Carolina Electric & Gas Company (SCE&G) and national political tensions with presidential administrations seeking to fully privatize the production and distribution of electricity by eliminating or dramatically reducing federal financial support for rural electricity programs. These latter tensions reached a peak during the years of the Reagan administration. Though generally popular in South Carolina, the Reagan administration's oft-stated opposition to "big government" included opposition to the Rural Electrification Administration (REA), the cooperative system, and the very existence of public sector involvement in the generation and distribution of electricity.

At the state level, the political and business tension between the investor-owned utilities and the cooperatives diminished for a time after the passage of the Territorial Assignment Act in 1969. To be sure, while localities still quarreled over how territorial lines were drawn, by the early 1970s, most territorial maps had been completed throughout the state, and a general if fragile détente seemed to exist between investor-owned companies and member-owned cooperatives. It would be another fifteen years before battles over territory resumed, and when that fight finally resurfaced, it was fierce. But during the 1970s, the cooperatives and their private sector competitors enjoyed a comparatively peaceful coexistence in South Carolina.

Similarly, by 1976, the cooperatives seemed on the verge of victory in the fight over Trotters Shoals on the Savannah River, later known as the Richard B. Russell Dam and Lake. *Living in South Carolina* touted that achievement by reprinting the resolution adopted unanimously by the South Carolina Electric Cooperative Association (SCECA) at its December 1975 meeting. After hailing the environmental benefits of hydropower over nuclear and fossil fuel plants, the resolution underscored SCECA's unanimous support for Russell Dam project "for the reasons that such construction will provide many jobs for the unemployed [a key issue during the recession of 1973–79], an increase in recreational lands and wildlife for the use of citizens of this state and other states, and the electric power to be generated upon completion of the project will provide a lower energy cost than is presently available in South Carolina." The resolution also petitioned the governor, the General Assembly, and members of the federal delegation from South Carolina for their support for construction on the Russell Dam project.[1]

There were good reasons behind SCECA's support of the Russell Dam project. As SCECA executive vice president R. D. Bennett's editorial highlighted in January 1976, during the middle years of the 1970s, the United States faced a significant energy crisis involving its reliance on fossil fuels due to the Organization of the Petroleum Exporting Countries (OPEC) reduction in oil production and the related embargo. The 1973 oil crisis resulted in a four-fold increase in global oil prices over the span of six months, with prices substantially higher in the United States. These factors strained production of coal and other fuels, as Americans sought ready alternatives to oil, thus forcing rapid price increases in other fuel categories. Coal, for example, which was the primary source of electricity generation in the 1970s, nearly doubled in price from 1973 to 1974, thus driving energy prices even higher.[2] Bennett underscored the possibilities for South Carolina residents if alternative sources of fuel were not sought and utilized:

Already the use of electricity for nonessential purposes is being curtailed in some parts of the country. Rationing of electric power is a frighteningly real possibility in the very near future. Every knowledgeable person admits that the electric power situation in

America has reached a critical stage. If this nation is to maintain its
position of world leadership, and if our people are to retain their
existing level of living . . . if our American culture is to survive as
we know it . . . then we must generate every kilowatt of electricity
we can from whatever source we can devise.[3]

Bennett added that power generation from all possible sources remained essential to preventing the United States from falling behind the
Soviets, stressing that in the face of further proposed delays to the Russell Dam project, "The national security is a need that overrides all objections."[4]

The electric cooperatives' advocacy initially proved successful. By February 1976, a joint statement by South Carolina lieutenant governor Brantley Harvey and Representative Charles Powell emphasized the advantages
of the project for the state.[5] Even Senator Strom Thurmond, who had opposed the project in the early 1960s, now expressed his support. "I recognize there is some opposition to the Russell Dam project," Thurmond told
Living in South Carolina in 1976. "I am for the dam. We need the energy, the
employment, the recreation, the soil conservation and watershed measures it will provide. There's a tremendous demand coming for electric
power. We should take every step possible to meet that demand. The Russell Dam is part of it."[6] Similarly, Senator E. F. "Fritz" Hollings, a latecomer
in support for the project, also gave his endorsement. Angered by what
he perceived as the "smell of scandal" in relationships among the oil, gas,
and coal companies, Hollings expressed newfound support for the dam
project: "These are mammoth costs, but there's no question of feasibility
of the Russell Dam. It may have been a marginal project a few years ago,
but today the hydroelectric generation feature is of prime importance. I
support this project. It will be built."[7] Indeed, of South Carolina's six con-
gressmen that year, only James Mann of the Spartanburg-Greenville area
(Fourth District) opposed the project.[8] The project's most visible opponent remained South Carolina's first Republican governor of the modern
era, James B. Edwards.[9]

Despite this strong political support, the path forward for the Russell
Dam was far from a smooth one. Despite claims that the project was environmentally advantageous compared to fossil fuels and nuclear power,
the Russell Dam project had its detractors among environmentalists, who
expressed concerns over the project's ecological impact on native species,
water quality downriver from the project, and even concerns that earth-
quake activity could trigger a massive natural disaster once the lake was
stacked behind the dam.

The cooperatives, however, remained steadfast in their support of the Russell Dam and R. D. Bennett took off his gloves when criticizing the opposition. "Environmentalists, with a real interest in preserving our surroundings or improving them," Bennett claimed, "have endangered many worthwhile power producing projects. All Americans are concerned with the environment, but there comes a time when we must measure human progress against preservation of wildlife, of maintaining our level of living as against a rearranged wildlife habitat."[10]

That same month, Senator Thurmond introduced legislation that would boost pumped storage capabilities in the project to meet the objections of Governor Edwards that generating capacity was not sufficient to justify cost. Thurmond acknowledged the environmental objections but downplayed these concerns in comparison to the advantages of "energy production, recreational opportunities, and increased employment generated by construction."[11] Clearly the Oil Crisis and resulting recession had shifted the political landscape and the need for new electric generation capacity stood foremost in the minds of most politicians.

Interestingly, not all of Thurmond's relatives agreed with the popular senator. B. H. Thurmond of Edgefield wrote to *Living in South Carolina* expressing adamant opposition to the dam project, noting that "many power facilities now are not being used efficiently, [and] thousands of acres of timber would be flooded, ruining hunting in the area, eliminating trout fishing on the river forever."[12] SCECA responded by attributing rising costs to opponents of the project. "When the project is completed—and it will be completed," Bennett wrote, "the nation's taxpayers can blame these obstructionist groups for most of the additional cost."[13]

Criticism of environmental organizations often emerged from the SCECA and the cooperatives during the battle over the Trotters Shoals project. Robert W. Williams Jr., the manager of Pee Dee Electric Cooperative, devoted a portion of his April 1976 column to denouncing "this small, arrogant fraction" that was only interested in stopping new energy facilities without offering "any sensible alternative."[14] The outspoken Bennett went further, testifying before the Army Corps of Engineers in Elberton, Georgia, that the delays caused by environmentalists and conservationists were "nothing more than a rape of the taxpayer by these people who would deny the citizens of South Carolina and Georgia the benefits deriving from this project. . . . Rather than environmentalists, these people should be called obstructionists."[15] Two months later, Bennett even insisted that the proposed Russell Dam project was a "nonpolluting, environment-improving" project, a description not supported by the project's own environmental impact statement from 1974, which conceded that the loss of nearly twenty-seven thousand acres of bottom-land as wildlife habitat and the loss of more than fifty-nine thousand acres of timber resources as "adverse environmental effects."[16] When opponents suggested alternative energy projects—wind and solar in particular—the leadership of the cooperatives argued, with considerable justification, that such large-scale wind and solar projects would not be commercially viable for at least twenty to twenty-five years.

Bennett's frequent, often colorful, and sometimes off-putting comments about the environmentalists' objections to the Russell Dam became a staple of his public statements. Anti-communist rhetoric common during the Cold War peppered Bennett's remarks. Perhaps the most colorful and tendentious of Bennett's comments appeared in the Bicentennial issue of *Living in South Carolina,* when he proclaimed, "Nikita Khrushchev said the communists would bury America. Obstructionists are doing the spade work."[17] Bennett's style was replicated in columns by highly regarded local writers like Larry Young of the *Athens Daily News* and often reprinted in the cooperative publications. Writing in August 1976, Young critiqued efforts by groups like the Sierra Club, the Environmental Defense Fund, and the National Parks and Conservation Association to stop programs designed to export nuclear power generating technology—another favorite interest of the cooperatives in the 1970s—to other countries. "I suppose the need to be reassured is what motivates these people," wrote Young. "It has to be that or the fact that they want to live in a second-rate nation powerless to defend itself and afraid to step ahead in science, research, and technology."[18] In the eyes of Bennett, opponents of power generation projects seemed downright un-American.

Some cooperative members bristled at this kind of tendentious rhetoric. William Park Jr. of Seneca wrote to *Living in South Carolina* to excoriate the magazine for its coverage of the debate over the dam project. Referencing an October 1976 article, Park explained:

> Even though the Russell Dam will be a beneficial project from your
> viewpoint as a supplier of the state's electrical needs, it eludes me
> as to why you chose to print such an article. It seemed to me that
> this article is the typical, politically loaded, rhetorical emptiness
> that characterizes "debate" on so many controversial subjects today.
> Never once were any of the pertinent arguments concerning this
> project, pro or con, mentioned. The bulk of the article relied on
> name-calling to obtain the sympathy of readers . . . . Perhaps this is
> a politically effective method of swaying the public in your favor;
> I personally consider it high time the people in our nation began
> to divorce themselves from emotionalism about the issues and

appraise both sides of the problem intelligently and as dispassion-
ately as possible to arrive at decisions. Otherwise, they only end
up as puppets of the media and other rhetoricians.[19]

Nevertheless, the cooperative publications continued to pump out articles highlighting the benefits of the Russell Dam project. One 1977 article
suggested that completion of the dam project would mean that giant, re-
cord-sized reservoir trout, like those found at Santee Cooper, Clarks Hill,
and Hartwell, would result in similar catches behind the Russell Dam.[20]

The editors of the cooperative publications proved adept at presenting a persuasive narrative for cooperative members, repeatedly reminding them of the "good" the cooperatives were doing while also reminding
them of the flaws in their opponent's arguments. To contrast themselves
with the investor-owned utilities, SCECA also highlighted its many efforts
on behalf of local communities. A Kirby Able column in 1976, for example, emphasized that the cooperatives "have become vital parts of their
communities, not just as a utility, but as a concerned citizen of the community." Able went on to cite impressive statistics about nationwide cooperative participation in hundreds of community projects and emphasized
the cooperatives' role as job creators.[21]

The cooperatives seldom pulled punches when it came to defending
themselves against political attacks. During the 1976 presidential race, for
example, *Living in South Carolina* highlighted Republican incumbent Gerald Ford's opposition to the Rural Electrification Act in 1948 and his un-
favorable votes on 57 out of 68 bills related to rural electrification during
his lengthy service in Congress. As president, the magazine noted, Ford
also proposed a budget that capped the REA loan guarantee program.
Moreover, Ford's Agriculture secretary, Earl Butz, claimed that "the job
is done" in completing electrification in rural America. Democratic presidential candidate Jimmy Carter, by contrast, had long been a champion
of rural electrification.[22] While it is impossible to know what effect, if any,
the cooperatives' evaluation of the candidates had on the outcome, it is
worth noting that Carter was the last Democratic presidential nominee to
carry South Carolina, winning the state by a large margin, 56 percent to 43
percent in 1976.

Much to SCECA's surprise (and disappointment), however, President
Carter, concerned about the impact of federal spending on runaway inflation, came out against the Russell Dam project in 1977. Given the need
to pare federal spending to curb runway inflation, Carter decided to delay funding for the Russell Dam project. Carter asked for further study,
insisting that the delay would help balance the federal budget. Deficit
reduction was a pressing priority for the newly elected president trying

to combat "stagflation"—the twin devils of both inflation and unemployment. Congressman Butler Derrick, representing the district in which the Russell Dam was to be built, agreed with Carter's decision, much to the irritation of Bennett.[23] That irritation, however, did not prevent an outright endorsement of Derrick and most of the South Carolina congressional delegation just prior to the 1978 election. Declaring the featured elected officials "Friends All" for their open-minded approach to rural electrification, *Living in South Carolina*'s editors also reminded readers that former president Nixon—by then an easy foil in the wake of his 1974 resignation—had briefly abolished the REA program before Strom Thurmond fought to bring it back to life.[24] That same year, the editors of the cooperative publications reminded voters to support Question 2 on the statewide ballot, which proposed amending the state constitution to permit the electric cooperatives to negotiate with the South Carolina Public Service Authority to become joint owners of electric generation projects and transmission facilities.[25] That measure passed by a 55 percent to 45 percent margin.[26]

President Carter's sudden opposition to the Russell Dam nevertheless threatened to derail the project before it could be completed. Scrambling once again to defend the project, the colorful Bennett answered claims that hunting wild turkeys in the area would be diminished by the dam by holding aloft a bottle of Wild Turkey whiskey at a hearing in Anderson and insisting that it was the only wild turkey he had ever seen in the region before the Clarks Hill Dam project brought turkey stocking to the area.[27] Editorials later in the year attacked endangered species like the furbish lousewort, the snail darter, and the Appalachian monkeyface pearly mussel that had stopped various other energy projects, with SCECA writers concluding, "If it comes down to a choice, we opt for mankind."[28]

Other supporters of the Russell Dam project argued that, if it were abandoned, funding already invested in the project would be lost. Indeed, by May 1977, $17 million had already been spent, with another $21 million slated for that year's budget. The coffer dams at that point were nearly complete, meaning that the river flow would be diverted in short order. It was too late to stop the project, cooperatives and their allies argued, and if it were stopped, the waste would be unconscionable. WSPA-TV and Radio of Spartanburg also argued that the environmental claims were hogwash. "The Savannah was never noted as a trout stream," WSPA's editorial argued, "and all this talk of the environmentalists wanting to preserve the river for some species of fish is just so much smoke screen to delay the further development of a great river resource for electric power and water conservation."[29]

While the Russell Dam project floundered amidst disagreement over the approval of the additional funds needed to complete it, the cooperatives found themselves embroiled in other touchy political battles. Caught between advocacy for the Russell Dam project and President Carter's insistence that conservation was essential to America surviving the energy crisis, cooperative leaders like Bennett strained to navigate the nuances of debate. After months of preaching energy conservation in 1976 and 1977, for example, SCECA took a new approach in 1978, arguing that conservation might be somehow un-American. Criticizing closures at schools and universities in the fall and winter of 1977 in an effort to save energy, R. D. Bennett wrote, arguably engaging in hyperbole, "Is this the direction America wants to move? If we drastically cut the use of energy, we retard the growth and industrialization of this country."[30]

A month later, in the middle of a national coal strike, Bennett suggested just how dirty a word "conservation" had become: "*Conservation* of the nation's resources is the watchword of environmentalists and ecologists. *Wise utilization* is perhaps a more appropriate approach to our natural resources."[31] Such editorials inexplicably seemed to run in direct conflict with the articles that appeared in the same publications, such as one column encouraging customers to shop for appliances based on their Energy Efficiency Ratio (EER) in an effort to conserve energy and thus save money.[32] Yet Bennett seemed to jump back on the conservation bandwagon by mid-1979, urging customers to keep their air conditioners off until "you just *have to*" and pay attention to EER ratings and R-numbers on insulation. His concluding message: "Won't you start 'Thinking Conservation Now'?"[33]

The high-profile energy politics of the 1970s and early 1980s presented South Carolina's electric cooperatives with the challenge of championing hydroelectric projects as "clean" solutions to the energy crisis while also touting nuclear projects as safe and clean alternatives in an era when serious doubts about nuclear safety arose. Throughout the 1970s, the cooperatives advocated for the expansion of nuclear power, rightly arguing that supplies of oil and gas were rapidly dwindling and ultimately exhaustible as well as subject to the whims of international politics, while other alternative energy sources (solar, wind, etc.) could not be fully developed and implemented on a large-scale in time to meet pressing energy needs. "This means there is simply no way the world can get along without nuclear energy," *Living in South Carolina* writers argued in 1977. The argument likened opposition to nuclear power to advocacy for poverty, malnutrition, and disease: "Sincere and well-meaning people acting on emotions and insufficient information—people who would never in their wildest imaginations be aligned on the side of increasing poverty, suffering, and starvation in the world—are, through their opposition to nuclear energy development and their support of various restrictions and hindrances to other types of energy development, doing that very thing."[34] In November 1978, *Living in South Carolina* ran a feature story on how nuclear energy works, highlighting its affordability, reliability, and safety, in spite of growing doubts among the public over the wisdom of increasing reliance on nuclear power.[35]

Then in the early spring of 1979, the serious accident at the Three Mile Island nuclear plant in Pennsylvania shifted the dynamics of that conversation, at least for the short term. Located near Harrisburg, Pennsylvania, the Three Mile Island plant suffered a partial reactor meltdown on March 28, 1979, releasing xenon and iodine into the atmosphere (potentially affecting the health of some two million residents). The incident caused an estimated $2.4 billion in property damages and cost more than $1 billion to clean up.[36] The timing could not have been worse for the nuclear industry. Just twelve days earlier Hollywood had released the *China Syndrome*, which starred Jane Fonda and Michael Douglas as intrepid reporters who uncover and secretly film a nuclear power plant accident. The nuclear industry had dismissed the movie as a "character assassination of an entire industry" just days before the accident, with System Nuclear Research Engineer David Rossin of the investor-owned Commonwealth Edison Company of Chicago dismissing the film's premise entirely: "Frankly, I don't believe a serious accident could ever happen."[37]

The embarrassment of timing notwithstanding, the nuclear industry in general and the cooperatives in particular were not ready to abandon their support for nuclear energy. By the time the Three Mile Island incident occurred, South Carolina had the highest concentration of nuclear facilities in the United States—a trend that had begun with the construction of the Savannah River Plant near Aiken in the 1950s. By 1978, there were four nuclear plants operating in South Carolina, another six planned, and 40 percent of the state's power came from nuclear generation. One of those new plants was the V.C. Summer nuclear station at Jenkinsville in Fairfield County, which had been built by SCE&G but was one-third owned by Santee Cooper.[38] The serious accident at Three Mile Island also had little effect on the cooperatives' attitude toward and interest in nuclear investment. In December 1979, less than a year after the accident, thirty cooperatives in North and South Carolina announced their desire to buy part of the Catawba Nuclear Plant near Rock Hill from Charlotte-based Duke Power Company. The move was designed to remove Duke Power as a middleman between power generation and delivery and thus save money for the cooperatives and their members on electricity rates.[39]

Overall, Three Mile Island did little to lessen the enthusiasm of the cooperatives for nuclear power in South Carolina. The cooperatives continued to use their publications to make their position clear to their members. A February 1980 article, for example, highlighted that the electric power industry had "concluded that this nation must forge ahead with nuclear generation or face a grave economic slump in the 1990s."[40] The article went on to critique other power sources, concluding that coal facilities had too many environmental issues, water generation was limited, geothermal could account for no more than 2 percent of power production by the year 2000, and solar would not produce more than 6 percent of power needs.

In 1980, the Tennessee Valley Authority's (TVA) Clinch River Breeder Reactor Project in Roane County, Tennessee, faced pressure from federal authorities due to cost overruns. Originally approved and funded in 1972 at an estimated cost of $400 million, the Clinch River project escalated in cost each year so that by the time it was finally canceled in 1983, its estimated cost was $4 billion. While the energy industry had originally committed $250 million to the project in 1972, it refused to increase this investment, leaving federal taxpayers to carry the burden.[41] Nevertheless, the cooperatives continued to argue that they were on the right side of history, with the new executive vice president of SCECA, Al Ballard, appealing for the completion of the Clinch River nuclear project:

> The electric cooperatives have provided the kind of leadership that
> brought people to the halls of Congress, fighting first for light in
> dark areas, and later to defend many areas of agriculture. Coopera-
> tive people helped write and pass the first major rural development
> act, then used it to help rural America. They fought successfully
> to preserve the US Department of Agriculture and to expand the
> services of the Farmers Home Administration. . . . They are grass
> roots, people organizations.[42]

In addition to national issues, the cooperatives faced local public relations challenges on issues far removed from the controversies over nuclear power. In 1979, Robert L. Wingard, the general manager of Berkeley Electric Cooperative, pled guilty in the face of ten federal counts associated with "falsifying financial records to cover up unreasonable and improper expenditure of more than $750,000 in co-op funds."[43] US District Judge Solomon Blatt Jr. ultimately gave Wingard a six-month federal prison sentence, five years' probation, two years of public service, and a $7,500 fine.[44] In the wake of the case, Santee Cooper actually made a bid to buy out Berkeley Cooperative, but Berkeley's new leadership resisted. "Those were unfortunate things," new Berkeley Manager E. E. "Skip" Strickland explained in October 1980, "but they should be forgotten now. We have a big job to do." In an effort to limit any loss of public confidence, Berkeley touted its home energy audit program, its commitment to providing community services, its efforts to restructure electric rates to the benefit of members, and its initiative to send all of its trustees to training programs as examples of its obligation to do right by cooperative members.[45]

At the same time, the logjam on the Russell Dam project finally seemed to clear. With the dam already 30 percent completed by December 1979, local press reported that there were no longer funding roadblocks to the project. President Carter had signed off on the missing $45 million in funding in September 1979 (after vetoing the funds in 1978). Yet Third District congressman Butler Derrick remained opposed to the project. Derrick continued to call the appropriation "pork barrel" spending by the "Santa Claus committee." The only remaining obstacle, it seemed, was the lawsuit brought by environmentalists. The suit argued three objections to the project: diminished water quality, earthquake risk, and ecological devastation to areas impacted by the dam.[46] Additional problems surfaced two years later when archaeologists from the South Carolina's Institute of Archaeology and Anthropology identified six hundred prehistoric and historic sites, including significant Native American sites, an 1833 Calhoun family plantation site, and the remains of a Revolutionary War–era fort, Fort Independence, within the area to be flooded.[47] While these discoveries did little to slow the project, they did create yet another set of public relations issues for the cooperatives.

A federal judge finally thwarted environmentalist efforts to stop the opening of the dam in April 1982, affirming only that the US Army Corps of Engineers had failed to come up with a plan for mitigating fish and wildlife losses resulting from the project and giving the Corps sixty days to come up with a plan.[48] By that point, 90 percent of the dam and 65 percent of the project were complete.[49] The Russell Dam project faced another challenge in August 1982, when the City of Abbeville made plans to sue the Corps of Engineers, claiming that the Russell project would cause the Rocky River, which drained into the Savannah above the Russell project, to back up and thus reduce the generating capacity of their electric plant on Lake Secession.[50] Legislation introduced by Strom Thurmond and Butler Derrick eventually provided for federal reimbursement to the City of Abbeville for its losses.[51] Other challenges included a leak in the dam that began spewing eighty to ninety gallons per minute in May 1983;

the Corps of Engineers planned to fix that with the equivalent of caulking compound.[52] Ultimately, the Russell Dam structure was completed in September 1982, with plans for the first of eight generating turbines to go online in July 1984.[53] Actual power generation began in January 1985, with additional turbine units completed by 1992.[54]

Just as the cooperatives were finally wriggling free of the debate over the Russell Dam, new challenges surfaced in the form of new President Ronald Reagan's proposed 1981 budget changes to REA financing, which would have cut REA access to the Federal Financing Bank and limited the REA's access to low-interest loans. The cooperatives did not hesitate to speak out to inform their members. Writing in April 1981, SCECA executive vice president Al Ballard lambasted the proposed changes, highlighting the cooperatives' belief that the administration's opposition was essentially ideological:

> The Administration proposals for the Rural Electric program are inflationary, and they will do nothing to cut federal spending. . . . We have long suspected that REA was thrown on the chopping block primarily because of a philosophical opposition to the program. There is no other way to explain the present plans, which will destroy a great program and result in no benefit to the problem of inflation. . . . If adopted, rural people throughout America will have rate increases far beyond the normal increases [that] are predicted for the next few years. . . . We urge you to write or call your congressmen and senators and let them know of your concern over budget proposals for REA that do nothing but fuel inflation in rural America.[55]

The remainder of the April 1981 issue of *Living in South Carolina* was devoted to criticism of Reagan, not only on the proposed REA changes but also on his lack of attention to America's farmers. Larry Cribb, author of the monthly column "Across South Carolina," argued:

> If we have to subsidize the farmer, then so be it. Is that any different from subsidizing the automobile industry or the airline industry or big business in general? Big business calls their subsidies under different names like accelerated tax depreciation or tax-free revenue bonds or tax incentives—but regardless of what they are called, they are all the same. I think Americans would rather see their food supply protected at least equally to the manner that other segments of the business world are protected.[56]

Indeed, as 1984 dawned, it was clear that the fight between the Reagan administration and the cooperatives would continue. The January 1984 issue of *Living in South Carolina*, for example, led off with a profile piece on the December 1983 annual meeting, at which Democratic congressman (later senator) Tom Daschle of South Dakota told the assembled members, "Electric cooperatives have contributed as much to the success of this nation as any other program in the history of the country, and we must win this fight in order to be able to survive. . . . The administration would have you believe that electric cooperatives have done their job and should be dismantled. This is simply not so."[57]

The cooperatives spent the first part of 1984 lobbying the Congress to pass the Rural Electric Self Sufficiency Act, which was designed to raise the interest rates that electric cooperatives paid for loans from the REA, thus helping the REA to remain self-funding—an approach Reagan had consistently opposed.[58] The fight appears to have gotten especially ugly in summer 1984, when the Reagan administration allegedly coordinated a "media attack" designed to "cripple the rural electric program."[59]

In an effort to counter Reagan, cooperative publications borrowed a page from Reagan's own playbook, turning to Cold War–era patriotic appeals. Patrick T. Allen authored a guest editorial in 1984 that reminded members that Romania faced power shortages, and its communist government was cutting off power to its citizens. "We should all thank God for our democratic system of electric cooperatives," Allen concluded.[60] In an effort to mobilize their members, cooperatives' leaders also sometimes focused on stories that were clearly political in nature but did not have an obvious connection to the cooperatives. One such example was a feature story on efforts by a group of South Carolina legislators to drive a letter-writing campaign to the two 1984 presidential candidates, urging them to focus on the loss of domestic textile jobs in South Carolina because of cheap textile imports, before additional jobs evaporated. "We must convince both candidates of the importance of this matter to the people of our state and our nation," state Senator Robert Lake of Newberry insisted. "The President has the power to do something about this problem of textile import[s]."[61]

Reagan refused to back down, especially in the wake of his landslide re-election in 1984. By 1987, the cooperative publications were again running editorials about Reagan's proposals to eliminate the rural electrification program permanently.[62] Reagan's rhetoric, combined with his popularity, appears to have taken a toll on the cooperatives. In response to Reagan's relentless efforts to end the REA, the attacks on Reagan became more pointed as Reagan's second term drew to a close. "Unlike the Reagan

Administration," Larry Cribb wrote in June 1987, "the entire South Carolina Congressional Delegation is solidly in support of the Electric Cooperative Program."[63] A month later, Ballard criticized Reagan again: "Rural Electrification has offered the Reagan Administration a chance to cut the federal deficit by some $7.5 billion next fiscal year. And because one of the goals of the Administration has been to sap our program, the Administration officials oppose the offer. They are fighting it even though the ultimate benefit is to the cooperative member. . . . It's another clear signal to our South Carolina Congressional Delegation . . . that this Administration appears to have little concern about the problems of rural America."[64]

In that same issue appeared a lengthy article with detailed tips from the South Carolina congressional delegation about how to pen letters to one's representatives.[65] Ultimately, the cooperatives declared victory over the Reagan administration in late 1987. "We feel pretty confident the Rural Electrification Program is here to stay," Al Ballard wrote. "We've survived the most intense attack this program has ever witnessed—but the Reagan Administration has failed to do us in."[66] Nevertheless, lobbying of the congressional delegation for their support as a bulwark against the Reagan administration continued throughout 1988. "You're up against it when the administration is out to destroy your program, and that is exactly the situation we have now," York Congressman John Spratt told *Living in South Carolina* in June 1988."[67] With the Reagan presidency ended, the changeover to the George H. W. Bush administration did little initially to help the cooperatives. Beginning in 1989, the Treasury Department officials looked to impose prepayment penalties on loans that the cooperatives were trying to pay off early or refinance. This necessitated new legislation proposed by the South Carolina delegation to protect the cooperatives.[68] Occasionally, however, the Bush administration and the cooperatives found a few points of agreement. One example was the push for greater energy efficiency. After a 1990 IRS ruling that determined utility rebates for adopting energy-efficient appliances were taxable, the South Carolina cooperatives lobbied President Bush, through South Carolina Congressman Butler Derrick, to establish a tax exemption on such rebates through Bush's proposed "National Energy Strategy." To the surprise of the cooperatives, Bush agreed and added the exemption to his priorities.[69]

Still, the political relationship between the cooperatives and the Bush administration remained chiefly confrontational. The cooperatives battled with the administration over cuts in the 1990 Omnibus Budget Resolution Act, which eliminated funding for 25 percent of REA-insured loans and piggybacked on an additional 40 percent reduction in REA loan funds during the Reagan administration. In response, the South Carolina congressional delegation unanimously backed restoration of the REA loan funds to earlier levels. Other initiatives backed by the delegation included "support for long-range research to study the theory of global climate change."[70] In 1991, Congress determined that the REA should be categorized as a loan program rather than an expense item in the federal budget, forever changing the way the debate over the REA could be framed.[71]

While the cooperatives were taking on Reagan over loan funding earlier in the 1980s, a new fight emerged in South Carolina, again over territorial assignments. Beginning in January 1984, the South Carolina legislature considered two bills that would allow the electric cooperatives to retain their service areas after annexation of territory into cities. This issue arose due to the rapid growth of suburbs and exurbs in post–World War II South Carolina. As previously rural areas (long served by the cooperatives including after the territorial agreement of 1969), grew heavily populated, some of these areas were annexed into cities and towns, which cooperatives had previously not been allowed to serve under terms of the territorial agreement. Members were urged to write to their legislators to build support for the bills.[72] The SCECA even dug out a quote from Clyde Ellis, "a pioneer in rural electrification," that crystallized the issue: "We gain nothing and all of us waste resources by the bitter struggles which have always characterized the industry. . . . The first step must be for all electric suppliers to recognize the legitimacy and permanency of other types of suppliers. Then all of us could settle down to the task of serving our own areas, our own consumers, and the public interest, to the best of our ability."[73] The South Carolina Senate passed the bill in Spring 1984 on a rather lopsided 34–7 vote, and the bill passed the House shortly thereafter, and Governor Richard Riley signed the bill into law in June 1984.[74]

That measure would seem to have ended any renewed territorial controversies, but in 1989, rumors surfaced that South Carolina Electric & Gas Company (SCE&G) was jockeying for the opportunity to buy out several cooperatives in the state and thus take over their territories.[75] In the February 1989 issue of *Living in South Carolina*, Ballard characterized SCE&G as a "corporate predator [that] seeks to swallow up one or more Electric Cooperatives." Ballard was quick to underscore the paradox of SCE&G wanting to own territory that it had once adamantly refused to serve. At issue was a new bill introduced to the state legislature requiring a two-thirds vote of all cooperative members before a local cooperative could be dissolved. Under the state law then in effect, an investor-owned utility could dissolve a cooperative with the consent of as little as 3 percent of the members. Ballard again mobilized the letter-writing campaign, urging members to contact their representatives.[76]

South Carolina cooperatives also used their publications to communicate to members concerning the benefits of the cooperatives while also reminding them of the investor-owned utilities' dismissal of rural and underserved areas in the past. "Not long after World War II . . . I began construction of my house," wrote C. Richard Blackwell, a cooperative member from Little River. "[I] contacted SCE&G for service. I thought all was going fine until I looked up one day, and men and equipment were tearing down the line, and I said, 'Whoa! Wait a minute, I want you to connect me to your line.' They said, 'Sorry, material is needed worse somewhere else.'" Blackwell went on to explain SCE&G's choice to ignore rural folks or gouge them for connections when he was a child. The REA, he reminded readers, did the work for rural people that SCE&G would not. "Don't you ever, as a Co-op member, let somebody like SCE&G talk you into selling us out. This is our line—we own it."[77]

The cooperatives criticized SCE&G specifically for its takeover efforts, its insistence on raising rates while already turning a substantial profit, and its false claims that cooperatives did not pay any taxes. Ballard reminded cooperative members that SCE&G was seeking monopoly power in large areas of the state, and that, over the years, the utility had taken "millions of dollars in federal subsidies, and they enjoy them today . . ." Ballard emphasized how the company had dismissed the needs of rural people. "But not one can make up for the [SCE&G's] failure to pitch in and help rural people when they needed it," he concluded.[78]

In February 1989, Ballard held a press conference that was widely covered by the media and featured member speakers who recalled ill treatment by SCE&G in the early days of rural electrification. Henry Driessen Jr., a native of Hilton Head Island, touched a sensitive nerve when he told the story of Black residents of the island meeting with SCE&G to ask for power to be connected to the island, only to be told by SCE&G that doing so was not profitable because the residents were "only poor farmers, and they could not afford electricity."[79] Sonny Hanchel of Johns Island recalled SCE&G refusing to provide power to Johns Island when it was requested. "But [now that] Johns Island is growing, and developers have bought up land and want to develop the island," Hanchel explained. "We find ourselves now being invaded by SCE&G. We feel that it is illegal, and they're doing it very irresponsibly."[80] Columnist Charlie Walker, writing for Kingstree's weekly the News, summed up SCE&G's approach by comparing the company to the cow bird. Walter wrote:

SCE&G doesn't want to milk our cow. They want to butcher it. If we allow it to happen, your light bill is going to climb like a kite in a March wind. The reason I call this privately-owned utility a cow bird is because they have identical lifestyles. A cow bird doesn't build a nest, but they lay eggs in the nest of other birds. In 1939, the people of rural Williamsburg County had no electricity. The privately-owned power companies were not interested in running power lines. . . . In 1939, there were 10,000 pine trees for every house in Williamsburg County. But pine trees don't burn electricity, so the private utilities thumbed their noses at the people of rural Williamsburg County. Now where there was once nothing but forest there are populated areas. Today there are shopping centers where once there was nothing but open fields. Today the ugly duckling the private utilities once ignored has become a beautiful swan. And they are dumb enough to believe that the people they ignored are going to kill the fatted calf and welcome the prodigal power company?[81]

Such memories were ubiquitous among longtime cooperative members and families, and the stories they told were devastating to SCE&G's claims, motivating many others to come forward in support of the cooperatives. Even today, such sentiments linger. During a series of interviews completed between 2013 and 2015, numerous cooperative members recalled SCE&G's dismissal of potential rural customers. "They were just adamant about not putting wires out that far," Aiken Electric Cooperative member Shorty Caprell recalled, "because we wouldn't have sense enough, you know? [That] was the impression. Dumb farmers, they don't know how to use electricity anyway. When the power did come out from the REA, I think the power company then began to have second thoughts: 'Maybe we made a mistake, and maybe those people weren't as dumb as we thought they were. They're using power like crazy out there in the countryside.'"[82] Oscar Sadler of the York Electric Cooperative remembered Duke Power insisting on $500 per house for power to be strung along his road just after World War II. "Instead of telling us they didn't want to fool with us," Sadler recalled, "they just said, 'We'll charge you a rate we know you can't pay.'"[83] Bill Gibbons of Broad River Electric Cooperative described the cooperatives as completely changing the way rural people related to one another. "They changed the whole concept of who these people were," Gibbons said, "[And] when voting time comes, they get to the ballot box."[84]

In the face of SCE&G's hostile takeover attempts, the cooperative member community rose to defend itself. On March 6, 1989, when the House Labor, Commerce, and Industry Subcommittee held a public hearing on the proposed legislation in Columbia, more than 1,000 cooperative members showed up, even though only a small portion could be seated in the hearing room.[85] *Living in South Carolina* followed up in April with still more coverage, including a testimonial from Aiken cooperative member Ilene C. Harral.[86]

The tension that emerged from working for either the cooperatives or the investor-owned utilities and thus having to battle one's neighbors sometimes troubled folks on both sides. Robert Williams, who worked for York Electric Cooperative, remembered the territory battles with Duke even before territorial assignment. "Charlie Plemmons was their head guy outside at Duke Power," Williams recalled, "and he and I were good friends. We'd fight like you wouldn't believe during the day, then we'd go out to eat at night and have a good time."[87] Such tensions between friends and neighbors returned as SCE&G ratcheted up their competition with the cooperatives during the 1980s. Ultimately, a new law protecting the cooperatives passed in the Senate by a voice vote and in the House by a margin of 108 to 6.[88]

But territorial battles between SCE&G and the electric cooperatives were far from over despite the new legislation. In mid-1989, for example, representatives of the SCANA Corporation (SCE&G's parent company) appeared before a congressional subcommittee to ask that investor-owned utilities be eligible recipients of rural development funds, and that additional funds be made available by slashing loans to the cooperatives.[89] Almost simultaneously, Aiken Electric Cooperative took steps to protect a portion of its territory that had been annexed into the city of Aiken by offering to pay a 3.5 percent fee to the city for all power sales within the jurisdiction and thus discourage the city from turning the territory over to SCE&G. Aiken Electric Cooperative suggested that revenue from such a fee could top $44 million over ten years. SCE&G acknowledged Aiken Electric Cooperative's right to continue serving customers in the annexed area but noted that the City of Aiken was not obligated to protect cooperative customers in annexed areas. SCE&G also opposed the assignment of a franchise within city limits to cooperatives, even if they had once controlled that customer base before annexation.[90]

The territorial tensions increased to the point that the cooperatives announced: "investor-owned utilities have declared war." Speaking to the Board of Trustees of The Electric Cooperatives of South Carolina (ECSC) in the summer of 1989, attorney Crosby Lewis underscored the threat, citing evidence obtained in a lawsuit involving Berkeley Electric Cooperative: "Their objective is the acquisition of electric service territory. We discovered from their own business documents that SCE&G has been planning and implementing its long-range plans to oust the Cooperatives from the business of providing electrical service."[91] NRECA executive vice president Bob Bergland agreed. "It's the areas around the cities—Co-op territory—where the real growth is and the investor-owned utilities are going to try all they can to force you to sell out or to take you over," Bergland insisted. "They're coming at us hard, and they aren't going to let up."[92]

The fight over territory culminated in a November 28, 1989, ruling by the South Carolina Public Service Commission that state law prohibited investor-owned utilities from using annexation as a tool to claim new customers in areas controlled by the cooperatives. The case at hand specifically involved Johns Island in Berkeley Electric Cooperative's territory, where SCE&G had begun building power lines to serve a new shopping center on the island following Charleston's annexation of the island despite existing language in the state law that prohibited exactly this kind of duplication of service. Nevertheless, SCE&G announced their plans to appeal the ruling.[93] About a year later, Judge Luke Brown, a South Carolina Circuit Court judge, upheld the South Carolina Public Service Commission determination, noting, "This duplication activity [by SCE&G] was precisely what the General Assembly had determined was not in the public interest." Brown further added, "Cities have no right under the [South Carolina] Constitution to regulate electrical service. Any such right can be granted only by the Legislature."[94]

During the 1980s, electric cooperatives also focused attention on another critical issue: stimulating rural economic development.[95] As one article explained in 1989, "Electric cooperatives have an economic stake in . . . keeping customers on their lines, but the Co-ops also feel a strong social obligation to preserve a vital part of American society and a valuable way of life. This will not be possible unless these rural and suburban citizens have the same opportunities available to them."[96]

SCE&G bristled at such statements. For the better part of a year following Hurricane Hugo's landfall in South Carolina on September 21, 1989, hurricane recovery dominated the actions of cooperatives and investor-owned utilities alike. By September 1990, however, the conflict was on again, this time over proposed efforts to allow rural cooperatives to begin developing water and sewer systems in rural areas. In response, the National League of Cities testified to Congress that their plan—possibly in concert with SCE&G—was to expand through annexation and force the takeover of rural electric facilities. "The war is destined to start all over again," responded Al Ballard, the ECSC executive vice president.[97]

Also threatening to the investor-owned utilities was a new focus by the cooperatives in creating subsidiaries that functioned as real estate development corporations. As one article noted in November 1990, "One of [Aiken Development Corporation's] main current activities centers around the establishment of a state-of-the-art research park, which, when activated, is expected to attract some of the major names in high-tech industry."[98] Put simply, if the cooperatives were now in the business of commercial real estate and building industrial parks that would also be serviced by their power generation, the investor-owned utilities would be able to capture a smaller share of that pie. As of November 1990, Aiken, Black River, Coastal, Fairfield, Mid-Carolina, Pee Dee, Tri-County, and York electric cooperatives were either investors in or owners of commercial development buildings or industrial parks located in their service areas.[99]

This change in focus prompted some observers to caution the electric cooperatives about remembering their mission. Robert M. Hitt, then the managing editor of *The State* newspaper, told the December 1990 meeting of the state's electric cooperatives.

> You are generally perceived by the public as having an excellent relationship with your customer owners, . . . I do think, however, that it is important for you to continue to remember that you are an Electric Co-op. You're not in the real estate business, not in land development, not involved in a lot of businesses outside the realm of providing electricity. When you think about it, it is peculiar to Electric Co-ops that your greatest vulnerability is your own success. That's ironic.[100]

Undeterred by loss after loss in the courts and the legislature, SCANA and its SCE&G subsidiary continued to attack the cooperatives into the early 1990s. In early 1991, SCANA's focus was on lobbying Congress to restrict the cooperatives' ability to borrow money to expand infrastructure to serve new loads from development occurring in the cooperative territories.[101]

The cooperatives, meanwhile, continued doing what they did best—building goodwill with members and the public. In October 1991, for example, the City of Bennettsville announced that it had chosen to become the first municipality with its own electric utility to choose an electric cooperative (Marlboro) to serve as its wholesale power supplier. Bennettsville Mayor Wanda Stanton explained why: "The Co-op has attractive rates, but more importantly, we needed a power supplier that gave the city of Bennettsville a voice in decisions affecting its electrical service. With the co-op system, we now have that voice. Before we were at the mercy of the power company."[102]

By the mid-1990s, the South Carolina cooperatives had weathered innumerable storms, some of their own making, some brought on by competitors who had always opposed the existence of the cooperatives. In the end, it was probably the overall honesty and directness of the cooperatives, and their strong connection with their members, that allowed them to count on elected officials to support them. Bobby Tuggle, who served as vice president of customer service for Berkeley Electric Cooperative and was often involved in working with the state legislature, remembered the key to good relationships with legislators. "We were always straightforward with them," Tuggle said. "If you lie to somebody one time, you might do it again. We were never going to do that. . . . Sometimes, maybe the truth wasn't the most helpful, but we always told them the truth about any issue we were dealing with."[103] Tuggle's comment reflected what had always been the greatest strength of South Carolina's electric cooperatives: their members could trust what they said. That trust, and the cooperatives' commitment to serving their members, proved valuable as 2006 marked a turning point in the cooperatives' working relationship with the state's investor-owned utilities (IOUs). Thanks in part to the cooperatives' reputation and their trust in Keller Kissam, at the time SCE&G's president of retail operations, co-ops and IOUs were able to resolve remaining territorial disputes through a years-long mapping process of utility service in South Carolina. Such accomplishments deserved celebrating, but not for long as the state's electric cooperatives would face new challenges in the late twentieth and early twenty-first centuries.

From Water Closets
to Weatherization

s the membership of South Carolina's electric cooperatives expanded, so did the cooperatives' involvement in South Carolina's rural communities. Beginning in the 1970s, the cooperatives undertook new projects to address lingering rural issues. One of the largest issues targeted by the electric cooperatives was substandard housing. Even in the latter half of the twentieth century, many rural South Carolinians were still living in homes that were of significantly lower quality than those of their urban counterparts. Over the past fifty years, the cooperatives have strived to rectify that inequality through innovative housing programs. Two of these programs, "John's Johns" and Help My House®, have not only substantially improved the lives of South Carolinians but also indelibly impacted state and federal housing policy.

While the cooperatives' rural electrification project of the 1930s and 1940s dramatically improved the quality of life for rural South Carolinians, decades later many of their members still lived without modern amenities: most notably, indoor plumbing. The 1970 census determined that South Carolina was first in the nation for outdoor privies (i.e., "outhouses") and found that a staggering 149,300 homes in the state lacked adequate plumbing.[1] Governor John West's Privy Project (known among the governor's aides as "John's Johns") presented a creative solution to the problem in the form of affordable "snap-on" bathrooms.[2] Delivering these units would be a major step toward bringing rural South Carolina into the twentieth century. But as West acknowledged, tackling such an undertaking alone appeared unfeasible even for a governor. Only by partnering with the state's electric cooperatives was Governor West able to implement his plan and help thousands of South Carolinians who were languishing in substandard housing.

To fully understand the Privy Project, it is necessary to understand the political context for Governor West's administration. His groundbreaking housing initiative was built upon the groundwork laid by two fellow South Carolina politicians: his predecessor, Governor Robert McNair, and US senator Ernest "Fritz" Hollings. On April 21, 1969, Governor McNair addressed the Carolinas Council of Housing and Redevelopment Officials, promising what West—at that time lieutenant governor—called, "[a] new commitment at the state level to solving the housing problems of South Carolina."[3] West viewed McNair's speech as a "turning point" for housing in the state. A few months later, McNair would appoint the Advisory Commission on Housing, which West described as, "[the] primary vehicle for mobilizing support and resources [for housing projects] at the state level." McNair made West the chairman of this new commission, which he served on through his last year as lieutenant governor.[4] It was here that West "became deeply and personally aware of the critical housing situation which exists [in South Carolina]." While he admired McNair's efforts, West saw that, on the whole, they were "doing little more than holding our own, and perhaps not even that much."[5]

Incited by what he saw during his lieutenant governorship, when West became governor himself, he "placed the issue of housing high on the list of priorities for [his] administration" and pledged in his inaugural address that "we can, and we shall, in the next four years, initiate new and innovative programs which will in our time provide adequate housing for all our citizens."[6] As one of the first acts of his administration, he worked towards this end by appointing Charleston banker Hugh Lane Sr., to the chairman seat he had once held. Lane, who West described fondly as a "bulldog," would soon prove indispensable to the administration and provide the idea for a "snap-on" bathroom that turned into the Privy Project.[7] If not for the work of Governor McNair and his establishment of the Advisory Commission on Housing, it is possible that Lane never would have worked for West and nothing would have come of his idea.

Concurrent to Governor McNair's reinvigoration of South Carolina's housing efforts, Senator Hollings took similarly catalytic action. In 1968 and 1969, Hollings toured through impoverished areas of South Carolina accompanied by various NAACP officials.[8] On these "hunger tours," as they would later be called, he was shocked by the conditions in which so many were still living. In February 1969, Hollings recounted his findings to the US Senate Select Committee on Nutrition and Human Needs, and his testimony drew considerable attention. Senators, members of the press corps, and visitors packed in the hearing room watched and listened in disbelief as Hollings dictated dozens of tragically poignant scenes of human suffering. Several of these scenes were a result of poor sanitation and insufficient restroom facilities. In one particularly disturbing case, he described a part of Greenville where, "88 families were required to use one toilet, the seat of which had been burned for firewood."[9] Hollings argued that unless underlying living conditions were improved, broader initiatives to address issues like public health were futile. "There is no use to get the child with the worms and give him shots [if] he is back out in the fecal matter, without toilets, and he has the worms back in 48 hours," he said.[10] After eloquently making his case for change, Hollings concluded with a call to action. "We've got work to do in our backyard . . . ," Hollings declared, "and I'd rather clean it up than cover it up."

Hollings's "hunger tours" and subsequent Senate testimonies were extremely effective, allowing the Senator to successfully advocate for the expansion of food stamps and other federal aid programs.[11] Recognizing this, when Governor West took office in 1971, he decided to take his own tour.[12] While Hollings's policy goals were primarily focused on starvation and malnutrition—he published *The Case Against Hunger: A Demand For A National Policy* in June 1970—West was more concerned with housing.[13] To make his "housing tour" a reality, West recruited a young Jim Clyburn as his aide. Clyburn, who had been working on housing issues as the executive director of South Carolina's Commission for Farm Workers, proved more than up to the task.[14] "After he brought me into the Governor's office [as his aide for human resources]," Clyburn recalled, "I organized a tour of communities that had been left behind, suffering from persistent poverty, hunger, and substandard housing." On what West called a "raw February day" in 1971, he, Clyburn, and Senator Hollings embarked on their tour.[15] Clyburn's efforts proved to be crucial. West said he was "instrumental in calling attention to the problems" in Charleston, specifically, where Clyburn had lived before joining the governor's staff.[16] Given his experience as chairman of the Advisory Commission on Housing, West was well aware of South Carolina's housing situation, but even he was not prepared for what they saw on the tour. "The housing was atrocious," West said. "Old people were living in almost huts. People were just appalled by the conditions." It was clear to West that there were many critical housing issues that needed to be addressed, but he was struck by one in particular that was all too common, "A lot of the people did not have indoor plumbing."[17]

Governor West understood that housing issues like insufficient plumbing were at least partially a consequence of funding sources prioritizing urban areas of the state over the rural ones. "[M]any of our housing problems exist in rural areas," West said in a speech to the Carolinas Council of

Housing and Redevelopment Officials in April 1971, "Many of them far-removed from programs which might exist in urban sections of the state."[18] He noted that while improvements had been made on the indoor plumbing issue since the 1960 census, the state's progress was woefully slow and not something to celebrate.[19] At the time, most cities and towns in South Carolina did not have a housing authority, which West believed handicapped the speed of the state's housing efforts and prevented assistance from reaching the rural areas that needed it most.[20] However, when he proposed the State Housing Authority—which he would establish in June of that year—he did so with the intention that the organization would coordinate federal, state, and local efforts and complement existing housing initiatives.[21] In order for it to work, and for West's administration to successfully confront the indoor plumbing issue, he needed a strong partner, one that was a zealous advocate for rural South Carolina. A few weeks earlier, he had found one: South Carolina's electric cooperatives.

In March 1971, Governor West met with R. D. Bennett, executive vice president of the South Carolina Electric Cooperative Association, and Al Ballard, the SCECA's director of industrial and community development, and issued a statement pledging his full support to their Stand Tall Commission.[22] This commission was a rural development program that Bennett and Ballard had founded at the cooperatives the previous year. As Bennett wrote in a column titled "Bring Our Kids Home" in the July 1970 edition of *Living in South Carolina*, the goal of the Stand Tall Commission was to revitalize rural South Carolina and stem the exodus of young people by providing communities with, among other things, "good job opportunities, modern housing, water under pressure, recreational facilities, and other modern conveniences."[23] One of the primary functions of the commission was as a conduit between rural communities and the state and federal governments. For example, volunteers for the Stand Tall subcommittee on housing would seek out poor housing, survey the residents, and help them apply for home improvement loans from the Farmers' Home Administration and other governmental entities.[24]

West was quite taken with the cooperatives and the Stand Tall Commission. In a May 1971 speech to the Rural Electric Statewide Managers Association (RESMA)—where Bennett was elected president—West referred to the cooperatives as a "full-time partner" in his housing endeavors and called the Stand Tall Commission "one of the most ambitious programs of human resource development our state has seen," encouraging the other state associations' managers to organize commissions of their own in their home states.[25] The governor continued to shower praise on the Stand Tall Commission when he addressed the cooperatives that December, saying that the work of the commission in the intervening months since his last address proved that his "confidence [had] been more than justified."[26] West believed that the Stand Tall Commission could be the key to reaching the rural areas that had gone overlooked: "The Stand Tall Commission has emerged as a visible and effective organization carrying out the type of valuable grass roots work so necessary to reach the people of this state most in need. It has been the same self-help approach which first brought electric power to rural South Carolina, and I am convinced that it is this approach which can also bring many, many more everyday necessities and conveniences to those South Carolinians who live away from the metropolitan areas."

When Governor West needed assistance to tackle the state's indoor plumbing crisis, the cooperatives and the Stand Tall Commission were the obvious choices for the undertaking. In fact, the Stand Tall Commission had already been working on the issue, helping people apply for Farmers' Home Administration loans to install "modern bathrooms" in their homes.[27] However, the governor's new bathroom initiative would be different. Hugh Lane brought West the idea of a prefabricated "snap-on" bathroom that could be attached to homes without indoor plumbing.[28] This would be an affordable, simple, and quick solution to the problem that plagued thousands of people in the state. But these units were more than just bathrooms, they also included a bathtub, wash basin, hot water heater (which could be connected to the kitchen), and an overhead electric heater—all things that many homes still lacked—all for the price of $1,000.[29] If these units could be manufactured and delivered at that price, it would be a gamechanger for rural housing in the state. There was just one problem: the State Housing Authority was broke. The state legislature had not appropriated any funds for it. Through dogged effort, Lane was able to secure $500,000 in federal funds over the course of the agency's first year, but for the first snap-on bathroom West sought an alternative source of capital: the electric cooperatives.[30]

"The Governor's Office called once again," reads the first line of a July 1972 article from *Living in South Carolina*. "And once again the electric cooperatives of South Carolina responded."[31] Governor West asked Bennett and Ballard at the Stand Tall Commission for their help on the snap-on bathroom pilot. The two men then took it up with W. H. Norris, manager of Tri-County Electric Cooperative, and convinced him that the cooperative should donate the pilot unit. Norris agreed and, after securing approval from his board of trustees, did just that. The result was not only the first snap-on bathroom in South Carolina, but the first in the entire nation. When the cooperatives held a dedication ceremony at recipient and Tri-County member Almeta Dunlap's home, the governor was effusive in his praise for the cooperatives. "Again the electric cooperatives have played a leading roll [sic] in making better life for all the people in rural South Carolina," said West, ". . . through the Stand Tall Commission . . . they have worked with us anytime, day or night."[32] West envisioned this pilot unit as the first of many to be used throughout the state. "It is better to light one candle then [sic] to curse the darkness," said West. "This is not a single candle, but the first of many hundreds of thousands to make better life for our people." That August he would highlight the success of this pilot in a grant request to the US Department of Housing and Urban Development (HUD), asking for $190,000 to put a demonstration model in every county in South Carolina.[33] However, in his remarks at the dedication ceremony, West concluded that government alone could not make this initiative successful, but emphasized that "as long as we get team work, we will gain our goals."[34]

This was far from the end of the cooperatives' involvement in this project. As West noted at the dedication (and later in his grant request to HUD), to bring these bathroom units to people's homes, there needed to be "technical education centers to train people to install" them.[35] The cooperatives, which already provided education opportunities through the Stand Tall Commission, were once again the ideal partner. "The co-ops were instrumental in bringing electricity to many rural communities," recalled Clyburn in 2021, "and this initiative sought to tap their expertise to connect households in need with a pre-fabricated bathroom."[36] When President Richard Nixon placed a moratorium on housing subsidies in 1973, West testified before a Senate subcommittee that April about the cost-effectiveness of his snap-on bathrooms and claimed that if he relied on the cooperatives to provide technical education, then the cost of the initiative could be even lower than previous estimates. "This is an example of involving more and more people to solve the problem that really is the toughest part of our housing program," testified West.[37]

Thanks to the immense support of the cooperatives jumpstarting the initiative, Governor West's Privy Project—the humorous "John's Johns," a riff on the name of popular port-a-potty company, Don's Johns—was a resounding success. By July 1973, the University of South Carolina's School of Engineering, contracted by the governor's office, had produced a prototype of the snap-on unit that could be mass manufactured. By that point, many units had already been installed and three hundred more applications were pending.[38] Under West's administration, the state went from first in outdoor privies to first in snap-on bathrooms.[39] The public was grateful for his efforts and even gave him an endearing new nickname.

"I was called the privy governor at the time," West humorously recalled many years later.

The Privy Project is one of the premier examples of the cooperatives successfully sparking change through government partnership. If the cooperatives, with their expertise, resources, and manpower, had not partnered with Governor West and his struggling State Housing Authority, it is possible the idea for the snap-on bathroom may have remained just that, an idea. But because of the cooperatives' investment in improving their communities, they were able to change lives. This is more than just hyperbole. When Governor West retraced his "housing tour" steps in August 1973, he observed there was "tangible evidence" of progress in the communities he visited.[40] His housing programs had significantly increased standards of living, but it was the Privy Project that had been especially impactful. One of West's stops was at the two-room frame house of Eliza Palmer, an eighty-year-old blind woman.[41] She was the recipient of, in her words, the "wonderful" experimental toilet the governor's office was testing in Berkeley County. This chemical-based alternative to the regular snap-on model would allow even people without running water to have a sanitary toilet for the first time. When West stopped by Mrs. Palmer's home, she was so overwhelmed with gratitude that, in what *The State* called the "most dramatic moment of the day," she clasped Governor West's hand and spontaneously began reciting Psalm 23 (with West soon joining her). This tender moment speaks to the profound significance that a toilet, an amenity people living in cities had taken for granted for decades, represented to people in rural South Carolina who for so long went without one. The work the cooperatives did on West's Privy Project was about more than just bathrooms, it was about giving rural people a sense of pride and, in the words of the Stand Tall Commission's housing manual, "[creating] in their mind a whole new concept of the future available to their children."[42]

The impact of the initiatives the cooperatives and Governor John West jumpstarted would reverberate into the coming decades. Rural housing improved significantly, and many people were able to enjoy substantial quality-of-life improvements that would have been unattainable only a generation prior. However, even well into the early 2000s, there were rural South Carolinians who remained in low-quality, energy-inefficient housing who had to choose between paying reasonable power bills and keeping their homes at a bearable temperature in the state's volatile climate—often getting neither. The cooperatives themselves also faced a serious dilemma. The state was growing in population. Cooperatives needed new electricity generation assets. However, the environmental agenda of the incoming

Obama administration complicated the cooperatives' predicament and had the potential to make the generation of electricity more expensive. This put the cooperatives in a bind: they needed a way to meet their members' needs and ensure they were living comfortably while also keeping rates low and reducing carbon dioxide emissions. In 2009, they developed Help My House® as a common sense, member-oriented solution to this Catch-22. Much like John's Johns, Help My House, which sought to weatherize and retrofit members' energy-inefficient homes with a novel funding mechanism called on-bill financing (OBF), soon gained national attention and became the basis for state and federal legislation.

During the first decade of the twenty-first century, the cooperatives found themselves in a dilemma. South Carolina was growing and the state's energy needs grew alongside it. From 1998 to 2008, the cooperatives' total load (the cumulative amount of energy their members used) increased an average of 5.2 percent every year; if the trend held for another five years, total load would be double its 1998 level.[43] To avoid brown-outs (throttling member energy use), the cooperatives weighed whether new generation assets, specifically, new nuclear power facilities near Jenkinsville and a coal power plant in Johnson should be built. If possible, the cooperatives wanted to avoid reliance on expensive nuclear facilities, which were estimated at the time to cost $4 billion—with members footing the bill.[44] However, coal, while a cheaper alternative to nuclear, was not an easy sell, either. If constructed, it would be one of the last new coal-fired plants in the country and, given heightened awareness of coal's negatives environmental impact, the building of a new coal-fueled plant loomed as highly controversial.

While the cooperatives' energy needs continued to grow rapidly, environmental law and politics evolved as well. In 2007, the Supreme Court held in *Massachusetts v. EPA* that carbon dioxide (CO_2) qualified as a pollutant under the Clean Air Act, which meant that the Environmental Protection Agency (EPA) could regulate it.[45] Though the EPA under the George W. Bush administration seemed willing to run out the clock on the issue without taking action, cooperatives believed the next administration was unlikely to follow suit. At the time, Senator Barack Obama was campaigning for president on ambitious promises of "hope and change," declaring his intent to cut CO_2 emissions by 80 percent and invest $150 billion in clean energy if elected. While the Bush administration was content to take a hands-off approach to environmental policy, Senator Obama promised to develop a firm plan to limit carbon emissions.[46] When President Obama entered office in 2009, one of the first bills to come to a vote was the American Clean Energy and Security Act (otherwise known as the Waxman-Markey bill, or "cap and trade"), which passed the House on a close 219–212 that June. Among other things, the bill targeted CO_2 by setting a goal of reducing emissions by 17 percent from 2005 levels by 2020.[47] To achieve that goal, generating entities would be given an allowance of how much CO_2 they could emit. To exceed that limit would require permits, an economic disincentive intended to help reduce pollution.

The legislation had major implications for the cooperatives. At the time, more than 80 percent of the electricity delivered by Santee Cooper and Central to the cooperatives came from coal plants, which emitted significantly more CO_2 than plants fueled by other sources.[48] If the bill were to pass (and especially if other more restrictive bills followed), cooperatives would have to pay significantly more for wholesale power purchased from generating entities and those additional costs would inevitably trickle down to their members in the form of higher electric bills. This prospect further complicated the cooperatives' challenge with the generation of electricity. Given the options at that time, no matter what they chose, it was going to raise the unit cost of electricity to members. Mike Couick, CEO of the cooperatives' statewide association, The Electric Cooperatives of South Carolina (ECSC), took those concerns to US Representative John Spratt, the same hometown congressman for whom he had worked as a legal aide in the early 1980s. "I sat down with Congressman Spratt lamenting that everything Congress had looked at was going to be a lot more expensive for co-op members," Couick recalled. "He said, 'We've got to do something to help these folks. Bring us back some ideas.'"[49]

One option the cooperatives had been exploring for several years before Couick's meeting with Congressman Spratt was energy efficiency and use reduction. In 2007, Central Electric Power Cooperative, the power supply aggregator for the state's cooperatives, passed a resolution to, among other things, commit to offering "conservation and energy efficiency programs designed to reduce the growth in demand and energy on our system" and to "encourage partnerships which promote research to limit emissions from power generation, encourage conservation and enhance energy efficiency."[50] Ron Calcaterra, CEO of Central, and the Renewable Resources and Energy Efficiency Committee (R2E2) convinced the board to adopt these measures with the help of GDS Associates, Inc., an engineering consulting firm. "We wanted a third party to come in, an independent party to come in and talk to the board," said Calcaterra. "I didn't want it coming from Central staffers. I wanted an independent party to support or give [reasons] why this would be good."[51]

In the study GDS conducted and subsequently reported to the board, they outlined over a hundred energy efficiency measures that would be cost-effective for the cooperatives to implement.[52] This was the genesis of several cooperative energy-efficiency initiatives, including the distribution of one million energy-efficient CFL lightbulbs to members, and confirming the installation of 150,000 switches to control members' water heaters during peak demand periods.[53] However, to offset growing demand and the prospect of stiff penalties for CO_2 emissions, the cooperatives needed to develop a more comprehensive program, one that could tackle whole-house efficiency on a large scale. Couick observed that seven of GDS's top-ten energy-efficiency recommendations had to do with making living spaces more energy efficient (termed space-conditioning).[54] This was significant because, as Couick pointed out, "52 percent of a house's use of electricity in South Carolina at that time was for space-conditioning." Targeting these seven measures could be the key to ameliorating the cooperatives' generation and emission issues.

Wanting to put a face to the GDS report, Couick, much like Senator Hollings and Governor West before him, took a tour of some of the troubled homes.[55] He had the local cooperatives guide him through some of the houses that had the highest power bills, and he interviewed the affected homeowners and renters. What he found was that many of the poorest people were paying the highest power bills—primarily for heating and cooling—while reaping the fewest benefits. Some were paying several hundred dollars a month in the peak seasons and still could not keep their homes at a decent temperature.[56] "I would hear people tell me, 'It is so cold in this house,'" Couick recalled, "'that when I get the kids up to go to school in the morning in the winter we all stand in front of the oven while it's on in order to be warm enough to get dressed.'"[57] Many of these problem houses were manufactured homes (otherwise known as double-wides or mobile homes), which housed 24 percent of cooperative members. These homes had air leaks, poor insulation, inefficient electric heating, and other issues that were costing the homeowners thousands of dollars a year in wasted energy. South Carolina needed a creative solution.

In 2009, Couick asked Ron Calcaterra to help determine the most effective way to reduce CO_2 emissions and keep electricity affordable. Calcaterra and the engineers at Central concluded that the best course of action was to lower system-wide energy use and reduce peak demand. They estimated that, over the course of ten years, improving the efficiency of 225,000 homes would reduce energy use by 5.6 million megawatt-hours, enough to offset the need for new generation and reduce CO_2 emissions by 6.7 million metric tons. In addition, the efficiency measures would collectively save members up to $270 million a year and create as many as 1,500 new jobs statewide.[58]

To illustrate that implementing the energy-efficiency measures outlined by GDS would be a cost-effective solution, the cooperatives decided to do a proof-of-concept project. In the fall of 2009, the cooperatives ran an advertisement in *South Carolina Living* magazine for a Help My House home makeover contest. Out of four thousand entries, seven were chosen to receive complimentary efficiency upgrades in their homes. In early 2010, under the supervision of the cooperatives, contractors got to work on these seven houses doing everything from plugging leaks to adding insulation and a new heat pump. The project showed immediate results. One of the recipients, Linda Butler, enjoyed significant benefits from the efficiency upgrades. Before the makeover, Butler, a Tri-County member much like the recipient of the first snap-on bathroom Almeta Dunlap, was paying $400 to $500 (with one bill that was almost $800) a month in the peak-season heating and cooling bills, yet it still was not enough to keep her 1,296-square-foot home at a bearable temperature. After receiving the upgrades, not only was her home a more comfortable temperature but also her electric bills were reduced by an average of $188 a month. As a part-time teacher's aide, she had struggled to pay utility bills, but now they seemed more manageable. This trend of savings was true for the rest of the makeover recipients as well. Over the course of ten months, those homes saved a total of 33,016 kilowatt-hours and $4,296.29. This proved that not only could a larger scale efficiency program work, but that it would be an invaluable service for struggling cooperative members.[59]

While it was clear that these efficiency measures could be cost-effective, the cooperatives lacked the large, independent cash reserves needed to help members pay for the upgrades. This was a major challenge. There was no way that someone like Linda Butler, for instance, could pay the several thousand dollars upfront cost necessary to pay for home efficiency upgrades. This was true for many of the lower-income cooperative members who would most benefit from the efficiency upgrades. The average household income in the service territories of the cooperatives was 14 percent below the national average.[60] So not only would they not be able to afford the cost of home improvements, they would also be unlikely to have the credit to qualify for a bank loan. The cooperatives needed a way to help these members afford these upgrades that circumvented conventional funding methods. Couick then discovered a potential solution: on-bill financing (OBF).[61] On-bill financing allowed the cooperatives to offer long-term, low-interest loans that members could pay back on their monthly electric bills.[62] Theoretically, even with the added expense of loan payments, members would still save money as, due to the efficiency upgrades, they would be paying for less electricity. Cooperatives in Kansas had experimented with on-bill financing, but the South Carolina coopera-tives would be the first in the country to use it for whole-house efficiency and to use it on such a large scale.[63]

For the cooperatives to make the on-bill financing program work, they needed government funding to finance the loans. Couick took the idea back to Representative Spratt and House Majority Whip James Clyburn, who had previously been indispensable to the John's Johns project. "I fell in love with the idea and then introduced the concept to the members of Congress on both sides of the aisle," Clyburn said. "Everybody felt like this was a great thing to undertake."[64] In 2010, Clyburn introduced the idea as the Rural Energy Savings Program Act (RESP) and advocated for it, using testimonial videos the cooperatives had collected during the home makeover contest.[65] "These people had these incredible testimonials . . ." remembered Mike Hacker, Clyburn's former floor director and senior ad-visor. "So we put together kind of a greatest hits of those videos and we showed them at the press conference when we introduced the bill and when Clyburn testified before the agriculture committee in support of the bill." The bill received bipartisan support, with fifty-five cosponsors, including South Carolina Representatives Spratt, Bob Inglis, Joe Wilson, and Henry Brown. Spratt commented that the economic benefits the bill would have for South Carolina were a "grand slam" and said that RESP would "work" and would have "multiple winners."[66] The bill passed the House handily by a vote of 240–172.

Meanwhile, the South Carolina legislature passed a law in 2010 that al-lowed "utilities to offer OBF to homeowners, to tie the repayment of the loan to the meter and not the borrower, and to disconnect power if loan payments [were] not made."[67] This was especially important because by tying repayment to the meter, the co-ops could forgo credit checks and give loans to members who would not otherwise be credit-worthy. Fur-thermore, attaching loans to electric bills protected credit-providers from default as less than one-quarter of 1 percent of cooperative electric bills were not collected in 2010.[68] Everything was shaping up for the on-bill financing program to go into effect. But when the bill came before the US Senate, it stalled. "We were fighting everybody to get [RESP] passed . . . ," said Couick. "And everybody was trying to love our bill to death."[69] Despite the efforts of the cooperatives, the bill never came to vote. The session ended. The cooperatives were back to square one.

Undeterred, Couick went back to the drawing board. He wanted to conduct a pilot program that could serve as a model for national policy to follow. When RESP fizzled out in the Senate, Clyburn sent Couick and Hacker to the US Department of Agriculture (USDA) office to secure funding to continue doing the on-bill financing retrofit program independently.[70] There they were able to get a loan from the Rural Economic Development Loan & Grant Program (REDLG) to do another energy efficiency pilot program. "They allowed us to get a loan for end-use energy efficiency, something they had never done before," said Lindsey Smith, vice president for education at ECSC, "But when they heard the ideas, they said 'We'll try that.'"[71] Although the USDA originally approved only $740,000, it soon increased the amount to $1 million to better meet the cooperatives' needs. "The original loan that Central got was . . . $740,000 because that was the cap [for REDLG loans] at the time . . . ," said Smith. "[but] USDA, the federal government, changed their program to fit ours." Around this time, Carol Werner of the Environmental and Energy Study Institute (EESI), whom Couick had met when pitching his OBF plan in Clyburn's office, secured funding from the Doris Duke Charitable Foundation for program design and outreach. Werner would serve as a sort of conduit between the cooperatives' pilot program and interested parties in Washington.[72] With all the funding secured, the cooperatives could start their pilot in earnest.

In early 2011, the cooperatives started their Help My House pilot with the intention of retrofitting one hundred member houses and studying the results on energy-efficiency and savings as well as the efficacy of OBF.[73] The pilot was done in collaboration with numerous agencies. ECOVA, a firm that implemented energy efficiency programs for utilities, was brought on to help with planning, management, and analysis, and ECOVA partner Integral Analytics assessed cost-effectiveness. Carton Donofrio Partners, a marketing and consumer research firm, developed messaging, created marketing materials, conducted surveys, and reported on the views of program participants. 1st Cooperative Federal Credit Union prepared and processed loan documents—the terms of the loans were 2.5 percent financing over ten years. KW Savings Co., a new nonprofit created by Central Electric and ECSC, paid contractors and managed loan payments in perpetuity.[74]

Eight cooperatives (Aiken, Black River, Broad River, Horry, Palmetto, Pee Dee, Santee, and Tri-County) participated in the pilot. These cooperatives conducted outreach and screened participants, looking for those in homes with high power bills. A cooperative energy advisor performed walkthrough audits of the homes and reviewed energy use data with Central to see which homes could be cost-effectively upgraded. Comprehensive audits were performed on candidates' homes to make sure the energy savings would exceed the cost of the loan payments. "Our contractors [would] go in and make an energy-efficiency assessment . . . ," said Calcaterra, "And we would turn over [the results] to the homeowner showing the savings." Contractors then competed for bids. After members picked their preferred contractor, 1st Cooperative Federal Credit Union drew up the loan contract and the energy advisor presented it to the member for their signature. "Once the work was done," said Calcaterra, "we, on behalf of the member, would send [an energy auditor] to their home to make sure all the work was implemented as scheduled or as approved."[75] At first the post-work audits revealed some challenges. "That was kind of tough in the beginning," Calcaterra observed, until the contractors realized that the cooperatives were determined to run an effective program. "If you agree to do this," Calcaterra continued, "by gosh you're going to do it or you don't get paid." The cooperatives provided this service to protect the members—most of whom did not have the expertise to assess the quality of the retrofit services provided—from being taken advantage of by the contractors. "They didn't pay for it until it was approved by the co-op," said Calcaterra.

The Help My House pilot program was a resounding success. By the time the cooperatives finished, they had retrofitted more homes than they had originally intended. "We started out aiming for 100 but we ended up going past that [to 125 homes] because Tri-County Electric had so many people, so many members interested in getting their houses retrofitted and Central voted to allow them in [to the pilot]," said Smith.[76] Just like in the home makeover contest, the pilot recipients of the retrofits enjoyed substantial energy and cost savings. Among those 125 retrofitted homes, there was a 34 percent reduction in energy use, and participants saved an average of $288 a year after loan payments.[77] Those homeowners were understandably pleased with the results, with survey results indicating 96 percent of the pilot's participants were satisfied or very satisfied with the work done on their homes.[78] Some participating co-ops were fans of the program, too. Before the pilot, none of them intended to launch an ongoing OBF program, but, after the pilot, seven cooperatives expressed interest in doing so.

The pilot program also had ripple effects outside of South Carolina. Calcaterra and Couick both got inquiries from policymakers in Washington, including Clyburn, and were invited to speak about the pilot. "It's hard to overstate how much the program has impacted federal policy and federal programs as it's taken life . . . ," said Smith. "That pilot was talked about all over the country," Couick recalled. Clyburn in particular proved to be a steadfast ally to the Help My House project. "When Clyburn ran for re-election, he had people showing [the Help My House pilot] putting in extra insulation and stuff," said Couick. "He was championing this."[79]

Eventually, in no small part thanks to the strident efforts of the cooperatives, Clyburn was able to get RESP included with the 2014 Farm Bill with the program itself launching in 2016.

In 2017, nearly eight years after Couick first took his concerns to Congressman Spratt, the South Carolina cooperatives finally received their first loans from RESP.[80] Since the pilot program in 2011, Help My House had already weatherized a total of 887 member homes. The $13 million awarded to the cooperatives through KW Savings Co. in new zero-interest loans would allow them to retrofit an estimated 1,250 more homes. Much like Governor West retracing his "hunger tour" steps with Clyburn in 1973, Couick and Clyburn visited one of the beneficiaries of the Help My House program. Martha Scott, eighty years old and blind, suffered harsh temperatures when her heat pump broke, and the meager wages she made cleaning houses were insufficient to replace it. Not only did Santee Electric's Help My House program replace her heat pump, but the co-op's Operation Round Up program also funded a new roof for Scott's home installed by volunteers from HomeWorks of America, a faith-based non-profit based in Columbia. In an image strongly reminiscent of the photo of Governor West and Eliza Palmer forty years prior, Scott is seen clasping Clyburn's hand in gratitude. In a way, these two moments are bookends to each other, showing the fruits of a lifetime of partnership between the cooperatives and the government, and Clyburn in particular. "Jim Clyburn's legacy is, at least to me, the very best evidence of where cooperatives excel—at innovation and community commitment," said Couick. "The results have been an improvement in members' quality of life, dollars saved, and carbon emissions avoided."

Over the years, several factors have slowed the momentum of the Help My House program. The pressure of growing total load began to level off after the 2008 financial crash, which made an energy crisis seem less imminent, and the cooperatives eventually invested indirectly in next generation nuclear generation anyway. President Obama's environmental program was never fully adopted. After Waxman-Markey's Cap and Trade bill failed in the Senate, the Obama administration slowed its drive for new CO_2 regulations. It was not until June 2014's Clean Power Plan that the EPA proposed regulations on existing power plants, and it did not complete the final versions until 2015.[81] These regulations were still being litigated when the Trump administration entered office in 2017. Later that year, the new administration left the Paris Climate Accords and began repealing the Clean Power Plan with the intention of replacing it with Trump's own Affordable Clean Energy Rule (ACE).[82] These economic and political shifts made the program less of a priority for the government and made hitting an ambitious target like retrofitting 225,000 homes un-likely.

However, the pendulum may swing the other way. In early 2021, the District of Columbia Court of Appeals ruled that ACE violated the Clean Air Act, leaving the new Biden administration, which had already rejoined the Paris Climate Accords, with a blank slate.[83] "It's like deja vu all over again for me," said Couick.[84] He believes that with Biden in office, Help My House will "be even more active now," as the administration recognizes the "need to find something that works in South Carolina." Perhaps Biden will take a more aggressive approach to environmental policy than his predecessors, catalyzing a new groundswell of federal support for the Help My House program. But even if that does not happen, the cooperatives will continue to run the program and continue their work to improve members lives.

Their work on John's Johns and Help My House are two important examples of the cooperatives going above and beyond their responsibilities as electric utilities to improve the lives of their members. They are also examples of how investments can snowball over time. In other words, the programs show how a single event, the installation of a snap-on bathroom, could spawn a partnership that more than forty years later would culminate in a multi-million-dollar federal program. Housing in South Carolina still presents many challenges, but with determined effort from the cooperatives, political and community leaders, and many others, it is hoped that such problems may one day seem a distant memory.

Cooperative Principles and Member Services

n South Carolina, the cooperatives adhere to the seven cooperative principles adopted by the International Cooperative Alliance: voluntary and open membership; democratic member control; members' economic participation; autonomy and independence; education, training, and information; cooperation among cooperatives; and concern for community.[1] Each of these principles is vital to a cooperative's mission and purpose, but it is "concern for community" that speaks to the heart of the organization. For years, modeling this principle in the communities they serve has distinguished cooperatives from investor-owned utilities (IOUs) in the state. It was concern for their communities that led the cooperatives to electrify rural South Carolina after the IOUs had abandoned the venture, deeming it unprofitable, and the same principle continues to drive co-ops to meet the needs of their members.

For nearly a century, the cooperatives have gone above and beyond their basic responsibilities by providing a number of groundbreaking services to members. Like electrification, these services have addressed needs endemic in rural South Carolina that have otherwise been neglected. Because of their business model and the principles that they adhere to, the cooperatives have been uniquely equipped to meet these needs. The principles of "autonomy and independence" as well as "cooperation among cooperatives" in particular have given the cooperatives the flexibility to experiment with new services and the ability to adopt the successful services of fellow cooperatives for their own members. This chapter serves to highlight the origins and history of four of the cooperatives' most impactful initiatives: the Washington Youth Tour, Operation Round Up, Honor Flights, and Rural Broadband Internet Access.

In the early 1970s, the cooperatives were taking a more active approach to rural development. As noted in the previous chapter, R. D. Bennett, executive vice president of the South Carolina Electric Cooperative Association, intended to reverse the exodus of young people from rural South Carolina.[2] This was a primary goal of the Stand Tall Commission and part of the reason for his partnership with the governor on the John's Johns project. One of the other ways the cooperatives reached out to young people was by offering unique opportunities. One of these opportunities introduced during Bennett's tenure was the Washington Youth Tour. WYT is a member service program that coordinates an annual all-expenses-paid trip for exceptional high school students to visit the nation's capital and learn about the workings of their government. Like many cooperative services, WYT started out small with the involvement of only a few cooperatives, then gradually became a cooperative tradition statewide.

WYT originated more than sixty years ago, when Lyndon B. Johnson (at that time a US senator from Texas) delivered a speech to the National Rural Electric Cooperative Association (NRECA) in 1957, declaring, "If one thing comes out of this meeting, it will be sending youngsters to the national capital where they can actually see what the flag stands for and represents."[3] That summer and for the next few years, cooperatives in several states independently sent students to work in or tour the capital each summer, some for a few days and others for several weeks. In 1964, NRECA began coordinating these annual trips so that cooperatives across the country could have students together in the capital for the same week in the summer and participate in joint activities. The national Washington Youth Tour was born. In the first years of WYT (at the time called the "Rural Youth Tour"), South Carolina's cooperatives and co-ops from many other states did not send a group to the capital. South Carolina was first represented on the tour in 1965 by Mary Olis Brooks, a Clemson student and at the time reigning "Miss Rural Electrification." Brooks served as the official host of the Rural Youth Tour and was photographed by newspapers meeting President Lyndon Johnson on the south lawn of the White House.[4]

In June 1971, eleven months after R. D. Bennett published his column, "Bring Our Kids Home," in *Living in South Carolina* announcing his intentions to give new opportunities to rural young people, the South Carolina cooperatives sent five students to the capital to participate in WYT.[5] Three cooperatives (Mid-Carolina, Pee Dee, and Santee) each invested slightly less than $300 for these students to stay in Washington from June 14 to 18.[6] Though the trip itself was brief, it was full of unique experiences for the students, who barely had a moment's rest that week. Over the course of

five days, they visited national monuments and historic landmarks including Mount Vernon, Arlington Cemetery, the Lincoln and Jefferson memorials, the Capitol rotunda and Senate chambers, the Library of Congress,
the Smithsonian Institute, the National Geographic Society, Ford's The-
atre, the Bureau of Engraving and Printing, the FBI building, the National
Archives, the Wax Museum, Washington Cathedral, Embassy Row, and
the Pentagon. They took a boat ride down the Potomac, danced with students from other states to the music of a live rock and roll band, and ate
at multiple area restaurants. Students visited Senator Strom Thurmond in
his office, competed with other students in a quiz competition, listened
to speakers hosted by NRECA, and even met President Nixon.[7] Under-
standably, sore feet were a common complaint throughout the week.

It is difficult to fathom how monumental an opportunity the trip was
for this first class of students. None of them had even flown on a plane before, much less shaken hands with the President of the United States.[8] In
the July edition of his regular column, "Thoughts From The Editor's Desk"
in *Living in South Carolina*, Walt Riddle remarked that the students would
"never forget" the myriad of experiences they had in Washington, and that
as a consequence of the trip, they would "become better citizens." In the
years since that first trip, the WYT has become a staple of the South Carolina cooperatives' member services and hundreds of students have followed in the footsteps of that first class. It has also grown substantially year
after year, going from five students in the class of 1971 to seventy-seven in
2020.[9] The ongoing success of the program is a testament to its impact on
rural students. To them, it is more than just a trip. "The chief mission there
is educating these young people . . ." said Van O'Cain, director of public and member relations at The Electric Cooperatives of South Carolina
(ECSC) as well as South Carolina's Youth Tour coordinator, "But in addition to that, it's the socialization. I've always heard this from the Washington trip, that 'It's great that we're in DC and get to see all the monuments
and everything, but just being able to meet people, meet *new* people [is
meaningful].'"[10] O'Cain explained that many of the students have never
left the state and, if not for the cooperatives, they may not be able to go on
a trip like WYT. "So the socialization part is really big," concluded O'Cain.
Brent Towery, who participated in WYT in 2014, made similar comments
after returning from the capital. "It's pretty cool being around so many
other kids who have big goals for the future," he said. "After the first day of
the trip, it's like we had all known each other forever."[11]

When the coronavirus pandemic and public health threat of COVID-19
limited public interactions in 2020, the in-person Washington Youth Tour
was cancelled. "We were in the middle of interviewing students for the

Washington trip when everything shut down . . . ," said O'Cain. "[It was] kind of depressing."[12] However, instead of canceling the event altogether, the South Carolina cooperatives organized their first Virtual Youth Experience (VYE).[13] Students who participated were able to hear from and interact with a stellar lineup of South Carolina leaders including Governor Henry McMaster, Senator Lindsey Graham, Congressman Jim Clyburn through online video conferencing. "It was not a passive screen experience," wrote Mike Couick, who was in attendance for the event. "They asked poignant questions of our speakers that illustrated their concerns and attitudes." O'Cain emphasized that even though the event was online, students were still able to socialize. "[T]hey were able to talk to these [speakers], but more importantly, they were able to chat with each other," he said.[14] Using the platform's chat function, students were able to type comments to one another during the live sessions and socialize, developing those friendships virtually.

Not only did the students hear from speakers and socialize, cooperatives also devised a new way for them to learn and engage on current issues.[15] During the virtual conference, students were trained in journalistic skills, so the podcasts they produced (audio recordings no longer than eight minutes) answered the question, "How have the events of 2020 have impacted me?" Small teams of three to four students competed for a grand prize of a $5,000 college scholarship for each member of the winning team. Twenty podcasts were submitted for judging by a panel of journalists including opinion editor Cindi Scoppe and reporter Avery Wilkes of Charleston's *Post and Courier* newspaper, Craig Melvin of NBC's *Today* show, and ABC News co-anchor and correspondent Kenneth Moton. Scoppe lauded the work of all the students for articulating "very grown-up perspectives" and for showcasing "resiliency" while "adapting to a very different kind of world."

Despite the obstacles faced during the Virtual Youth Experience, it was a resounding success. In 2021, keeping in mind the lessons learned, the cooperatives hosted a hybrid Youth Experience—with four days virtual and the final day in person.[16] They eagerly anticipated that they would be able to return to the traditional format for the 2022 Youth Tour and continue to provide this service that has grown to be so beloved by cooperatives and members alike.

———————————

In the late 1980s, Palmetto Electric Cooperative launched one of the cooperatives' largest and most ambitious member services to date: Operation Round Up. This member service originated late one night in 1989 when Tom Upshaw, then Palmetto Electric's CEO, was struck by an idea:

what if cooperative members rounded-up their monthly electric bills to the next dollar to support people in need?[17] This was "one of those four-o'clock-in-the-morning-when-you-can't-sleep ideas," said Upshaw.[18] It was an elegantly simple idea that had the potential to do enormous good for the cooperative's members. If implemented, it would only cost individual members a few cents a month, or an average of $6 a year, but multiply that by the total number of cooperative members and that would produce thousands of dollars annually for philanthropic projects. Upshaw pitched this "Round Up" program to Palmetto Electric's board. They approved the idea and established the Palmetto Electric Trust, a subsidiary charity with a separate board, to process requests for Operation Round Up funds. To date, the trust has distributed over $8 million in Palmetto Electric's service area.[19]

This money has funded multiple projects beneficial to the local community. In the early years, Operation Round Up disbursed funds to important community projects including the construction of a helipad for the Hampton General Hospital, the establishment and installation of Jasper County's 911 system, and ongoing partnerships with local philanthropic organizations like Second Helpings, a food pantry.[20] Tray Hunter, vice president of marketing and public relations at Palmetto Electric, pointed out that those early community investments are still bearing fruit. Hunter noted that the helipad, for instance, which was built in January 1990 "is still in use today."[21] He also pointed to more recent disbursements their Operation Round Up program has made, like the $30,000 they donate annually to the Bright Ideas Education Grant Program, which provides teachers with $1,000 mini grants for "innovative and effective classroom education curriculum that cannot be covered by traditional school financing," or the college scholarships they give to college students in both two- and four-year programs.[22] Each of these projects and programs funded by Palmetto's Operation Round Up have had an indelible impact and continue to benefit members and nonmembers alike in or near Palmetto Electric's service area.

Though Palmetto Electric developed Operation Round Up to meet local needs, it was quick to share the idea when other cooperatives across the country expressed interest. "[W]hen we saw it was going to be such a great program, we decided to let electric cooperatives that are under the NRECA umbrella adopt the program," said Martha McMillan, senior executive assistant at Palmetto Electric.[23] South Carolina cooperatives also took advantage of the opportunity by starting their own Operation Round Up programs, with sixteen of the state's cooperatives participating and a total of $33 million in Round Up funds dispersed across the state by

2014.[24] As of 2019, 327 cooperatives nationally offered Operation Round Up. Telephone companies and other organizations are now offering similar programs, as well.[25] Palmetto Electric has even been contacted about the program by organizations in Canada, England, and Australia.[26] "We had no idea it would spread like it has," said Tom Upshaw. "I'm absolutely amazed." While Palmetto Electric does not track disbursements of Operation Round Up programs outside of South Carolina, the total amount of funds disbursed nationwide is undoubtedly massive. "I'm sure it's got to be half a billion [dollars] or more," says Hunter.[27]

As impressive as Operation Round Up's disbursement figures are, the enormity of the program's effect on people's lives cannot be quantified. Take Joyce Davis, for example. Davis, a Palmetto Electric member, applied for Operation Round Up funds to repair her mobile home.[28] When Martha McMillan assessed the damage to the home on behalf of Palmetto Electric, she found it irreparable. Instead of granting Davis's initial request, McMillan offered to buy her a new home. According to McMillan, Davis jumped up and down in excitement, so much in fact that she broke right through the floor of her house. Operation Round Up changed Davis's life for the better. "When I found out my home was too unsafe to live in, Palmetto Electric and Operation Round Up gave me hope and told me to not worry," said Davis. "Because of Palmetto Electric, I now have a decent mobile home to live in and can focus on my health."[29]

Davis's story is just one of thousands of similar Operation Round Up stories from across the country. The program has, with great flexibility, been able to provide meaningful support to all kinds of people and organizations with all manner of problems—whether it be food or housing insecurity, medical emergencies, or other problems altogether. The reason it has been able to do so successfully is because it has stayed attuned to members' needs. The program does this by making members a core component of the program itself. When cooperatives set up a trust to run Operation Round Up, they put member volunteers on the trust's board. "That trust board meets once a month, usually, to look over requests and make allocations," said Lou Green, executive vice president of ECSC. "So it's members making decisions about member money on behalf of the members."[30] This member-driven, member-focused approach helps ensure that Operation Round Up allocates money in the most beneficial way possible. Members know what they need, and they know what other members need and know what will make a difference in people's lives.

The program's runaway success aside, at its core, Operation Round Up is simply doing what the cooperatives have always done: helping people. Leigh Smith, retired communications coordinator for Lynches River

Electric Cooperative, argued it is aligned with the seventh cooperative principle, "concern for community."[31] "Co-ops were organized to bring power to the rural areas of our state, but the broader aspect of that is to improve the lives of the people we serve," summarized Smith. "You couldn't find a better program to do that than this one."

In the early 2010s, the cooperatives ushered in a new era of member services by forging an historic partnership with Honor Flight of South Carolina and offering a well-deserved opportunity to the state's rural World War II veterans. The original Honor Flight program was started in 2004 by Ohio-based physician assistant and Air Force veteran Earl Morse.[32] Several months after attending the opening of the World War II Memorial on the National Mall in April of that year, Morse became concerned that many veterans of the war would not be able visit it. "I would see my World War II veterans some three, six months later, and I'd ask them if they'd gone to see [the memorial]," Morse said. "Three hundred of them, and not one of them had been to it. Reality set in. They were never going."[33] It was then that he had the idea for Honor Flight (now known as the Honor Flight Network), an organization that would provide VIP flights for World War II veterans to the capital to see their memorial. Since the first flight of twelve veterans from Ohio in May 2005, the organization has spread across the country, with chapters being opened in forty-five states and some 81,000 veterans served by 2012.[34] In 2007, Bill Dukes, owner of the Blue Marlin restaurant in Columbia, established Honor Flight of South Carolina and that same year sent their first flight of veterans to the capital. Over the next few years, many more Honor Flights flew out of South Carolina. However, as the decade ended, Dukes grew increasingly concerned that many veterans, especially in rural parts of South Carolina, would never hear about the program in time and have the opportunity to participate in a flight. By one contemporary estimate, World War II veterans were passing away at a rate of 670 per day nationwide, and as of September 2010, South Carolina only had 29,300 of these veterans left.[35] "No question, the window for this program is beginning to close," said Dukes at the time.[36] He needed to reach those veterans and fast.

In 2011, Dukes spoke with Mike Couick, CEO of The Electric Cooperatives of South Carolina, about his dilemma.[37] That October, Couick proposed to the ECSC board that the cooperatives form a unique partnership with Honor Flight of South Carolina.[38] Previously, each Honor Flight in the state had been sponsored by several organizations and private donors. The cooperatives made state history by donating $60,000 to independently fund an entire flight.[39] "It was an answer to our prayers," said

Dukes. In addition to the money, the cooperatives brought expertise to the table. Previous South Carolina Honor Flights had drawn heavily from urban areas; the cooperatives would be able to identify and reach out to rural veterans who had previously been overlooked. "I think they'll find the vets we haven't been able to reach," Dukes said.[40]

In order to find them, all hands were needed on deck: every cooperative would have to search their service areas for veterans. At the ECSC Winter Conference in December 2011, Couick spoke to the state's cooperative leaders about "Honoring Our Homegrown Heroes," announcing the cooperatives' partnership with Honor Flight and highlighting some of the unsung World War II veterans from rural South Carolina.[41] One of the stories he shared was that of Strom Thurmond. When the war started, Thurmond, at the time nearly forty years old, was in no danger of being drafted and had no obligation to serve.[42] Nevertheless, he volunteered to fight and ended up serving in one of the most consequential operations of the war: D-Day. As Couick recalled the story, he shared the podium with an oddly poignant visual aid, the late Thurmond's jump boots, on loan from Thurmond's daughter-in-law. Couick's presentation jumpstarted the cooperatives' search for more rural heroes to honor. A month later in the January 2012 edition of *South Carolina Living* magazine, the state's most widely circulated publication featured cover art of Uncle Sam in his iconic pose with his figure pointing at the reader. The slogan now read, "We want YOU for the co-op Honor Flight."[43] Inside, readers found a multipage article about the program and an application for any South Carolina World War II veteran who wanted to attend the next Honor Flight.[44]

Given how swiftly the number of surviving World War II veterans had dropped since 2007, Dukes speculated that 2012 might be the last year for South Carolina Honor Flights.[45] He suggested to Couick that there may not even be enough World War II veterans left for a full flight and that the cooperatives might have to expand their search criteria. "Bill Dukes didn't think we could do it. He said, 'Well, Mike, we may have to fill in with [veterans of other wars],'" said Couick. "I said, 'Bill, we can do it.'" Not only were they able to successfully fill the flight, they exceeded their goal. "We did [that first flight], and we did that in April," recalled Couick. "We turned right around and did another one in September . . . [and] we did a third flight in December." Because of the cooperatives' strong rural network, they were able to reach scores of veterans that Honor Flights of South Carolina might have otherwise completely missed.

The first of the cooperatives' Honor Flights was documented in the May 2012 edition of *South Carolina Living*.[46] On the morning of April 11, one hundred World War II veterans from all over the state flew out of

Columbia to Washington, DC. On the flight and throughout the trip, the veterans were accompanied by volunteer guardians from their home cooperatives, each of whom paid $500 for the privilege.[47] When they got to Washington, the veterans had a packed itinerary. They visited the Lincoln, Korean War, Vietnam War, Marine Corps War, and US Air Force memorials; the Arlington National Cemetery; and the Tomb of the Unknown Soldier where they observed the Changing of the Guard. Throughout their visit, the veterans fielded questions from reporters and at every stop received an outpouring of gratitude from passersby.[48] "They treated us like kings," remembered Marine veteran Don O. Daniels. Couick recalled that along the way, they crossed paths with a group of eighth grade students on a field trip.[49] Their teacher approached one of the veterans, Richard I. Damron, and asked if he could share his war experience with her class. Damron, who had been quiet for much of the trip, opened up and began to recount incredible stories about his time serving in Iwo Jima. For that class, this was surely an unforgettable experience. "These students were meeting someone who lived history," said Couick. When they visited the World War II Memorial itself, each veteran processed it differently, touching the South Carolina pillar or looking on at the wall of stars commemorating the 400,000 military personnel lost in the war.[50] But perhaps the most moving part of the trip was the return. When the veterans returned to Columbia Metropolitan Airport that night, they received an ecstatic welcome, with a band playing patriotic songs and hundreds of South Carolinians chanting "USA! USA! USA!" Former seaman Haskell Harbin was moved to tears. "I was surprised to see how many people were interested in World War II veterans," he said. "I thought they'd forgotten about us."

This trip on its own was already a historic accomplishment for the cooperatives, but they continued to set themselves apart even after it was completed. In addition to flying those one hundred veterans to the memorial that April, the cooperatives also released a book in May documenting the trip with anecdotes and photographs and featuring each veteran telling his story in his own words.[51] As Couick wrote in a forward to the book subtitled, "The Quiet Heroes of World War II," many of the veterans had kept to themselves about the war over the years.[52] "Those who survived often chose not to talk about their experiences on the battlefields of Europe, North Africa, Asia, in the Atlantic and across the Pacific," wrote Couick. "When they returned to civilian life, they went on to quietly raise families and build a nation that had no equal." The book gave war veterans the unique opportunity to share their extraordinary experiences, some for the first time. "If anyone tells you he wasn't scared," said former infantryman Aubrey M. Anderson, "he was never there."[53] "We did what was expected of us," said retired Marine William L. Hartley. "Most of us don't look at ourselves as heroes. We're just veterans."[54] These veterans took incredible risks for their country, and the book served as a long-overdue tribute to them and their incredible accomplishments and sacrifices.

The cooperatives' unique partnership with Honor Flight of South Carolina continued a tradition of going the extra mile for their members. Cooperatives made Honor Flight history by funding entire flights independently, and they successfully located and signed up the rural veterans that they were told may not even exist. They not only honored these brave heroes of the Second World War but also immortalized them in the pages of the cooperative magazine and in a book about the veterans' service and sacrifice.

In the early 2020s, many cooperatives were amid developing one of their most ambitious member services yet: rural broadband internet access at high speeds. Throughout South Carolina, there were still many people who had slow or no internet connectivity; 344,000 did not have access to a high-speed wired broadband connection (then defined as greater than 25 megabits per second) and roughly 171,000 South Carolinians had no internet access at all.[55] The surprisingly high numbers were mostly the result of internet service providers choosing not to make the capital investments necessary to build high-speed cable to people's homes, especially in rural areas. Much like the investor-owned electric utilities nearly a hundred years before, internet service providers have determined that it is not financially advantageous for them to provide service to certain parts of the state. Consequently, rural counties were particularly underserved in South Carolina. Four of them—Allendale, Bamberg, McCormick, and Marlboro—each had less than 45 percent broadband coverage, with one of them, Allendale, only having 19.5 percent coverage.[56] The internet providers' approach in these sparsely populated rural areas grew from their for-profit business model. "[Y]ou can't blame them," says Bob Paulling, CEO of the Mid-Carolina Electric Cooperative, headquartered in Lexington. "It's their prerogative to make money. And to make money you need [population] density."[57] The enormous expense of deploying high-speed cable and the limited potential return-on-investment had deterred internet service providers from expanding into rural markets. These disincentives seemed unlikely to change for some time. But when Paulling became aware of the dilemma several years before, he did not become resigned to it. Instead, he saw an opportunity for a cooperative solution.

Several years before the Mid-Carolina Electric Cooperative hired Paulling as its CEO in 2013, the foundation for the cooperative's rural broadband initiative was already being laid. In 2005, the Mid-Carolina Electric Cooperative was exploring new means to monitor and communicate with its electrical substations.[58] At the time, radio technology was still commonly used for this purpose, but it had a couple of crucial drawbacks. "[The] radio [frequency] spectrum is very busy, and, so, weather dependent," explained Paulling.[59] To maintain a consistent connection with its substations, the cooperative needed technology that was more reliable. The cooperative eventually chose the Supervisory Control and Data Acquisition (SCADA) computer system, which would allow them to constantly monitor their substations in real time. As a component of this system, the cooperative built a network of high-speed fiber optic cables between the substations and their dispatch center, the hub of operations. Unbeknownst to the cooperative, this fiber would soon serve as the core for their yet-to-be-introduced rural broadband program.

Over the next few years, cooperatives became more experienced with fiber, building out further from their substations and deeper into their electric distribution system to communicate with downline devices.[60] In addition to increasing the useful range of the SCADA system, this new infrastructure also inadvertently put the cooperatives in a prime position to provide broadband to their members. With only a few adjustments, the cooperative could theoretically extend their lines directly to members and provide them with high-speed internet. When the American Recovery and Reinvestment Act was passed by the Obama administration in 2009, it offered grant money for the development of rural broadband through the Broadband Initiatives Program (BIP). Recognizing the opportunity, Mid-Carolina Electric Cooperative decided to try to make their first foray into rural broadband by partnering with a local telephone company and applying for BIP funds. Although they made a case for the need for rural broadband and provided evidence for the feasibility of such a project in their service area, the cooperative's application was rejected. In 2011, the cooperatives applied again for another round of grant funding, but their application was rejected for a second time. As a result of these two defeats, the cooperative's broadband ambition would remain dormant for the next few years.

In 2014, a few months after he became CEO of Mid-Carolina, Paulling met with the cooperative's board for a strategic planning meeting.[61] "One of the things that kept popping up" in that meeting, Paulling recalled, was the members' need for "true high-speed internet." The board asked him to look further into the issue. "I found out ... [that] we proved the feasibility and the need for it with the grant applications," said Paulling. With this in mind, in the next budget year, Mid-Carolina's manager of engineering

Lee Ayers proposed setting aside more money to build fiber, and Paulling knew how the cooperative could offset the cost. "We just came back to the board and said, 'We know our membership needs high-speed internet and we need fiber optic cable for our electric distribution . . . Let's just kill two birds with one stone and utilize the excess capacity in this fiber and start an internet company.' So that's what we did," Pauling remembered. In February 2016, the Mid-Carolina board voted to create a stand-alone internet cooperative, and CarolinaConnect Cooperative was born.

Later that year, after setting up necessary equipment in the cooperative substations to connect their fiber to the internet, CarolinaConnect started signing up test customers. As word-of-mouth spread, interest in the company grew rapidly. "To get the first thousand customers for Carolina Connect, it took 449 calendar days from the day we began and went into business," said Paulling. "The second thousand took 98 calendar days, the third thousand took 62 calendar days, and the fourth thousand took 42 calendar days."[62] CarolinaConnect not only attracted cooperative members, but other cooperatives as well (cooperatives made up of cooperatives as members is common). In August 2017, Newberry Electric Cooperative joined CarolinaConnect. Keith Avery, Newberry CEO, said the response was overwhelming.[63] "I have more questions asked today about 'When are you going to get it to me?' than I do power," said Avery. He said for some, rural broadband service has been just as impactful as rural electrification. "I had one lady who was probably 82 years old, and she called me one day and said, 'I just want to say thank you for the internet service because that's how I keep up with my grandkids,'" said Avery. "And she said this kind of equates back to when the lights were turned on, and I thought that was kind of an appropriate analogy." Though it hasn't yet had the impact of rural electrification, CarolinaConnect had a measurable impact on parts of South Carolina's Midlands, providing high-speed internet service for 10,500 Mid-Carolina Electric members and 3,500 members of Newberry Electric by April 2021, with more signing up all the time.[64]

While those Midlands-area cooperatives had been involved the longest with internet service, they were not the only South Carolina cooperatives working on rural broadband. In October 2019, Lynches River Electric Cooperative founded its own internet company, RiverNet Connect.[65] In June of 2020, Tri-County Electric followed suit with TriCoLink.[66] And in February 2021, Aiken Electric Cooperative joined CarolinaConnect. Other electric co-ops partnered with local telephone cooperatives, allowing them to be the service providers while using electric co-op polls to deliver high-speed internet service.[67] In fact, most of the state's co-ops are involved, in some way, in providing rural broadband. "The only ones where they're not doing it," says Couick, "is where there's pretty much already full deployment of broadband." Though many of these programs were in their infancy, a new law had potential to expedite their growth. In September of 2020, Governor Henry McMaster signed Act 175 into law.[68] The statute gave cooperatives permission to provide internet service, which had until then been a legal gray area.[69] "It's not something that was expressly written into the law in the '30s when they formed the co-ops," said Betsy Hix, government relations director of operations for The Electric Cooperatives of South Carolina, "and it wasn't clear if we were allowed to or not." This law also expanded the domain of co-op easements. Before rural broadband, co-ops already had easements, legal permission to run their electrical lines across privately-owned land. However, when the co-ops began their rural broadband project, they needed new easements for their fiber optic cables—despite the fact those cables were run on the same poles as the electrical lines. With the new law, the pre-existing easements for cooperatives' electrical lines could be applied to fiber as well, instantly severing miles of bureaucratic red tape. The law reduced the barrier to entry for cooperatives interested in becoming internet providers and could encourage others to take the leap.[70]

In addition to the law, there were also new sources of government funding on the horizon. "The General Assembly has previously appropriated $30 million, which will flow through ORS [the Office of Regulatory Staff]. That money is already out there," Hix explained. "And what they have been doing is a matching grant program. So, if a co-op [says,] 'I'll send $500,000 [to provide broadband to underserved census blocks],' they'll match it."[71] The matched funds would allow the cooperatives to greatly expand their rural broadband services, but an even bigger program was possible. President Joe Biden's administration had proposed a $2.3 trillion infrastructure plan that included $100 billion for broadband.[72] The plan dubbed high-speed internet "the new electricity" as a callback to the Great Depression-era Rural Electrification Act. According to Couick, such a windfall could be a gamechanger.[73] "[According to ORS estimates,] you could establish rural broadband in the state for $1.4 billion," said Couick. He explained that with the pre-existing matching grant program in South Carolina, the federal government would only have to provide $700 million to fully fund broadband development across all of South Carolina. With that funding, the cooperatives would be the best equipped organizations to use it effectively and reach the underserved rural areas of South Carolina.

The cooperatives were changing lives and altering the fabric of rural South Carolina with their broadband program. In the 2010s and 2020s, internet access had become crucial. "It's something you gotta have to sur-vive," argued Paulling, "especially in rural areas."[74] Lack of access to the internet disadvantaged students who needed to attend online classes or conduct research, working adults who needed to attend online meet-ings or send emails, elderly adults who relied on telemedicine appoint-ments, and anyone who wanted to connect to the rest of the world. "It just touches every part of your life," said Paulling. Similar to what R. D. Bennett observed in the 1970s, the dearth of opportunities that scarce access to the internet created led young people to leave rural areas. "We have a brain drain right now from rural South Carolina," Couick noted. "Younger people are moving away. They're moving away for economic op-portunity."[75] To keep people from leaving and to keep rural South Caro-lina alive, broadband efforts like those of the cooperatives were critical. "Internet service is now a necessity of life," summarized Paulling. "It's no longer a luxury."[76] This is the reality not only for residents of South Caro-lina, but Americans everywhere. While hundreds of cooperatives across the country have made strides in this area over the past several years by adopting their own broadband programs, it is evident based on the over six million households in cooperative service areas nationwide without access to high-speed that there is still much work to be done.[77] Complet-ing the rollout of rural broadband in South Carolina specifically will take herculean effort and cost millions more dollars, but as with every project cooperatives undertook on behalf of the people they serve, they would continue to push as hard as possible to help ensure a better life for their members. Paulling put it succinctly: "We're spending a lot of money, and it's a huge capital investment, but it's the right thing to do."[78]

As they proved time and again, the cooperatives took their principles seriously. "Concern for community" was not just a platitude, it was the motivation driving every action the cooperatives took. Cooperatives were invested in their members. They existed to make those members' lives better. The member services highlighted in this chapter represent a frac-tion of what cooperatives do in their communities. Beginning with rural electrification, the cooperatives' goal was to offer a better quality of life to rural people. Through their Washington Youth Tour, Operation Round Up, Honor Flights, Rural Broadband, and a host of other initiatives, they were doing much the same thing. Rural communities continued to face endemic challenges and certain disadvantages, but the cooperatives that serve them were working tirelessly to make things better.

10

Transparency, Accountability, and the Power of Democracy

n the latter half of the 2010s, South Carolina's electricity providers were in the spotlight for two failures that called into question their transparency and accountability. One was the discovery of the troubling practices of Tri-County Electric Cooperative's board of trustees, which damaged the community's trust in that cooperative and others across the state. The other was the abandonment of two nuclear reactors under construction at the V.C. Summer Nuclear Station in Fairfield County, a project that accrued billions of dollars of debt for South Carolina Electric and Gas (SCE&G) and Santee Cooper while customers were left to foot the bill—much of which came out of cooperative members' pockets. While the two scandals were not explicitly linked, they were similar in that they both involved rules not followed, and customers charged for benefits they would not receive.

The Tri-County story was launched by intense news media coverage of an annual membership meeting gone wrong, but it was fueled by the brazenness of misconduct that altered the public's perception of electric cooperatives and incited both legal and direct action against the cooperatives. The benefit of extensive scrutiny, however, was a refreshed and more urgent approach to managing electricity rates and a preparation for the increasing electrification of the economy, as the transportation sector turned from gasoline- to electric-powered vehicles.

In the fall of 2017, a consultant with the National Rural Electric Cooperative Association (NRECA), was brought to the Tri-County Electric Cooperative headquarters in St. Matthews to examine potential issues with board policies. The review revealed that Tri-County's trustees were compensated more than any other cooperative's board members in the Southeast.[1] In fact, the Tri-County board members received nearly twice as much annual per diem payments as their counterparts in other South Carolina cooperatives, averaging $52,000 a year—the chairman made nearly $79,000 in 2016—while the other cooperatives' trustees averaged just $28,000.[2] The board members secured this compensation primarily by exploiting a loophole in the cooperative's per diem policy. Every time the board met, each board member was given a $450 per diem (a per-day payment). While this was similar to the average board meeting per diem given to other cooperative trustees around the state, Tri-County held meetings much more frequently than other cooperatives.[3] Generally, co-operatives averaged a little over one board meeting per month. The board at Mid-Carolina Electric Cooperative, for example, met thirteen times in 2017. That same year, Tri-County's board met fifty times, often only for a few minutes.[4]

The trustees also gave themselves lifetime health insurance funded by the cooperative and, before the investigation upset the plan, the Tri-County Electric Cooperative board chairman, Heath Hill, asked the co-operative to look into providing a pension for board members.[5] "I knew as the CEO that just wasn't legal," said Chad Lowder. "[They] just can't do that because they're not [employees] of the co-op."[6] The electric coopera-tives are not-for-profit businesses designed to keep the price of electricity low for members. The costs of Tri-County trustees would be passed on to members. While the trustees were collecting the payments, Tri-County members were paying one of the highest rates in the state at 15.2 cents per kilowatt hour, higher even than SCE&G's oft-criticized rates.[7] The mem-bers have the authority to elect trustees and hold them to account. How-ever, financial documents and meeting minutes were not made public, so members were in the dark and accountability was thwarted.

In October 2017, Lowder, conflicted about the request made of him by the chairman, contacted the NRECA. It recommended bringing con-sultant Monica Schmidt to Tri-County to help address board compensa-tion.[8] Lowder brought this proposal to the board which, at the time, was amenable to the idea of outside accountability and told him to extend the invitation to Schmidt.[9] "What I told the board was [Schmidt] was going to come in and talk with them about good governance, but also about bene-fits . . ." said Lowder. "Well, at that time, the chairman, in his mind, he was hearing, 'Oh, well she's going to tell us we can get a retirement package. Have her come down.'"[10] However, instead of being offered additional compensation, the board was confronted with the fact that the compen-sation that they already received was excessive and placed them among the highest-earning board members in the country. "I do think it shocked them," said Lowder. "I do think for an instant there it was a sheer shock of just how exorbitant [compensation] had gotten . . ."[11] After this meeting, the board turned to Lowder for a solution; however, he was skeptical of their motives. "I think their intention was not to fix it as in 'reduce [the] per diems,'" said Lowder. "[It was] 'how do you make it look better than what it is?'"[12]

The board mandated that Lowder draft new bylaws to be delivered by January and, despite his suspicions about the board's motives, he quickly complied. Lowder, Aaron Christensen, a Charlotte-based lawyer Schmidt recommended with broad experience in cooperative governance, and the cooperative's general counsel, John Felder, worked through the holidays drafting new bylaws in order to meet the deadline. When they delivered the bylaws at the beginning of 2018, Lowder feared for his job. "I felt like I was going to be terminated on the spot," he recalled, "because, essentially, they were being told 'This is wrong.'"[13] However, much to Lowder's surprise, after making minor changes, they accepted the new bylaws and he was able to keep his job.[14] The new bylaws would have required the cooperative to have: a committee of members to supervise elections, new procedures to allow any members of the cooperative (customers and employees) to run for the board, rules for conflicts-of-interest and standards of conduct regarding trustees, and the strictest rules in South Carolina for limiting board compensation and keeping governance costs low.

Though the board accepted the changes internally, Tri-County's members still had to vote on implementing the new bylaws. The bylaws were scheduled to be mailed to members in April with the vote set for the cooperative's annual membership meeting in May.[15] At the board's monthly meeting just before the bylaws were mailed, some trustees began to reconsider their approval.[16] "[W]e're getting ready to go with the annual meeting in May to have the membership approve the bylaws," said Lowder, "but there's actions being taken behind the scenes between January and May to try to derail that process." At that monthly meeting, a motion was made to rescind the bylaws, and there was discussion about rejecting them altogether. Lowder and Felder reaffirmed their support for the changes and attested to their quality.[17] The board eventually relented and allowed the bylaws to be mailed to members.[18]

On Thursday, May 17, the day of the annual meeting, the opportunity for reform deteriorated as the afternoon wore on. The first issue was logistical. The cooperative was not prepared for the more-than-usual two thousand members who showed up to vote. There was traffic congestion and long lines for both registering and voting. Lowder suggested that this issue was being exploited to reduce voter turnout. "[There were] cars backing up traffic on purpose, stopping in the middle of the road, just so people couldn't come in to vote."[19] The second issue was voting interference outside the ballot box. "[In line to vote, my wife and I] got confronted, face to face, with an absolute disgraceful campaign to undo the new bylaws the board approved," recalled Joe Strickland, a firefighter and a concerned Tri-County member.[20] Family and friends of some of the trustees passed out "Vote No" cards to attendees in an effort to block the reforms.[21] "That was an insult," said Barbara Weston, another Tri-County member, "because they were on the property, and they shouldn't have been doing that anyway."[22] Seeing what was transpiring, two trustees resigned the day of the vote, and another resigned soon after. The "Vote No" blitz was successful, and the vote to approve the new bylaws failed 1,075 to 1,045.[23] This defeat demoralized many of the cooperative employees, but Lowder remained hopeful. "I told them, 'This is not over . . . You just have to have faith.'"[24]

After the annual meeting, CEO Lowder and state Representative Russell Ott, whose legislative district included part of Tri-County's service area, received comments and questions from upset members and employees. They were concerned that the new bylaws, referred to as "the gold standard" for cooperative governance, had been rejected even after the board put them before the membership.[25] The resignations of the trustees had also raised suspicions, and not just among members of the cooperative.

A few days after the bylaw vote, *The State* newspaper published an article by Avery Wilks headlined "SC utility's part-time board enriched itself while customers paid high power bills," which revealed much of the information about Tri-County's practices that had been previously withheld.[26] In the article, Wilks detailed the above-average pay the trustees received, the relatively high costs for electricity the cooperative's members were charged, and the excessive number of board meetings that the trustees held. Additionally, Wilks highlighted the unusual lifecycle the proposed bylaws went through, with the CEO and trustees first approving the measures before the members were urged to reject them.

Lowder went on record with Wilks to give insight on the peculiarity of the frequent board meetings, saying he had never "known any boards to meet in that level of excess" and pointing out that many of their sessions were only fifteen to twenty minutes long and could have been combined with the required monthly meetings to limit costs. He also gave his reasoning for the bylaw vote's outcome, claiming that "false information . . . was being spread telling members that the bylaws would eliminate the board [and] that all the authority would go to the CEO." Barry Hutto and Jeff Reeves, two of the trustees who resigned, told Wilks that after accepting the bylaws, the trustees actually implemented some of the new policies before a few of the board members began to campaign against the changes. In contrast to some board members, Hutto and Reeves were compensated less than $45,000 each by Tri-County in 2016.[27]

Wilks's article got attention among Tri-County members. The cooperative received over three hundred calls with many callers inquiring about the board's compensation and how to have trustees removed, a process authorized by the existing bylaws.[28] Lowder was supportive and advised them on this process. "I instructed the members [who came to my office], 'Here's what you can do . . .'" he said, "'you can get a petition up and call for a special meeting [to have a vote of removal]. This is your power as a member.'"[29] Members, including Barbara Weston, took his advice and soon began collecting signatures. One member went a step further and filed a class-action lawsuit against the board charging the trustees with violation of S.C. Code of Law 33–49–630, which states that "compensation shall not be paid except for actual attendance upon activities authorized by the board."[30] The suit highlighted that Tri-County's trustees grossed over $6 million since 2004, and it aimed to curb the cooperative's "excessive compensation" as well as award members with reparations for any "incurred monetary damages."[31] Lowder was committed to keeping both of these processes out in the open and made sure to notify the board of the members' intentions.

Other cooperatives were jarred by the news from Tri-County. Douglas A. Reeves, chairman of The Electric Cooperatives of South Carolina (ECSC), the cooperatives' state trade/service association, assembled a Governance Task Force designed to "examine issues of transparency and accountability."[32] Representative Ott, continuing to hear from people angered by the story, assumed a more active role by commencing work on legislative proposals that would require boards to be more transparent.[33] The task force, composed of each cooperative's CEO, board chair (except Tri-County's), and local lawyer, met multiple times in the following weeks, including one meeting with Representative Ott to discuss his ideas for legislation he was planning.

With the number of signatures on a petition to remove the six remaining trustees steadily growing and the ECSC board calling for them to resign, Tri-County's CEO, board, and general counsel held a meeting on June 21 to discuss the situation. They also allotted time for an open forum to allow cooperative members to speak. Minutes of the meeting show that the guest speakers were upset and began condemning Tri-County's trustees for "enriching themselves" and "deceiving" the cooperative's members, who "trusted [the board] to look out for [their] best interests."[34]

Members questioned the justification for the board's per diems, the number of meetings, and the insurance benefits. The trustees responded that CEO Lowder collaborated with the board and engineers to set the pay for meetings, but later in the discussions Lowder stated that the per diem met the state average.[35] The CEO also explained that Aaron Christensen, the bylaws attorney, had suggested a policy that would have capped the board members' pay when their compensation met the state's average trustee income, even if they continued to meet.[36] Only two representatives of Tri-County addressed the frequency of meetings. Jake Moore, an attorney who had been retained by the trustees to represent the board specifically, said that the board met more often because it was "integrally involved in the operation of the co-op."[37] Lowder noted that the frequency of meetings was what caused concern, not the per diem rate.[38]

The discussion also covered the bylaw vote, and multiple perspectives were offered on the matter. One trustee felt that the changes had been "rammed down [their throats]" by Felder, the cooperative's attorney, and Christensen, while another mentioned their desire to "straighten . . . stuff" out themselves.[39] Moore argued that the bylaws were too complicated and that the board preferred to work things out internally, without "the big shot from Charlotte" helping.[40] One member concurred that the bylaws were unclear because "the content and detail . . . was not adequately communicated" and "the script was so small [on the copies that were sent out] no one could read it."[41] Lowder opined that "those were good bylaws" that would "clean up" the cooperative, adding that he felt "hurt" when they were rejected after everyone had "ample time to review" them.[42]

The meeting concluded with a discussion about the removal petition. If 10 percent of Tri-County's membership signed the petition, it would force a meeting where members could vote to remove the current trustees from the board.[43] At the time, they had confirmed 705 of a required 1,368 signatures.[44] By July 9, over 1,400 had been obtained.[45] In the approximately eighty-year history of South Carolina cooperatives, this procedure had never been initiated.[46] The next step was to schedule the special meeting, which almost seven hundred members would have to attend to achieve a quorum and permit a valid vote.[47]

Even with more than 1,600 petition signatures and after weeks of being called on to resign, Tri-County's trustees remained. At another July 19 meeting, they were met with about eighty angry members wanting to hear the board's responses to the signature threshold having been achieved.[48] Throughout the session, trustees "seldom addressed the crowd's questions directly . . . did not respond to periodic calls for their resignations . . . [and] left the meeting room quickly after adjourning."[49] "[W]e asked questions [and] they would just ignore us . . ." said Tri-County member Joe Strickland. "It was totally disgraceful. They would not answer to their bosses, the [member-]owners of the co-op."[50] Moreover, the board avoided deciding on when to hold the removal vote on the grounds that "attorneys [were] going to have to look over all this stuff."[51] Felder then gave the crowd a tentative date: August 18, 2018.[52]

In the period leading up to that day, as people wondered whether objectionable compensation practices afflicted other cooperatives, *The State* brought new information to light. Avery Wilks wrote two more articles reporting other instances of questionable practices at South Carolina's cooperatives. The first piece pulled data from an October 2010 audit at Santee Electric Cooperative, which found evidence that Santee trustees were also collecting more than the average amount in per diem payments and travel reimbursement.[53] The audit had highlighted the policy of providing health insurance to former board members, which many cooperatives stopped in 2010 after being advised that state law prohibited it, and even more did so after the Tri-County board came under fire.[54] Additionally, *The State*'s research discovered that a few cooperatives were providing retirement plans worth over $100,000. The story pointed out that most cooperatives spent over $100,000 on sending boards to conferences and training sessions as well. Some members claimed these got turned into vacations, but cooperative officials insisted the trips focused on education with direct benefits to cooperative members. One official noted he attended meetings "ninety percent of the time" while on business trips.[55] Finally, Wilks detailed how some boards filled board candidate nominating committees with their family members and friends.[56]

The second article, released just four days before the removal vote on August 18, included more details about the Tri-County Board of Trustees. Aside from specifics about trustee compensation, Wilks found records of lavish board dinners costing Tri-County nearly $1,000, Christmas bonuses, and discrepancies in the hours some trustees claimed to have worked (including some nonexistent dates like February 30 and September 31).[57] Wilks also discovered that before their full monthly meeting on January 18, 2018, the trustees assembled for four committee meetings.[58] Lowder, the CEO, told *The State* that none of the four were longer than half an hour and that $11,600 would have been saved had they been scheduled alongside the full meeting.[59] Board attorney Moore insisted that the meetings were all "substantial and held for legitimate reasons," and that his clients were "country people" (a characterization later mocked by

Representative Ott and other members) who had been "stabbed in the back" by Lowder and Felder.[60] The board intimated that it was their CEO's fault for complying with the payments, however Lowder noted that he had "no legal authority to refuse payments to the board that hires and fires him."[61]

The regular monthly board meeting was scheduled to occur on Thursday, August 16, two days before the unprecedented vote on removing the cooperative's board. This one was unique, however, because none of the trustees attended.[62] Roughly sixty frustrated customers did show up and used the assembly "as a forum to discuss their plans to fire the six remaining trustees" that weekend.[63] The members also questioned whether the board members would resign or attend the specially called meeting to defend themselves.[64]

The following day was just as eventful. Unlike on Thursday, when an announced session was attended by dozens of members but no trustees, the board was planning an unannounced meeting to try to undermine the vote of removal planned for that Saturday. Wilks explained in another article for *The State* that the board convened to discuss a letter sent to CEO Lowder from attorney Moore that "raised the issue of whether Saturday's special meeting [was] legal, accused Lowder of refusing to comply with the board's requests and hinted the board could move to suspend or fire Lowder 'and other advisory staff.'"[65] It was apparent to Lowder that he was going to be removed as CEO—in fact, the board had had his termination papers ready as early as the June 21 meeting—and he called his wife to give her the bad news.[66] His wife, however, was undeterred. "[I told her] I'll be terminated pretty much on the spot and that'll be that," said Lowder. "She said, 'No you won't. We'll do something.' [And] she starts calling her friends and members she knows." The board's nefarious plan to sack Lowder quickly got around. "I got a call [that] morning saying, 'Joe, the board called a special meeting and they're going to fire Chad . . .'" said Strickland.[67] He immediately began rounding up as many people as he could to stop the meeting. "At this point, I had a network lined up of people, and I got on the phone and started calling [them] . . . [Then] I rode up my road to people I couldn't get in touch with on the phone," said Strickland. "I [even] walked across a field to get a farmer off his tractor to come to the meeting."[68] Weston, too, made efforts to get as many people as she could to attend the meeting. "[W]e just called everybody and said, 'You need to be there . . . because [of] what [the board] has planned," she said.[69]

By the time the board meeting was set to begin, there was a crowd of more than 225 people—and not just members, but over two dozen

Tri-County employees, too.[70] "[W]e had all the community there [and then] here come all the linemen for Tri-County," said Strickland. "And they walked in the back of the room ... and made a strong presence known [and showed] how they felt about the process without saying a single word."[71] In response to the potential "retaliatory measures" that were being planned, several people, including Lowder, Strickland, Weston, and the sheriff, went to the board room to confront the trustees. "[T]he sheriff said, 'Knock, knock. We've got the paperwork for you,'" said Strickland. "And we walked in and [the sheriff] served them [a temporary] restraining order."[72] This order prevented the board from firing or suspending any of Tri-County's staff.[73] The trustees, meeting in the boardroom, did not address the crowd that had gathered in the cooperative's community room, and they communicated minimally with the small contingent that had served them the restraining order. "[They] would not look at you, not answer you, [and] just stare off into space," said Strickland.[74] The trustees' disengagement, however, did not keep Strickland from giving them a piece of his mind. "[Joe] was very poignant when he said, 'If you really had the membership at heart, you would resign,'" recalled Lowder.[75] After this confrontation, the meeting ended, and the board reluctantly agreed not to attempt to stop the removal vote.[76]

That Saturday, more than 1,500 members showed up to cast their votes at the St. Matthews venue—a huge truck parking building at the cooperative now set with chairs like for other membership meetings.[77] Two questions were on the ballot: "Shall the remaining members of the Board of Trustees be removed from office?" and "Shall the proposed bylaws be approved?" No one on the board used the allotted opportunity to take the microphone and explain why they should remain in office, instead opting to not attend the special meeting at all.[78] Tri-County's trustees were removed from office by a vote of 1,453 to 30 and the bylaws were approved 1,322 to 155.

In Avery Wilks's article summarizing the results of the meeting, ECSC CEO Mike Couick described the outcome as an outstanding victory for two American institutions: "a free media and ... a working ballot-box."[79] The ordeal concluded with the trustees' resignations the following Tuesday, which also settled a second class-action lawsuit that had been filed sometime after the initial May 21 article.[80] Under the terms of that agreement, all civil claims against Tri-County and its employees were dismissed, but trustees were required "to resign, never again seek reelection or seek to elect their spouse or family member, and to not challenge the outcome" of the vote on August 18.[81] Members were invited to reconvene on November 17 to elect nine new directors.

With the Tri-County situation mostly resolved, ECSC Chairman Reeves and his Governance Task Force set out to establish a set of principles that would prevent similar occurrences in the future at any South Carolina electric cooperative. These principles were designed to improve five areas of cooperative policy: nominations, credentials, and elections; board vacancies; voting, campaigning, and quorum; transparency; and board and executive compensation. The first category focused on removing any influences that incumbent trustees up for reelection could have on the credentialing and nominating of other trustees. The board vacancies principle tied in to the first, adding that new trustee positions should not be filled by anyone with "a close degree of kinship" to current or recent trustees and that the election process should "promote transparency, foster democracy, and prevent nepotism."[82]

To make voting processes better, the voting, campaigning, and quorum principle sought to ensure cooperatives' members had "meaningful access to the ballot box," which meant "including a minimum number of hours to vote at the annual meeting, as well as an early voting opportunity." This third category also called for all votes to count toward the meeting quorum if voting were allowed before the announced meeting day. Regarding transparency, co-ops would guarantee members notice of meetings and opportunities to raise comments and concerns should they attend. Need-to-know details like meeting agendas, notices, and approved minutes would be available online for members. The final principle suggested that "board and executive compensation should be transparent and understandable for members," and that this would best be achieved by posting compensation and expense summaries online. The Governance Task Force would begin acclimating cooperatives to the principles at the start of 2019 as they looked to put the Tri-County situation behind them.[83]

Less than a week after the removal vote, however, *The State* published another article with new information on Tri-County's board practices. Wilks informed readers that it was a regular occurrence for some trustees to direct cooperative employees to various odd jobs, ultimately amounting to "hundreds of thousands of dollars' worth of electric and landscaping work" that board members or their friends got "at huge discounts or for free."[84] Cooperative member Barbara Weston claimed that some people "had stopped calling [the co-op] Tri-County Electric and started calling it Hill Electric" because of board Chairman Hill's outsized influence over the cooperative's affairs.[85] Employees stated that crews had been urged to restore power to some households sooner than others, clear trees that would not have interfered with power lines, and check into electrical issues at trustees' houses—jobs they agreed to after seeing "other Tri-County employees reassigned or fired after crossing" the board. The most expensive chore mentioned was installing power lines to provide electricity to a farm's irrigation system, a $300,000 endeavor that reportedly cost the trustee only $2,677.[86]

Upon hearing these findings, more legislators publicly shared their input on potential reforms for electric cooperative regulation. State Representative Gary Clary believed that there was a "lack of worthwhile information" provided to cooperative members, and state Senator Marlon Kimpson said the situation was "another example of abuse and misuse in positions of power," declaring, "you can't have too much transparency in these types of organizations." Senator Kimpson also stated he would file a proposal similar to Representative Ott's. If passed, Ott's bill "would require all cooperative boards to post online their board meeting agendas and minutes; publish online all board pay, including mileage, travel and per diem; and make it easier for co-op members to vote at annual elections."[87]

Not everyone agreed. Some House members felt that forcing alterations to cooperative policies could be counterproductive. Representative Roger Kirby thought that many cooperatives were "doing a great job," and he did not want to see any "knee-jerk legislation" that would penalize all twenty of them.[88] Likewise, Representative Wendy Brawley wrote a column in *The State* applauding Tri-County's members for utilizing the bylaws that "empowered" them and "[holding] the former board accountable."[89] She also referenced the expensive, lengthy legal battles that government-regulated utilities SCE&G and Santee Cooper faced after the V.C. Summer construction failure and concluded that the cooperative model expedited problem resolution.[90] ECSC's Mike Couick mentioned that, after meeting with cooperatives following the Tri-County news, "their level of awareness of deficiencies" had increased and all of them desired to be "part of the solution."[91]

Couick, hoping to avoid "one-size-fits-all" legislation that he opined could make progress more difficult for cooperatives, explained the changes the Governance Task Force supported.[92] The reforms directly addressed common concerns by ensuring that incumbent board members could not influence elections, ending the practice of filling board vacancies with trustees' relatives, making elections easier on members, and making vital information about boards more accessible. However, legislators who did not "have much trust for anyone in the utility business" following the failed nuclear project and the Tri-County board's removal still contended that "a new law [was] the only way to ensure co-ops [stayed] in line."[93]

While lawmakers shaped their proposals, nine new members, including Strickland and Weston, were elected to Tri-County's board of trustees on November 17, 2018. Several of the new trustees had been at the forefront of the efforts to remove the previous board, and they quickly began making improvements.[94] By the end of the year, the board had "elected officers, named delegates to state and national co-op groups, reviewed safety reports" and reduced its expenses by 30 percent. Tri-County also got a new logo and website, added the Help My House!® energy efficiency loan program and residential solar opportunities, and joined Touchstone Energy®, the national brand of cooperatives. Board meetings were scheduled at 6 p.m. so working members could attend, and subcommittee meetings were to be held on the same day as the required monthly meetings to save time and money. Additionally, Lowder promised that the cooperative's financial documents and tax forms would be included on Tri-County's website, accessible by its members.[95]

On January 8, the House of Representatives began deliberating on Ott's bill, H.3145. Several legislators voiced their opposition, agreeing with Brawley's belief that cooperatives are most effective when they are governed by concise bylaws, but Ott responded by assuring them that the bill would take no "power from co-op customers . . . [and] simply will empower a watchdog to have their backs."[96] In March, the bill passed through the House with a 104 to 6 vote, and, in May, the Senate with a 42 to 0 vote.[97] Governor McMaster subsequently signed the legislation one year to the day after the infamous annual meeting. He declared cooperatives as "vitally important to the past and future of South Carolina," and added that the legislation "will make things better for everyone."[98] Couick agreed with that statement, saying he considered the bill, which cooperatives helped draft and lobbied for, an "incredible affirmation that co-ops are committed to fixing issues that are of concern to their membership."[99]

The law established many new rules for cooperatives and made them accountable to the Office of Regulatory Staff—a state agency with the job of representing the public interest in utility regulation—and it generally followed the governance principles developed by the cooperatives' Governance Task Force. Among other things, these new rules included provisions that disallowed Trustee involvement in board elections, mandated that financial information and board meeting minutes be released regularly, made elections and meetings more accessible to members, and opened the cooperatives to inspections and audits by Office of Regulatory Staff and Public Service Commission.[100]

The new governance rules were made possible by the cooperation among all parties involved. The adversity led to modernization of all cooperatives' governance rules and enhanced their transparency and accessibility to their members. The way South Carolina cooperatives responded to their challenge became a national call to action. Electric cooperatives across the country observed the issues plaguing the South Carolina cooperatives, and many sought to learn how to avoid the same experience. Tri-County CEO Chad Lowder saw the entire ordeal as a victory for the cooperative business model. "What other business could see that . . . when something is wrong . . . the actual customers, in our case members, may say, 'Wait, that's not right. We're going to fix the problem,'" he said.[101] This win would give the cooperatives the momentum necessary to resolve their next dilemma: dealing with the failure of the Santee Cooper partnership with SCE&G to build additional nuclear generators at Jenkinsville.

During the Tri-County scandal, when the situation was deteriorating at the May 17 annual meeting in St. Matthews, news of the afternoon's chaos spread quickly to the state association's Columbia-area office. In a phone call with Couick, the association's vice president of government relations, John Frick, learned what was happening at the meeting and declared, "There goes Santee Cooper reform!"[102] For a moment, it seemed that the public and government relations nightmare produced by the Tri-County board would impede the cooperatives' ability to effectively advocate for reform of state-owned utility Santee Cooper, which had recently abandoned two unfinished nuclear reactors in Jenkinsville. While the events at Tri-County cast a shadow over the cooperatives' reputations, they worked together to rebuild trust with both the public and legislators, and reestablished credibility with proactive measures that would prevent future misconduct and support for the law to reform their own governance. This newfound trust and credibility bolstered the cooperatives' ability to lead the transformation of Santee Cooper and to address the failed nuclear project that cost the state's cooperative members billions of dollars.

The electric cooperatives and Santee Cooper had a long and productive relationship for decades before the V.C. Summer nuclear project started. As mentioned in previous chapters, the state's electric cooperatives do not own generation assets, so Central Electric Power Cooperative—their wholesale power aggregator—buys most of the electricity distributed by the co-ops from state-owned Santee Cooper.[103] This relationship, crucial to the function of the cooperatives, had been generally amicable, but by the turn of the twenty-first century, the relationship had begun to grow contentious. In fact, journalist Avery Wilks went so far as to call the relationship "toxic." One cooperative executive would later note that, to some degree, it was understandable based on the structure of their operating contract—known as the Coordination Agreement—that Central Electric and Santee Cooper would appear to be in conflict, but, in his view, that was a misunderstanding of their unique dynamic. "Santee Cooper acts and Central reacts," explained Robert C. Hochstetler, CEO of Central, the power supply aggregator for the twenty independent electricity distribution cooperatives.[104] However, many cooperative leaders saw a more troubling undercurrent to this acting and reacting. In contrast to Hochstetler's perspective, they perceived Santee Cooper as not treating the cooperatives, their largest customer, fairly or listening to their concerns. "Either they don't hear us, or they don't care," said Couick, reflecting on that era of the utilities' relationship.[105] Santee Cooper's seeming inability or unwillingness to heed the cooperative's advice was extremely concerning, especially given the amount of money their unique contract obligated Central to pay it.

Under the Coordination Agreement between the two utilities, Central did not pay a fixed rate per kilowatt-hour (kWh) of electricity purchased, the way a typical buyer might purchase gasoline by the gallon or potatoes by the pound. Instead, it paid for a portion of Santee Cooper's costs for (1) variable expenses including fuel, (2) fixed costs including capital costs, and (3) an administrative "adder." Although Central purchased about 60 percent of the electricity Santee Cooper produced, it paid approximately 70 percent of its fixed costs.[106]

Due to its onerous financial obligation to and limited control of Santee Cooper, Central was not only stressed but actively burdened by the utility. A June 2015 survey of Central's board meeting minutes between 2005 and 2015 showed that Santee Cooper was one of the most frequently discussed topics and a consistent cause of issues for the cooperative.[107] For years, Central worried that it could not rely on Santee Cooper to make wise financial decisions and feared that the utility might someday endanger the state's cooperatives. Just two years later, the sum of fears was realized.

On July 31, 2017, after devoting nearly a decade to the venture, the board of directors of Santee Cooper voted to halt construction on two unfinished nuclear reactors at the Virgil C. Summer Nuclear Generating Station near Jenkinsville.[108] It would become the biggest business failure in state history and send financial and political shockwaves across the state.[109] "I'm disappointed today not just for Santee Cooper and its customers but for our country and the industry as a whole," lamented Lonnie Carter, then-president and CEO of Santee Cooper: "If you really believe we need to reduce carbon [dioxide emissions], this was the way to do it."[110]

The failure of the V.C. Summer project was disastrous not only for Santee Cooper, but for South Carolina's electric cooperatives. As the utility's biggest customer, Central Electric and by extension cooperative member-owners across the state were obligated to pay billions for two unfinished nuclear reactors that never produced a watt of electricity.[111] While the scope of the fiasco came as an unwelcome surprise to Central and many other South Carolinians, failure was not unexpected by the owners, Santee Cooper and its partner SCE&G. In fact, it knew for years that the project was in jeopardy and, as later court hearings would show, intentionally misled the public, including the cooperatives, and did not take advice from Central that could have mitigated the catastrophe.

While the collapse of the nuclear project may have seemed sudden, the disaster was nearly twenty years in the making. As discussed in Chapter 8, electricity use in South Carolina grew an average of 5.2 percent year over year between 1998 and 2008.[112] In the midst of that unprecedented growth, Santee Cooper and Central became concerned about their ability to meet future demand. Santee Cooper projected that, if current trends held, demand would exceed its generation capacity by 2013, and system-wide "brown-outs" would be inevitable.[113] It was clear to both Santee Cooper and Central what needed to be done: they needed to construct new power generation assets, and quickly. Ronald J. Calcaterra, then-CEO of Central Electric, perceived that there were not many viable options on the table. So, when Santee Cooper proposed building a new coal-fueled power plant along the Great Pee Dee River in Florence County, Calcaterra felt that, given Central's position, "We can't say no."[114] In April 2006, Santee Cooper officially announced its intention to build the nearly $1 billion power plant. The project would be one of the last new coal-fired power plants in the country and was immediately unpopular, drawing strong criticism from environmentalists.[115] Soon Central, too, would join the opposition.

In 2007, the cooperatives grew more sensitive to environmental concerns about the Pee Dee coal-fired generator, especially considering new proposals at the federal level to tax carbon dioxide (CO_2) emissions, which threatened to make electricity made with fossil fuels much more expensive.[116] As a result, in September Central adopted a new environmentally friendly mission statement with goals of pursuing renewable resources that could offset or reduce CO_2 and other emissions. One avenue it considered to better align with this new mission statement was reduction of demand through energy efficiency initiatives, including the then-nascent retrofit program, Help My House featured in Chapter 8. The other, more relevant avenue it explored was directly reducing use of fossil fuels. Given its environmental goals, it was clear to Calcaterra that Central "had to try to avoid the Pee Dee unit while still meeting the obligation to serve."[117]

Central's opposition to the coal-fired plant was not strictly based on principle; it was common sense, too, according to Couick. "[I]t wasn't an environmental decision only," he said, "It was a dollars and cents decision to stop Pee Dee."[118] With Santee Cooper's permission, as required in their contract, Central began looking "to see if we could find some avenues to take advantage of that they couldn't," said Calcaterra.[119] As Central searched, Santee Cooper moved on to its next project: V.C. Summer.

In May 2008, Santee Cooper and SCE&G announced that they had signed an engineering, procurement, and construction contract with the Westinghouse Electric Corporation to build nuclear reactor units 2 and 3 on Lake Monticello, where another nuclear unit had been operating since 1984.[120] Santee Cooper, which owned a 45 percent stake in the new units, estimated it would pay approximately $4.4 billion to complete the project, with the first unit coming online in 2016 and the second in 2019.[121] Executives believed that both the Pee Dee plant and the V.C. Summer nuclear units would be necessary to meet rising demand, but Central and its member cooperatives found this to be excessive. "We always wondered if their numbers were really right . . ." said Couick.[122] Soon, the generation assets would go from excessive to unnecessary.

While Santee Cooper was taking preliminary steps to begin building the nuclear units, Calcaterra was in confidential talks with Duke Energy.[123] In the summer of 2009, Central announced that it had reached an agreement to buy some of its power needs from Duke, an arrangement that would phase in between 2013 and 2019 when demand was projected to exceed generation capacity. Not only was this deal convenient, but it was also much less expensive than new generation assets. "[W]hat was going to be $3,000 per kilowatt capacity [from the Pee Dee coal plant], you could replace with $750 per kilowatt from Duke Energy," said Couick.[124] This diminished any fear of looming brownouts and made the construction of new generation assets wholly unnecessary. Consequently, Santee Cooper abandoned plans to build the Pee Dee plant, but they decided to move forward with the nuclear units, much to the chagrin of Central and the cooperatives.[125]

Around the time the Duke Energy deal was finalized, Central began telling Santee Cooper that 45 percent ownership of the nuclear units was too much, even suggesting the project be abandoned entirely.[126] In the fall of 2009, Santee Cooper began to acknowledge that its ownership percentage was too high, but it assured Central and the cooperatives that it would eventually be sorted out. "Santee Cooper conceded that they didn't need all of that [ownership stake], but they were going to sell some of it to people in other states . . . once it was completed," said Couick. "The problem with that is, they were building it with our checkbook, where, if it didn't get sold, the co-ops were on the hook for 70% of the cost."[127]

By April 2010, Central was urging Santee Cooper to reduce its ownership to between 5 and 15 percent.[128] In December, Santee Cooper CEO Lonnie Carter agreed that "[i]t is imperative" that Santee Cooper reduce its ownership stake, with a goal of reducing its ownership to 20 percent and "move more of the power through purchased power agreements to further reduce costs . . ."[129] The cooperatives tried to help facilitate the sale by connecting them with their new supplier. "[W]e tried to get Duke Energy into the nuclear units," said Couick.[130] Their initial interest was promising. In June 2011, it was reported that Duke Energy and Progress Energy Carolinas were in talks to buy 10 percent and 5 percent shares, respectively.[131] Over the next few months, those numbers increased. By April 2012, it was reported that, instead of taking 10 percent and 5 percent stakes in the nuclear project, Duke Energy and Progress Energy Carolinas might take 10 percent *each*.[132] Simultaneously, Santee Cooper was negotiating with Ohio-based American Municipal Power Inc. to sell up to 5 percent interest in the project and negotiating to sell electricity to South Mississippi Electric Power Association with an option for it to buy up to 7 percent interest in the project. On top of that, it had already been in ongoing talks with Florida- and Alabama-based utilities to sell power and up to 10 percent interest in the project.[133] For a brief time, it seemed that Santee Cooper could offload most, if not all, of its 45 percent share, cutting its risk substantially and placing it well within the ownership range that the cooperatives were comfortable with. However, that window quickly closed.

"At the same time we're saying, 'You don't need that much,' Santee Cooper is saying, 'Trust us, we've got it sold,'" said Couick. "Well, what happened was [those sales] fell through . . ."[134] The deals with American Municipal Power and South Mississippi Electric never materialized, nor did deals with the Florida and Alabama utilities. In July 2012, Duke Energy bought Progress Energy Carolinas, which reduced their desired stake from up to 10 percent each to 10 percent total, split 5.9 percent and 4.1 percent, respectively, relative to their size.[135] That year, Santee Cooper retained Energy Strategies, Inc. (ESI) to help it more effectively market shares of the nuclear project.[136] In 2013, ESI president Howard Axelrod reported that, aside from Duke Energy, "[n]o other utility that was approached by Santee Cooper has indicated an interest in either an outright asset purchase or the execution of a long term PPA [purchase power agreement]." He concluded that the main issue was that nobody wanted to take on the "risks and uncertainties associated with a $10 billion ongoing nuclear construction project."[137]

Throughout that year, even negotiations with Duke Energy began to deteriorate. In January 2013, Lloyd Yates, Duke's executive vice president for regulated utilities, described negotiations as being in a holding pattern.[138] In April, Duke allowed its statement of intent to buy 10 percent to expire but continued to negotiate.[139] "The key here is to find terms that are commensurate to the risk and appropriate to our customers and shareholders," said Duke Energy Nuclear president Dhiaa Jamil. "We are hoping we will be able to reach an agreement with them on a piece of the Summer plant." However, in January 2014, Santee Cooper's board met to discuss negotiations with Duke Energy, and by the end of the month the deal was dead.[140] "In the end, all of us involved just couldn't pull it together," said Santee Cooper spokeswoman Mollie Gore. As a consolation, SCE&G agreed to buy 5 percent of Santee Cooper's stake in the project; however, this deal would take effect after the second reactor went online—a day that never came. After that deal was made, Gore said that Santee Cooper was no longer interested in selling shares of the nuclear project.

While disappointing for Central and the cooperatives, Santee Cooper's failure to sell off any of the project was not surprising. There were clear warning signs even at the beginning of negotiations with Duke Energy. SCANA, SCE&G's parent company, found additional partners to be unnecessary. "We already have a partner in V.C. Summer," said SCANA president and CEO Kevin Marsh in May 2011.[141] That same month, Duke Energy's CEO Jim Rogers shared his own doubts. "I'm trying to work something out," said Rogers, "but the challenge is working something out."[142] Part of the difficulty, he said, was "coming late to the dance" after SCE&G and Santee Cooper had already started the project. Duke Energy may have been very interested in being involved with the project. "Duke wanted in Jenkinsville," suggested Couick. "They wanted to help manage it being built."[143] However, the partners either found Duke's involvement unnecessary or unfeasible.

Despite its inability or unwillingness to reduce its financial liability on the project, Santee Cooper continued with V.C. Summer. "With Duke out and construction underway," said Couick, "the co-ops felt that you have to build it in order to sell it."[144] In March 2013, Santee Cooper and SCE&G laid the first slab of concrete at the V.C. Summer site, making theirs the first nuclear project in the country to break ground in thirty years.[145] While this was an accomplishment of sorts, it was also a major error in judgment for two reasons. First, evidence was continuing to pile up that the reactors were unnecessary. Not only had Central already contracted with Duke Energy to meet the projected increase in need, but that projected increase itself never arrived. In fact, energy use nationwide from 2009 onward was and continued to be stagnate.[146] So by the time the first concrete slab was laid, the justifications for the project were moot. Second, before that slab was even laid down, there had already been a series of delays that threatened the integrity of the project's timeline and endangered the project itself. The issues that caused these delays were so numerous that they could take up an entire chapter on their own.

The delays of modules CA20 and CA01 provide an illustrative example. Submodules for the nuclear units were being fabricated off site at a facility in Lake Charles, Louisiana, and were to be shipped to Jenkinsville to be assembled into larger modules such as CA20 and CA01.[147] The modules were scheduled for "hook-in" on November 18, 2011, and March 29, 2013, but the schedules soon proved unreliable. When Michael Crosby became Santee Cooper's vice president of nuclear operations and construction in October 2011, Santee Cooper and SCE&G were already anticipating that the CA20 and CA01 hook-in dates would be missed.[148] In August 2012, the contractor sent a revised schedule, delaying hook-in dates by fourteen months to January 19, 2013, and May 28, 2014. On January 11, 2013, Crosby sent an email saying that "[p]roduction work in Lake Charles is still in the ditch." In June, the contractor announced another delay of between nine to twelve months. Carter and the CEO of SCE&G emailed Westinghouse on September 6 that the frequent delays had placed "potentially unrecoverable stress on the milestone schedule approved by the SC Public Service Commission."[149] Westinghouse gave Santee Cooper and SCE&G a revised schedule for the nuclear project in August 2014, claiming that the two reactors would be substantially completed in June 2019 and June 2020.[150] Most people involved knew the schedule was unachievable.

Around this time, there was public speculation that the V.C. Summer project may be off schedule and over budget, but SCE&G and Santee Cooper offered reassurance.[151] "We [were] believing [Santee Cooper] when they [told] us that Westinghouse is doing a good job, they're overcoming obstacles, they've got a good plan, [they've] vetted the plan . . ." said Couick. "Only SCANA and Santee Cooper knew how difficult things were."[152] In April 2015, Santee Cooper delivered an optimistic 2014 Annual Report to the Governor and government officials to assuage fears that the project would not meet its deadlines.[153] However, Santee Cooper knew it would not meet the production deadlines, and it knew by extension that the project's $2.2 billion in federal production tax credits, which required the two reactors to be in service by January 1, 2021, were "in jeopardy."[154] Losing the credits would likely mean the end for the V.C. Summer project.

In the summer of 2015, Santee Cooper and SCE&G, fully aware of how dire their situation was, secretly retained the Bechtel Power Corporation, which has extensive experience designing and constructing nuclear power plants, to do an independent assessment of the V.C. Summer project.[155] In November of that year, they provided a draft report of their findings, concluding that "[t]he V.C. Summer Units 2 & 3 project suffers from various fundamental EPC [engineering, procurement, and construction] and major project management issues that must be resolved for project success."[156] These issues included but were not limited to: "a lack of a shared vision, goals, and accountability between the Owners and the Consortium [Westinghouse and subcontractors]"; inability to make a realistic schedule or accurately assess progress; a design that was "often not constructible"; low productivity due to "changes needed to the design, sustained overtime, complicated work packages, aging workforce, etc."; high turnover; and low morale. On top of all these issues, the report claimed that with existing conditions, the nuclear units would not be operational until at least June 2022, almost a year and a half after the cutoff date for the project's production tax credits.[157]

Santee Cooper and SCE&G wanted to make sure that the report did not become public. They even questioned the need to have a written report to begin with. Crosby's notes from a January 2016 meeting about the report included the question, "Do we really need a formal written report ... [t]hat stakeholders can use to throw rocks at us[?]"[158] Before the report was finalized, the damning revised schedule was deleted, removing one of the biggest rocks that could be thrown. While internally Santee Cooper and SCE&G were expecting the worst, they continued to project confidence to the public. "[A]t the same time they've got the Bechtel Report," said Couick, "they were reassuring Wall Street and the co-ops that everything was good and that things were getting better."[159] None of the documents (emails, graphs, reports, etc.) covering the project setbacks and delays were shared with Central.[160] When Central finally learned about the existence of the Bechtel report in late 2016 and requested a copy from Santee Cooper, they were denied. Soon, however, Santee Cooper and SCE&G's facade would crumble.

In late 2015, Santee Cooper and SCE&G negotiated a fixed-price agreement with Westinghouse that was meant to force the contractor to stick to a set budget.[161] "We intervened in the PSC proceeding considering SCE&G's participation in the fixed-price agreement," recalled Couick, "and we worked with the Office of Regulatory Staff to really tighten down the screws on that to where there were no exceptions."[162] Unbeknownst to the cooperatives, Westinghouse was already under incredible financial strain, and the fixed-price agreement was liable to force them into bankruptcy, a risk fully understood by Santee Cooper and SCE&G. The agreement went into effect in November 2016; in March 2017, Westinghouse filed for bankruptcy. "I truly think that's what led Westinghouse to file for bankruptcy. They no longer had a blank check," explained Couick.[163] This would end up being the final setback for the project, and just four months later Santee Cooper pulled the plug when its board voted to stop construction.

When the construction project was officially halted on July 31, 2017, Santee Cooper had already spent $4.7 billion—$2.8 billion of it from cooperative member-owners—and it estimated that completing the project would cost $7 billion and take another seven years.[164] Despite a report from SCE&G earlier that year claiming that 65 percent of the project was completed, it would become clear that only 35 percent was finished when construction stopped.[165] Since starting the project, Santee Cooper had raised electricity rates six times—by the project's end, each customer was paying $5 a month (4.5 percent of their bills) for the nuclear project—without delivering any extra benefit.[166] Less than a month later, following public outrage, Santee Cooper CEO Lonnie Carter resigned.

On September 2, 2017, amid investigations by the South Carolina House and Senate about how the project had gotten off track, Governor Henry McMaster demanded a copy of the Bechtel Report from Santee Cooper.[167] The next day, Santee Cooper sent a copy of the report, but urged McMaster to keep the document under wraps.[168] In a letter attached to the document, Santee Cooper's vice president and general counsel, J. Michael Baxley Sr., said, "[W]e request that the document provided to you not be copied, distributed, or given to any other individual, even those within your office . . . [W]e respectfully request that any contents of the document not be released to the media or any business, legal or financial entities." On September 4, Governor McMaster ignored Baxley's request and released the report, which was published in its entirety online by the *Post and Courier*.[169] This was the first time the public, including Central and the cooperatives, were able to see the extent of how poorly Santee Cooper and SCE&G had managed the V.C. Summer project. Public outrage spread and lawsuits were prepared.

The most significant of these lawsuits, *Cook v. Santee Cooper, et al.*, was filed just days prior to the release of the Bechtel report. On August 29, 2017, it was reported that two Santee Cooper customers, Horry County residents Chris Kolbe and Ruth Ann Keffer, were filing a class action lawsuit against the utility to recover money from their electric bills that had gone towards the failed project.[170] The case would soon be taken up by attorneys representing Jessica S. Cook and other plaintiffs and named SCE&G (which was renamed Dominion Energy South Carolina after its parent company, SCANA, merged with Dominion Energy in 2019) and Central as additional defendants.[171] While this lawsuit was ongoing, South Carolina's government was debating whether to reform or sell Santee Cooper. "A bunch of different legislative study committees convened . . ." said Wilks, who was one of the journalists who had covered the issues related to V.C. Summer for *The State* and later the *Post and Courier* newspaper, "[The House and Senate] took turns hiring consultants, or going through official processes to field offers . . . to determine what Santee Cooper's value [was]."[172] Because of "their contract to purchase Santee Cooper's power" the cooperatives had "a seat at the table" and became closely involved with these proceedings. "We said we didn't know if [Santee Cooper] needed to be sold or not," said Couick, "but we thought you needed to test the market" to see whether there would be interest in the state-owned utility if the state chose to pursue the time-consuming and costly effort to sell it.[173]

To test the market, the cooperatives worked with investment bankers to design a process for lawmakers to consider. Wilks described how, in essence, this process assigned the Department of Administration to "field official offers for Santee Cooper, hire consultants to evaluate them, then decide which one was the best offer and then present that to lawmakers."[174] The Department of Administration deemed the best offer to be from Florida-based electric company NextEra, which bid $9.46 billion to purchase Santee Cooper.[175] Legislative acceptance of the bid was unlikely from the start for several reasons. Some politicians opposed the sale option before an offer was made. "[T]here were some lawmakers, especially in the Senate, who would never ever agree to sell Santee Cooper," says Wilks, "and they made it difficult from day one for that to even be a possibility."[176]

Another reason was that many saw NextEra's offer as detrimental to ratepayers. One condition attached to its bid required that the legislature pass a law to pre-approve 2,400 megawatts of new generating assets, a stipulation that sounded to many like the Base Load Review Act, which had since lost favor with the General Assembly and a newly alert public.[177] The Department of Administration itself found that NextEra's bid was problematic. "[Its] analysis essentially found that NextEra's bid included a number of risks," said Wilks. "It wasn't really going to wipe out all [of Santee Cooper's] debt, because rates were actually going to go higher under NextEra."[178] From his perspective, this bid missed "the whole point of selling," which was "so rates would go down" and customers "would not have to pay for V.C. Summer." Because of the Department of Administration's report, the General Assembly was ambivalent about the option of selling to NextEra. "[Y]ou could really make the case that the NextEra sale offer was essentially dead the minute that analysis came out," said Wilks.

Concurrent with the sale discussion happening in the General Assembly, activity picked up in the class action lawsuit. In February 2018, Central Electric, which had been named as one of the defendants, filed a cross claim against Santee Cooper.[179] In 2019, after reviewing discovery documents, Central filed additional court documents (partially composed of notes from that Bechtel report) that showed with great clarity Santee Cooper's calamitous management of the V.C. Summer project as well as the lengths they went to conceal their mistakes from Central. Throughout that year, the plaintiffs mediated with Santee Cooper and SCE&G.[180] As settlement of the lawsuit began to seem more likely, the NextEra offer to purchase gained more relevance. "As that number comes out, [retired Chief Justice Jean] Toal, who was mediating the *Cook* case, appears to have used that NextEra bid as a target amount to be paid in a settlement," said Couick.[181]

In March 2020, the case was settled for $520 million with SCE&G paying $320 million and Santee Cooper paying the remaining $200 million.[182] In November, the money was distributed via refund checks to ratepayers, including hundreds of thousands of cooperative members who had been charged for the failed nuclear plants.[183] As part of the settlement agreement, Santee Cooper would freeze rates for four years, which was estimated to be worth another $510 million.[184] This was, in the opinion of Toal herself, "quite a win for the ratepayers in the plaintiff class."[185] The settlement would eventually end serious consideration of selling Santee Cooper—NextEra officially withdrew its bid in April 2021—and allow the cooperatives and General Assembly to redirect their focus to reform.

The cooperatives worked with other reform advocates throughout the reform debate, hoping to increase accountability and prevent disasters similar to the V.C. Summer incident from happening in the future. After it became "pretty clear that the path that this was going was the path of reform," the cooperatives helped "put together what we thought was the best package of reform" for Santee Cooper, said John Frick.[186] Much of it was designed to answer the question, as Couick put it, "How do you reform [Santee Cooper] to where they have to listen?"[187] So, the reform package included Public Service Commission hearings on proposed rate increases or new construction projects (with a quorum of the board present) to allow ratepayers input and so Santee Cooper, in Couick's words, could "be held accountable to cross examination."[188] According to Wilks, previously "Santee Cooper just kind of did whatever they wanted and customers were handed the bill at the end of the day," but the reforms meant that "[a]ny co-op members who don't like what Santee Cooper is planning to do will have more of a chance than ever to . . . bring their concerns to the state and try to do something about it before it actually goes into effect."[189]

The reforms altered the "best interests test" for Santee Cooper. "[The Santee Cooper board's] job is to make decisions that are in the best interests of Santee Cooper, and they have a statutory definition of how to do that," said Frick. "One of the . . . [first reforms that was proposed] . . . is making customers a priority within that best interests test."[190] The reforms would not only make Santee Cooper more accountable to ratepayers but to the cooperatives themselves by giving Central ex officio members on the board. Those people "will be able to share Central's perspective with the board before the board makes decisions, which we think will be helpful," Frick said.[191] It helps ensure that Santee Cooper communicates directly with Central, reducing the likelihood that information could be withheld as occurred during the V.C. Summer project. The existing requirement that two full board members must have electric cooperative experience was unchanged. Further, the legislation mandated that a new group of board members would be appointed over several years. Legislators would also have oversight on Santee Cooper's ability to issue bonds and would have the authority to investigate other issues as they arose.

After a long, contentious and complex process, the General Assembly's session came to a close and the Santee Cooper reform law was passed with broad support in the House and Senate.[192] While no provisions regarding the utility's sale were included in the final bill, Governor McMaster, who was a zealous advocate for selling Santee Cooper, signed the bill into law on June 15, 2021, bringing to an end one of most difficult chapters in the state's history.[193] Santee Cooper reform echoed that of Tri-County, which came to a close twenty-five months earlier in Governor McMaster's State House office when he signed the new cooperative governance bill into law—much to the relief of the legislators, Tri-County Electric Cooperative's new board of trustees, and other cooperative leaders who were in attendance. "We could not have done this without the sincere dedication of all of us working together—legislators and the co-ops," said Doug Reeves, the state cooperative association's chairman who had appointed the Governance Task Force.[194]

In the small audience was one of the most forceful proponents of changes to cooperative governance, state House Representative and

Tri-County member, Russell Ott. Now, he was ardent in his support of the cooperative model and his hope for the future of the cooperatives. "What I have come to learn is that I believe this model, the cooperative model, is the best one that we possibly have," declared Ott to applause:

> It's the one that's the closest to the people. It's the one whose leadership is elected by the customers, and that's the way it should be. We've made sure the customers are going to have the information they need, the transparency they should have . . . to make sure they're treated fairly. And that's all that anybody . . . wants, is to be treated fairly. So, I'm very proud of it, proud of everyone in this room. I look forward to its implementation, and I look forward to the cooperative system being strong for many, many years to come.[195]

EPILOGUE

South Carolina's electric cooperatives are more than just electric utilities, they are custodians of community and agents of change that have sparked a social movement in South Carolina. From rural electrification to broadband, the cooperatives have now spent more than eighty years transforming rural South Carolina and improving quality-of-life for their members. As a result, the cooperatives have become synonymous with the areas they serve, performing crucial functions for local communities. By providing reliable and affordable electricity, democratic control through local cooperative meetings, vital statewide and local communications via publications, and, today, broadband, cooperatives have helped connect members with each other, their community, and their state. A cooperative's members are not just consumers of electricity, they are co-owners of the cooperative with a genuine stake in its health and success as a community enterprise.

The cooperatives have been effective in rural South Carolina not based on the efforts of any one exceptional leader (though there have been many of them), but because of the effectiveness of the cooperatives' operating model. Member-ownership and the cooperative principles that flowed from it have helped fuel the cooperatives long-term success. While for-profit utilities serve investors' interests, the cooperatives exist to serve the needs and interests of their members. The cooperatives have consistently invested substantial capital in communities throughout South Carolina. Those investments help ensure that cooperative members enjoy many of the same advantages and opportunities as those living in urban and suburban areas. Those opportunities have changed countless lives.

In the 1930s and '40s, rural electrification transformed the way an entire generation of South Carolinians lived. Seemingly overnight, they joined the modern world with amenities like running water, refrigeration, washing machines, and, most importantly, electric lights. The "light line" was a lifeline for rural communities. The new conveniences, now taken for granted, revolutionized every aspect of their daily lives, rescuing them from dark homes and grueling manual labor and empowering them to pursue their dreams. In the years since, the cooperatives have built on their original commitment to rural South Carolina, expanding their focus and offering philanthropic services to further improve the lives of members. Services such as Operation Round-Up and Help My House have reached out to hundreds of families. Those and many other cooperative programs and services provide strong evidence that, to the cooperatives, "concern for community" is not just an abstract principle, it is their modus operandi.

President Franklin D. Roosevelt opened the door for electric cooperatives with the creation of the Rural Electrification Administration (REA). A few years later in 1943, Roosevelt observed, "I think the forward march of electric cooperatives has an even more profound significance in terms of our fight to preserve democracy, for it represents an extension of business enterprise, one in which the individual finds his greatest gain through cooperation with his neighbor."[1]

Just over a decade later, Senator Strom Thurmond expounded upon the significance of the cooperatives. In October 1955, Thurmond addressed an annual meeting crowd at Newberry Electric Cooperative, saying the REA, which catalyzed the rural electrification effort, had "more profound effects upon the economic and social history of our nation than almost any other single act" and that electrification had made life "more enjoyable and comfortable" in rural South Carolina.[2] In January 2021, over eighty years after the first electric cooperatives formed in South Carolina, longtime cooperative supporter US House Majority Whip Jim Clyburn eloquently summarized the contributions of South Carolina's electric cooperatives, noting that they have "been an important partner in my pursuit of making America's greatness accessible and affordable for all."[3]

With the strength of their member-ownership and the cooperative model fortified by recent tests of its strength and vitality, South Carolina's electric cooperatives seem well positioned to meet the challenges of the future and poised for many more decades of doing what they do best: using their cooperative and democratic model to serve their members.

NOTES

Introduction

1. The authors hope that this slender volume will provide a brief, popular and readable history told from the electric cooperatives' point of view rather than an exhaustive scholarly study of all the issues involved.

2. Janet G. Hudson, *Entangled by White Supremacy: Reform in World War I-Era South Carolina* (Lexington: University Press of Kentucky, 2009), 282–305; David L. Carlton, "Unbalanced Growth and Industrialization: The Case of South Carolina," in Winfred B. Moore Jr., Joseph T. Trip, and Lyon G. Tyler Jr., eds., *Developing Dixie: Modernization in a Traditional Society* (New York: Greenwood Press, 1988), 111–30.

3. Hubert Waldrop interview by Rachel Despres and Van O'Cain, July 22, 2013, transcript (in possession of the Electric Cooperatives of South Carolina). Hereinafter the Electric Cooperatives of South Carolina, Inc., will be referred to as ECSC. ECSC is also the current repository for oral history interviews and transcripts with South Carolina electric cooperatives members and employees cited in this and subsequent chapters.

4. Theresa Hicks interview by Van O'Cain and Lacy Ford, June 4, 2014, transcript (ECSC). Hicks later went on to serve on the Lynches River board after retirement.

5. Keith Phillips, ed., *Honor Flight* (Cayce, SC: Electric Cooperatives of South Carolina, Inc., 2012).

6. Mike Couick, CEO of the Electric Cooperatives of South Carolina, as quoted in Avery G. Wilkes, "SC Utility's Board Thrown Out of Office by More Than 1,500 Customers at Meeting," *The State* (Columbia, SC), August 18, 2018.

7. For a history of the Santee Cooper project, see Walter B. Edgar, *History of Santee Cooper, 1934–1984* (Columbia, SC: R. L. Bryan Company, 1984).

Chapter 1: When the Lights Came On

1. For a larger perspective on cooperative movements, see John Restakis, *Humanizing the Economy: Co-operatives in the Age of Capital* (Gabriola, BC: New Society Publishers, 2010) and for a larger perspective on the electrification movement, see Thomas P. Hughes, *Networks of Power: Electrification in Western Society, 1880–1930* (Baltimore: Johns Hopkins University Press, 1983). For examples of rural electrification in other states, see E.F. Chesnutt, "Rural Electrification in Arkansas, 1935–1940: The Formative Years," *Arkansas Historical Quarterly* 46 (1987):

215–60; D. Clayton Brown, "North Carolina Rural Electrification: Precedent of the REA," *North Carolina Historical Review* 59 (1982): 109–24; and Brian Q. Cannon, "Power Relations: Western Rural Electric Cooperatives and the New Deal," *Western Historical Quarterly* 31 (2000): 133–60.

2. Interview with Frank Hart by Van O'Cain, March 17, 2015, transcript (in possession of the Electric Cooperatives of South Carolina).

3. Interview with William F. Robinson by Van O'Cain, March 27, 2014, transcript (ECSC).

4. Interview with Jack Morris by Van O'Cain, June 19, 2014, transcript (ECSC).

5. Interview with F.E. Hendrix by Rachel Despres and Van O'Cain, July 22, 2013, transcript (ECSC).

6. Interview with Sammie McKinley by Van O'Cain and Walter Allread, September October 18, 2013, transcript (ECSC).

7. Interview with Arthur James by Van O'Cain, October 14, 2014, transcript (ECSC).

8. Interview with Gary Roberts by Van O'Cain, February 26, 2012, transcript (ECSC).

9. Interview with Eunice Spilliards by Van O'Cain and Lacy Ford, June 4, 2014, transcript (ECSC).

10. Interview with Henry Norris by Van O'Cain and Campbell Shuford, October 26, 2013, transcript (ECSC).

11. Interview with Dargan Hodge by Van O'Cain, October 8, 2014, transcript (ECSC).

12. Interview with Marion Caldwell by Van O'Cain, March 26, 2014, transcript (ECSC).

13. Interview with Bob Parker by Van O'Cain, March 17, 2015, transcript (ECSC).

14. Interview with Madge Strickland by Van O'Cain, May 29, 2014, transcript (ECSC).

15. Hodge, interview.

16. Robinson, interview.

17. Interview with Dick Burrell by Van O'Cain and Lacy Ford, June 4, 2014, transcript (ECSC).

18. Strickland, interview.

19. Interview with Billy Catoe by Van O'Cain, February 14, 2014, transcript (ECSC).

20. Interview with David Eugene Carson by Van O'Cain, July 22, 2013, transcript (ECSC).

21. Interview with William Good by Van O'Cain, March 20, 2013, transcript (ECSC); Interview with Lula Mathews by Van O'Cain, c. 2013, transcript (ECSC).

22. Interview with Kirk Roberts by Van O'Cain, April 1, 2014, transcript (ECSC).

23. Interview with Lou Carson by Van O'Cain, March 15, 2015, transcript (ECSC).

24. Burrell, interview.

25. Interview with Winona Peagler by Van O'Cain, December 17, 2014, transcript (ECSC); Walter Sanders by Van O'Cain, Lacy Ford, and Harvey Teal, June 3, 2014, transcript (ECSC).

26. Lou Carson, interview.

27. James, interview.

28. Interview with LaVern Polk by Van O'Cain and Lacy Ford, June 4, 2014, transcript (ECSC).

29. Interview with Nancy Heustess by Van O'Cain and Walter Allread, October 18, 2013, transcript (ECSC).

30. Interview with Scottie Plummer by Van O'Cain and Walter Allread, October 18, 2013, transcript (ECSC).

31. Interview with Cleland Manning by Van O'Cain, March 15, 2015, transcript (ECSC).

32. Interview with Louise Clark by Van O'Cain and Blake Ward, March 15, 2015, transcript (ECSC).

33. Interview with Frances and Albert Freeland by Mark Quinn and Jackson Shuford, July 1, 2014, transcript (ECSC).

34. Interview with Jessie Mae Jordan by Van O'Cain, May 21, 2014, transcript (ECSC).

35. Spilliards, interview.

36. Harry Slattery, *Rural America Lights Up: The Story of Rural Electrification* (Washington DC.: National House Library Foundation, 1940), 65.

37. Interview with Bob Smith by Van O'Cain, April 30, 2014, transcript (ECSC).

38. Interview with Mildred Allen by Van O'Cain, February 19, 2014, transcript (ECSC).

39. Burrell, interview.

40. Interview with Willie Mae Wood by Mark Quinn and Jackson Shuford, July 1, 2014, transcript (ECSC).

41. Robinson, interview.

42. Interview with Jerry Vaigneur by Van O'Cain, June 1, 2014, transcript (ECSC).

43. Interview with Bobby Edmonds by Mark Quinn and Jackson Shuford, July 1, 2014, transcript (ECSC).

44. Interview with Hubert Waldrop by Rachel Despres and Van O'Cain, July 22, 2013, transcript (ECSC).

45. Interview with Mary Spigner by Van O'Cain and Sheila Rivers, November 15, 2013, transcript (ECSC).

46. Jordan, interview.

47. Allen, interview.

48. Interview with Charles Banks by Van O'Cain, April 4, 2013, transcript (ECSC).

49. Interview with Bill Gibbons by Van O'Cain, March 16, 2015, transcript (ECSC).

50. Interview with Jerry Vaigneur by Van O'Cain and Lacy Ford, June 16, 2016, transcript (ECSC).

51. Hendrix, interview.

52. Interview with Mammie Jones by Van O'Cain, May 16, 2014, transcript (ECSC).

53. Spilliards, interview.

54. Hart, interview.

55. Interview with Louise Nichols by Van O'Cain, May 15, 2014, transcript (ECSC).

56. David Junious to Irvine F. Belser, October 6, 1950, Irvine F. Belser Papers, South Caroliniana Library, University of South Carolina, Columbia, SC (hereinafter cited as SCL).

57. Robert B. Dinkins to Irvine F. Belser, September 16, 1950, Belser Papers, SCL. Dinkins was the manager of the Black River Electric Cooperative.

58. David Junious to Irvine F. Belser, October 6, 1950, Belser Papers, SCL.

59. Irvine F. Belser to R. B. Dinkins, October 20, 1950, Belser Papers, SCL.

60. See, for example, Henry Richardson to Irvine F. Belser, August 27, 1952, and

Dennis Adams to Irvine F. Belser, February 27 and March 1952, Belser Papers, SCL.

61. Interview with Laylon Davis by Van O'Cain, May 16, 2014, transcript (ECSC).

62. Interview with Randolph Mackey by Van O'Cain and Lacy Ford, June 6, 2014, transcript (ECSC).

63. Waldrop, interview.

64. Spilliards, interview.

Chapter 2: The Origins of Electric Cooperatives

1. Peter Coclanis and Lacy Ford, "The South Carolina Economy Reconstructed and Reconsidered: Structure, Output, and performance, 1670-1985," in Winfred B. Moore Jr., Joseph T. Tripp, and Lyon G. Tyler Jr., eds., *Developing Dixie: Modernization in a Traditional Society* (New York: Greenwood Press, 1988), 93–110.

2. Sarah T. Phillips, *This Land, This Nation: Conservation, Rural America, and the New Deal* (New York: Cambridge University Press, 2007), 59–148.

3. US Congress, Senate, Committee on Agriculture & Forestry, *Rural Electrification*, 74th Congress, 2d Session, 1936, S. Rep No. 1581. For an overview of rural electrification in South Carolina, including historical photographs of 1920s and 1930s era powerlines and rural living conditions, see D. Clayton Brown, "Modernizing Rural Life: South Carolina's Push for Public Rural Electrification," *South Carolina Historical Magazine* 99 (1998): 66–85.

4. Committee on Agriculture & Forestry, *Rural Electrification*.

5. Committee on Agriculture & Forestry, *Rural Electrification*. For more on rural electrification efforts before the New Deal, see Richard Hirsh, "Shedding New Light on Rural Electrification: The Neglected Story of Successful Efforts to Power Up Farms in the 1920s and 1930s," *Agricultural History* 92 (2018): 296–327.

6. The Rural Electrification Administration was created by executive order on May 11, 1935. Early funding for this rural electrification effort had come through Congress via the Emergency Relief Act with $100,000,000 on April 8, 1935. Congress then passed the Norris-Rayburn Act, or "Rural Electrification Act," on May 20, 1936, a bill that extended the Rural Electrification Administration for ten years. See Harry Slattery, *Rural America Lights Up: The Story of Rural Electrification* (Washington, DC: National House Library Foundation, 1940), 27–32. For more on the "Southeast's hydraulic waterscapes," and an exploration of the environmental and political history of dams in the South, see Christopher J. Manganiello, *Southern Water, Southern Power: How the Politics of Cheap Energy and Water Scarcity Shaped a Region* (Chapel Hill: University of North Carolina Press, 2015). For a general overview of public dams and power in the postwar South, see Casey P. Cater, "Public Dams, Private Power: Electric Energy and Political Economy in the Post-Second World War US South," in Alain Beltran, Léonard Laborie, et al., eds, *Electric Worlds/Mondes électriques: Creations, Circulations, Tensions, Transitions* (Brussels: P.I.E-Peter Lang S.A., 2016).

7. Jack Irby Hayes Jr., *South Carolina and the New Deal* (Columbia, SC: University of South Carolina Press, 2001), 75–84; David Robertson, *Sly and Able: A Political Biography of James F. Byrnes* (New York: W. W. Norton, 1994), 223–245. For a history of the Duke Power Company, see Robert F. Durden, *Electrifying the Piedmont Carolinas: The Duke Power Company, 1904–1997* (Durham, NC: Carolina Academic Press, 2001).

8. Hayes, *South Carolina and the New Deal*, 76–78.

9. Hayes, *South Carolina and the New Deal*, 76–78.

10. Hayes, *South Carolina and the New Deal*, 79; Robertson, *Sly and Able*, 206–39; and Walter B. Edgar, *A History of Santee Cooper, 1934–1984*, 5–8.

11. Marvin Leigh Cann, "Burnet Rhett Maybank and the New Deal in South Carolina, 1931–1941," (Ph.D. diss. University of North Carolina, 1967), 15–53; Hayes, *South Carolina and the New Deal*, 79–80.

12. David L. Carlton, "Unbalanced Growth and Industrialization: The Case of South Carolina," *Developing Dixie*, 111–30.

13. Carlton, "Unbalanced Growth and Industrialization," 111–30.

14. James F. Byrnes to Harold Ickes, December 14, 1934, James F. Byrnes Papers, Clemson University, Clemson, SC.

15. "Rural Electric Act Questioned," *The State* (Columbia, SC), November 6, 1935.

16. Slattery, *Rural America Lights Up*, 39.

17. *The State* (Columbia, SC), March 12, 1939.

18. Ernestine B. Law, *And Then There Was Light: A History of Aiken Electric Cooperative, 1938–1988* (Aiken, SC: Howell Printing Company, 1988), 8-9.

19. *The State* (Columbia, SC), March 12, 1939.

20. For a comprehensive account of opposition to the Santee Cooper project on environmental, conservation, and preservation grounds, see T. Robert Hart, "The Lowcountry Landscape: Politics, Preservation and the Santee-Cooper Project" *Environmental History* 18 (January 2013): 127–56.

21. *The State* (Columbia, SC), April 30, 1939.

22. See S.C. Code Ann. § 8555-121 (1942).

23. See S.C. Code Ann. § 8555-93 (1942). A cooperative could be formed by the joining of five or more persons or two or more cooperatives (S.C. Code Ann. § 8555-95 (1942). This is the same language in current code at §33-49-220, and it also required that the cooperative's name include the words "electric" and "cooperative" followed by "inc." See S.C. Code Ann. § 8555-94 (1942). It is also the same language in current code at § 33-49-240. Initially, electric cooperatives were created for the purpose of supplying electricity and promoting and extending its use in rural areas. See S.C. Code Ann. § 8555-92 (1942). By 1954, the purpose of the cooperatives was amended to include an obligation to "make membership available without arbitrary or unreasonable limitations thereon, to all coming within the purview of that purpose." See S.C. Code Ann. § 12-1037 (1954). The original statute, and the current statute, limits membership in a cooperative to the incorporators and those persons who agree to "use electric energy furnished by the cooperative when such electric energy shall be available through its facilities" (S.C. Code Ann. § 8555-98 (1942) and S.C. Code Ann. § 33-49-410 (2012)).

24. S.C. Code Ann. § 8555-93. This is the same language in current code at § 33-49-250 (2).

25. *The State* (Columbia, SC), April 30, 1939.

26. *The State* (Columbia, SC), March 12, 1939.

27. Records of the South Carolina Secretary of State indicate the Laurens Cooperative was chartered on May 15. *The State*'s coverage of their REA loan on May 12 represents that the cooperative was being formed, thus it seems the Laurens Cooperative received its REA loan for line construction as, or even just before, being fully chartered by the state. See *The State* (Columbia, SC), May 12, 1939.

28. *The State* (Columbia, SC), June 2, 1939.

29. *The State* (Columbia, SC), July 8 and July 22, 1939.

30. *The State* (Columbia, SC), August 16, 1939.

31. *The State* (Columbia, SC), July 22, 1939.

32. *The State* (Columbia, SC), August 9, 1940.

33. Records of the South Carolina Secretary of State; Quotation from The Electric Cooperatives of South Carolina, "Electric Cooperative Timeline," accessed December 1, 2016, https://www.ecsc.org/content/electric-cooperative-timeline.

34. *The State* (Columbia, SC), June 20 and July 14, 1939.

35. *The State* (Columbia, SC), June 24 and July 29, 1939.

36. *The State* (Columbia, SC), September 16, 1939.

37. *The State* (Columbia, SC), September 17, 1939.

38. See *The State* (Columbia, SC), November 11, 1939.

39. For legislation concerning line transfers see, *The State* (Columbia, SC), April 19, June 20, and August 1, 1940.

40. *The State* reported on August 24, 1940, that "To the Pee Dee Electric Cooperative; Darling. M line 36 miles; Chesterfield A. 17 miles; Florence X, 83 miles. Total number of customers served by these lines, 489. To Santee Cooperative: Williamsburg Line A, 16 miles; Williamsburg E and Georgetown X, 44 miles; Georgetown D. 44 miles; Florence network, 148 miles; Clarendon S, 31 miles; customers served by these lines, 996. To Marlboro cooperative: Marlboro A Line, 22 miles; Marlboro C line, 20 miles; Dillon C line, 38 miles; customers served 219. To Marion cooperative: Dillon E line, 27 miles; customers serve 99." See *The State* (Columbia, SC), August 24, 1940.

41. Edgar, *A History of Santee Cooper*, 11, 18.

42. This, too, began with an REA loan. In September 1941, the federal REA allotted one quarter million dollars for "construction of a transmission network to carry power from the Santee-Cooper development to 16 rural electric cooperatives. . . . The allotment was made to a cooperative as yet unnamed but with headquarters in Charleston county." See *The State* (Columbia, SC), September 13, 1941.

43. Law, *And Then There Was Light*, 15–16, 20; Hayes, *South Carolina and the New Deal*, 84; Edgar, *History of Santee Cooper*, 11, 18–20, 95, 121–25.

44. Figures from Public Service Commission Report. See *The State* (Columbia, SC), October 5, 1946.

Chapter 3: Working the Lines

1. Interview with Arthur James by Van O'Cain, October 14, 2014, transcript (in the possession of in possession of The Electric Cooperatives of South Carolina).

2. James, interview. In 1940, the average per capita farm income in South Carolina was $147. The $5 membership fee represented about two weeks of income. Of course, farm income varied widely around the average. See Ernest M. Lander, *A History of South Carolina, 1865–1960* (Columbia, SC: University of South Carolina Press, 1970), 119.

3. Interview with Dargan Hodge by Van O'Cain, October 8, 2014, transcript (ECSC).

4. Interview with Kirk Roberts by Van O'Cain, April 1, 2014, transcript (ECSC). For a discussion on electrification, lighting, wiring, and farm architecture, see

Sarah Rovang, "The Grid Comes Home: Wiring and Lighting the American Farmhouse," *Buildings & Landscapes: Journal of the Vernacular Architecture Forum* 23 (2016): 65–88. See also Sarah Rovang, "Envisioning the Future of Modern Farming: The Electrified Farm at the 1939 New York World's Fair," *Journal of the Society of Architectural Historians* 74 (2015): 201–22.

5. Interview with Jack Morris by Van O'Cain, June 19, 2014, transcript (ECSC).

6. Interview with N. L. "Shorty" Caprell by Rachel Despres, June 26, 2013, transcript (ECSC). For an economic analysis of the REA's impact on agricultural productivity, see Carl Kitchens and Price Fishback, "Flip the Switch: The Impact of the Rural Electrification Administration 1935-1940," *Journal of Economic History* 75 (2015): 1161–195. See also Carl Kitchens, "The Role of Publicly Provided Electricity in Economic Development: The Experience of the Tennessee Valley Authority, 1929–1955," *Journal of Economic History* 74 (2014): 389–419.

7. Interview with Ray Derrick by Van O'Cain and Muriel Gouffray, June 26, 2013, transcript (ECSC). For more on attitudes towards electrification on farms, see Audra J. Wolfe, "'How Not to Electrocute the Farmer': Assessing Attitudes Towards Electrification on American Farms, 1920–1940," *Agricultural History* 74 (2000): 515–29.

8. Derrick, interview.

9. Interview with Peggy Dantzler by Jackson Shuford, September 29, 2014, transcript (ECSC).

10. Derrick, interview.

11. Interview with Dickie Walker by Van O'Cain, December 8, 2014, transcript (ECSC).

12. Interview with Helen Martin by Van O'Cain,, February 27, 2014, transcript (ECSC).

13. Interview with Billy Catoe by Van O'Cain, February 14, 2014, transcript (ECSC).

14. Interview with Victor Wilform by Van O'Cain, September 17, 2014, transcript (ECSC).

15. Interview with Michael Dupree by Van O'Cain, December 10, 2014, transcript (ECSC).

16. Dupree, interview.

17. Interview with Leslie Tindal by Van O'Cain, October 14, 2014, transcript (ECSC).

18. Interview with Charlene Haynes by Van O'Cain, March 18, 2015, transcript (ECSC).

19. Derrick, interview.

20. Interview with Marion Caldwell by Van O'Cain, March 26, 2014, transcript (ECSC).

21. Interview with Walter and Maxine Baker by Van O'Cain, July 25, 2014, transcript (ECSC).

22. Interview with Lewis Ringer by Walter Allread, February 19, 2014, transcript (ECSC).

23. Walker, interview.

24. Derrick, interview.

25. Derrick, interview.

26. Dantzler, interview.

27. Dantzler, interview.

28. Dantzler, interview.
29. Dupree, interview.
30. Dantzler, interview.
31. Dantzler, interview.
32. Dantzler, interview.
33. Dantzler, interview.
34. Dantzler, interview.
35. Baker, interview.
36. Baker, interview.
37. Interview with Bill Gibbons by Van O'Cain, March 16, 2015, transcript (ECSC).
38. Interview with Joe Gibbs Sr. by Van O'Cain and Jackson Shuford, December 17, 2014, transcript (ECSC).
39. Interview with David Eugene "Gene" Carson by Van O'Cain, July 22, 2013, transcript (ECSC).
40. Martin, interview.
41. Martin, interview.
42. Interview with Bill Murray by Van O'Cain, December 17, 2014, transcript (ECSC).
43. Interview with Buddy Harvey by Van O'Cain, December 8, 2014, transcript (ECSC).
44. Interview with Hilda Lewis by Van O'Cain and Jackson Shuford, December 17, 2014, transcript (ECSC).
45. Interview with Jerry Brewer by Van O'Cain, December 8, 2014, transcript (ECSC).
46. Interview with Virgil Leaphart by Van O'Cain, December 5, 2014, transcript (ECSC).
47. Interview with LaVern Polk by Van O'Cain and Lacy Ford, June 4, 2014, transcript (ECSC).
48. Walter "Sonny" Sanders by Van O'Cain, Lacy Ford, and Harvey Teal, June 3, 2014, transcript (ECSC).

Chapter 4: Electricity and the Rural Home

1. Interview with Gladys Meetze by Van O'Cain, November 5, 2014, transcript (in the possession of The Electric Cooperatives of South Carolina).
2. Peter Coclanis and Lacy Ford, "The South Carolina Economy Reconstructed and Reconsidered: Structure, Output, and performance, 1670–1985," in Winfred B. Moore Jr., Joseph T. Tripp, and Lyon G. Tyler Jr., eds., *Developing Dixie: Modernization in a Traditional Society* (New York: Greenwood Press, 1988), 93–110; Robert J. Gordon, *The Rise and Fall of American Growth: The U.S. Standard of Living Since the Civil War* (Princeton: Princeton University Press, 2016), 1–24, 535–63; State Data Center of Iowa, "Urban and Rural Population for the United States and All States:1900–2000," accessed June 24, 2021, https://www.iowa datacenter.org/.
3. Gordon, *The Rise and Fall of American Growth*, 535–63; State Data Center of Iowa, "Urban and Rural Population for the United States and All States:1900-2000," accessed June 24, 2021, https://www.iowadatacenter.org/.
4. "One of the Best Credit Records," Editorial, *South Carolina Electric Co-Op News*, Black River Edition, February 1961.

5. "Half a Mile Off the Highway," *Living in South Carolina*, Aiken Edition, November 1963, 12.

6. "Downward Price Trend Makes Home Appliances Best Buys of the Year," *South Carolina Electric Co-Op News*, Black River Edition, February 1961.

7. "Wash, Rinse, and Spin," *Living in South Carolina*, Pee Dee Edition, February 1963, 22. For a classic study of "labor-saving" devices, household technology, and women's labor, see Ruth Schwartz Cohen, *More Work for Mother: The Ironies of Household Technology from the Open Hearth to the Microwave* (New York: Basic Books, 1983).

8. H. W. "Hub" Norris, "Take the Jump with a Heat Pump," *South Carolina Electric Co-Op News*, Mid-Carolina Edition, March 1961, 5.

9. "New! Terrific!" advertisement, *South Carolina Electric Co-Op News*, Mid-Carolina Edition, March 1961, 3, 7.

10. "The Electro-Warmth Opens a Marvelous New World of Luxury Sleeping Comfort to You," advertisement, *South Carolina Electric Co-Op News*, Horry Edition, November 1962, 3.

11. "A 1961 Frigidaire Frost-Proof Refrigerator," advertisement, *South Carolina Electric Co-Op News*, Mid-Carolina Edition, July 1961.

12. "Look at all 8 by Frigidaire before you buy any food freezer!" advertisement, *South Carolina Electric Co-Op News*, Laurens Edition, May 1962, 11.

13. Winifred R. Mullikin, "When the Lights Came On," *South Carolina Electric Co-Op News*, Aiken Edition, October 1961, 2.

14. "Members Talk about Their Cooperative," *Living in South Carolina*, Edisto Edition, February 1989, 6–7, 19.

15. Caldon King, "When the Lights Came On," *South Carolina Electric Co-Op News*, Lynches River Edition, August 1962, 2.

16. Mrs. H. D. Crook, "When the Lights Came On," *South Carolina Electric Co-Op News*, Laurens Edition, May 1962.

17. Hildegarde Popper, "In Electric Ranges, It's the Built-In Look," *Living in South Carolina*, Coastal Edition, March 1963, 7–8.

18. For example, see "Electric Heat: What Does It Cost?" *South Carolina Electric Co-Op News*, Mid-Carolina Edition, March 1961, 8. Economist and historian of technology Mark Aldrich argued that "especially for women in rural and farm households, kerosene provided an important bridge fuel to the newer age of gas and electricity. To ignore it is to ignore what was for many an important introduction to modern times." For more on the use of kerosene in rural homes, see Mark Aldrich, "The Rise and Decline of the Kerosene Kitchen: A Neglected Energy Transition in Rural America, 1870-1950," *Agricultural History* 94 (2020), 24–60.

19. "Rural Electrification Is 97 Percent Complete," *Living in South Carolina*, Pee Dee Edition, February 1963, 11.

20. For the full spread see, "School Time Is Eye Check-Up Time" and "Correct Light Means Comfortable Sight," *South Carolina Electric Co-Op News*, Black River Edition, March 1961, 1. The latter article included the offer of personalized assistance.

21. Edith Ann Byrd, "Light for Living: Recipes for Better Living Through Better Lighting," *South Carolina Electric Co-Op News*, Mid-Carolina Edition, September 1961, 1.

22. "Now See This!" *South Carolina Electric Co-Op News*, Little River Edition, March 1961, 7.

23. Jan Reynolds, "Good Lighting for A SAFER Home," *South Carolina Electric Co-Op News*, Black River Edition, September 1962.

24. "Dishwasher Fights Spread of Germs Through Family," *South Carolina Electric Co-Op News*, York Edition, February 1962.

25. Wisconsin REA News, "Guest Editorial: Silence Is as Silence Does," *South Carolina Electric Co-Op News*, Little River Edition, July 1961, 2.

26. Barbara Spadetti, "No Need to Swelter This Summer," *South Carolina Electric Co-Op News*, Little River Edition, July 1961. Such a figure works out to approximately $2.00 per day in 2017 dollars. For more on the history of air conditioning, see Raymond Arsenault, "The End of the Long Hot Summer: The Air Conditioner and Southern Culture," *Journal of Southern History* 50 (1984): 597–628 and Jeff E. Biddle, "Making Consumers Comfortable: The Early Decades of Air Conditioning in the United States," *Journal of Economic History* 71 (2011): 1078–94.

27. "Teenagers Find It's 'Hip' Helping with Dishwashing," *South Carolina Electric Co-Op News*, Laurens Edition, January 1962, np; and "Carefree, Automatic Oven Cooking," *South Carolina Electric Co-Op News*, Laurens Edition, January 1962.

28. "Home Owner's Question Box," *Living in South Carolina*, Coastal Edition, March 1963, 18.

29. "Fallout Shelter Is 4-H Project for Meetze Boys," *South Carolina Electric Co-Op News*, Coastal Edition, November 1961.

30. Untitled advertisement for light pole, *South Carolina Electric Co-Op News*, Lynches River Edition, April 1962.

31. "Gold Medallion Family," *Living in South Carolina*, Aiken Edition, November 1963, 13.

32. "Own Your Own Home," advertisement for Shell Homes, Inc., *South Carolina Electric Co-Op News*, Mid-Carolina Edition, March 1961, 7. While "Shell Homes, Inc." was initially a brand, the term came to describe any new home construction in which the builder provided the initial shell of the house, often with an unfinished interior that buyers were obligated to complete on their own. The term is still used in the industry today without brand attribution.

33. "Stylecraft Homes," advertisement, *South Carolina Electric Co-Op News*, Little River Edition, July 1961.

34. "Own Your Own Home," advertisement for Shell Homes, Inc., *South Carolina Electric Co-Op News*, York Edition, February 1962; "Own Your Own Home," advertisement for Shell Homes, Inc., *South Carolina Electric Co-Op News*, Blue Ridge Edition, March 1962; and "Wise Homes for Happy Family Living," advertisement, *South Carolina Electric Co-Op News*, Blue Ridge Edition, March 1962.

35. "It's New Home Time," advertisement for Jim Walter Homes, *Living in South Carolina*, Coastal Edition, March 1963, 21.

36. "Go Modern: Let Us Remodel and Modernize Your Home," advertisement for J. L. Nipper Construction Company, *South Carolina Electric Co-Op News*, Salkehatchie Edition, August 1961.

37. Modern Homes Construction Company, advertisement, *South Carolina Electric Co-Op News*, Horry Edition, November 1962.

38. "American Family Homes," advertisement, *Living in South Carolina*, Lexington Edition, March 1976, 5.

39. "More Home for Less Money," *Living in South Carolina*, Laurens Edition, March 1977, 2. Page four of this same issue carried news that circulation of *Living in South Carolina* had exceeded 201,000, making it the eighth-largest circulation among states in the country.

40. "The Tysons Build Their First New Home," advertisement for Jim Walter Homes, *Living in South Carolina*, Lexington Edition, March 1976, 7; and "Need a Home? Have 'They Said 'No'?" advertisement for Miles Homes, *Living in South Carolina*, Lexington Edition, March 1976, 13.

41. "Own a New Home for as Little as $5,160," advertisement for Carolina Model Home Corporation, *Living in South Carolina*, Lexington Edition, March 1976, 21.

42. "The Finest Traditional Log Homes That Modern Technology Can Produce," advertisement for Southland Log Homes, *Living in South Carolina*, Little River Edition, April 1981, 25.

43. See, for example, "The Insulated Mobile Home Roofing System," advertisement for WeatherMaster, *Living in South Carolina*, Lynches River Edition, March 1989, 25.

44. "Mobile Home Owners," *Living in South Carolina*, Little River Edition, March 1992, 21.

45. "Why Buy Half a Pool?" advertisement for Pools by Ace, *Living in South Carolina*, Lexington Edition, March 1976, 29. The frequency of ads for pools waned during the early 1980s, but they appeared more frequently in the late 1980s and early 1990s.

46. "Hold It," advertisement for Wickes Buildings, *Living in South Carolina*, York Edition, March 1978, 9. Multiple manufacturers, including Butler, Arco, and Morton Buildings, ran such ads throughout the period.

47. "Amazing Super-Growing Species Soars into a Magnificent Tree in Just One Year!" advertisement for West-Bond Nursery Sales Co., *Living in South Carolina*, Laurens Edition, March 1977, 7. Advertisements for various plantings, fruit trees, and similar products were common in the co-op publications during the 1970s, but few pitched the tree or planting as an improvement to lifestyle at home, as the Royal Paulownia ads did.

48. "Spectacular Flowering Walnut," *Living in South Carolina*, York Edition, March 1978, 5. Not mentioned was the fact that black walnuts (*juglans nigra*) take at least four to six years to fruit and twenty years to produce a large crop. Each year seemed to focus on a new tree of choice, often with the same drawings modified to show the shape of the new tree. In 1981, for example, the Canadian (or Carolina) Poplar was the featured tree. See "Zooms Roof High in Just One Single Year!" *Living in South Carolina*, Little River Edition, April 1981, 23.

49. Larry Cribb, "Exotic Flower or Weed?" *Living in South Carolina*, April 1990, 4.

50. "White Roofing Foils South's Blazing Sun," *South Carolina Electric Co-Op News*, Laurens Edition, January 1962.

51. D. A. Wilcox, "You'll Say 'Electric Heat Can't Be Beat,'" *South Carolina Electric Co-Op News*, Lynches River Edition, August 1962.

52. "Electric Heating Both Practical and Economical," *South Carolina Electric Co-Op News*, Santee Edition, October 1962. For an example of an article clearly aimed

at co-op members who straddled the electric/flame fuel divide, see "Converting to Electric Heat Is Easy, Economical," *Living in South Carolina*, Coastal Edition, March 1963, 19.

53. "Save Money If You Install Dishwasher" and "Insulation is Good Insurance," *South Carolina Electric Co-Op News*, Horry Edition, November 1962.

54. "How Come Chicken's So Cheap?" advertisement, *South Carolina Electric Co-Op News*, Black River Edition, September 1962.

55. Sean Wilentz, *The Age of Reagan: A History, 1974–2008* (New York: HarperCollins, 2008), 49–126.

56. "Energy Conservation Requires Discipline," *Living in South Carolina*, York Edition, March 1978, 17.

57. R. D. Bennett, "Think Conservation," *Living in South Carolina*, York Edition, June 1978, 23.

58. "Energy, Water Saving Device Offered Free to Santee Cooper and Electric Cooperative Customers," *Living in South Carolina*, Tri-County Edition, September 1979, 16–17.

59. "Intertherm Hot Water Electric Baseboard Heating," advertisement, *Living in South Carolina*, Pee Dee Edition, September 1976, 26.

60. "Checklist of Ways to Save Money While Keeping Warm," *Living in South Carolina*, Laurens Edition, March 1977, 13; and "Chances Are There's a Heat Pump in Your Future," *Living in South Carolina*, Laurens Edition, March 1977, 16. Another column on how to save energy in both water use and heating ran just two months later. See "Energy Saving Ideas," *Living in South Carolina*, Santee Edition, May 1977, 20.

61. "A New Approach," *Living in South Carolina*, Aiken Edition, June 1977, 23.

62. "Low Cost, No Cost," *Living in South Carolina*, Little River Edition, April 1981, 19–21.

63. "Alcoa ½ Price Siding Sale," advertisement, *Living in South Carolina*, Aiken Edition, February 1980, 5.

64. "Solar House," *Living in South Carolina*, Berkeley Edition, October 1977, 10–11.

65. Liesl C. Clarke, "'Do-It-Yourself' Solar Heating," *Living in South Carolina*, Aiken Edition, May 1978, 25.

66. Margaret Callison Pridgen, "Clemson Prof Co-Inventor of New Solar Energy Cells," *Living in South Carolina*, Tri-County Edition, September 1979, 26–27.

67. Robert D. Partridge, "Cooperative Month: October 1977," *Living in South Carolina*, Berkeley Edition, October 1977, 32.

68. Al Ballard, "We Must Speak Out," *Living in South Carolina*, Berkeley Edition, December 1981, 3.

69. "Rural Electrification: It Works," *Living in South Carolina*, Black River Edition, December 1984, 24.

70. "Co-Ops Have More Line Than All Other Utilities," *Living in South Carolina*, Horry Edition, October 1990, 5.

Chapter 5: South Carolina's Electric Cooperatives
and the Changing Role of Women

1. Interview with William F. Robinson by Van O'Cain, March 27, 2014, transcript (in the possession of The Electric Cooperatives of South Carolina).

2. Interview with Walter and Maxine Baker by Van O'Cain, July 25, 2014, transcript

(ECSC); Interview with Kirk Roberts by Van O'Cain, April 1, 2014, transcript (ECSC).

3. Mrs. N. D. Clayton, "When the Lights Came On," *South Carolina Electric Co-Op News*, Broad River Edition, December 1961, 2.

4. For one such example, see Virginia Ruth, ed., "For the Ladies," *South Carolina Electric Co-Op News*, Mid-Carolina Edition, March 1961, 6. Just one page of this issue offered details on how to make an Easter egg pyramid, how to bake cookies with a waffle iron, how to use crispy bacon in other applications, how to make shrimp mariniere, and how to use foil preparations to improve the flavor of ham. For discussions of American farm women and the significant technological, cultural, and social changes in rural women's lives in the twentieth century, see Dorothy Schwieder, "Education and Change in the Lives of Iowa Farm Women, 1900–1940," *Agricultural History* 60 (1986): 200–215; Katherine Jellison, *Entitled to Power: Farm Women and Technology, 1913–1963* (Chapel Hill: University of North Carolina Press, 1993); Ronald R. Kline, *Consumers in the Country: Technology and Social Change in Rural America* (Baltimore: Johns Hopkins University Press, 2000); Jenny Barker Devine, "'Hop to the Top with the Iowa Chop'": The Iowa Porkettes and Cultivating Agrarian Feminisms in the Midwest, 1964–1992," *Agricultural History* 83 (2009): 477–502; and Chrissy Lutz and Dawn Herd-Clark, "'No One Was on Their Own': Sociability Among Rural African American Women in Middle Georgia during the Interwar Years," *Agricultural History* 93 (2019): 437–51.

5. "Fabulous 'No-Frost' Foodarama by Kelvinator," advertisement, *South Carolina Electric Co-Op News*, Mid-Carolina Edition, April 1961. The Foodarama's twelve cubic feet of refrigeration and six cubic feet of "freezer space *right in your kitchen!*" must have seemed massive to the consumers of the day, but today's top-of-the-line side-by-sides dwarf the Foodarama with their standard, combined capacity of 26 cubic feet. For comparison, a 1961 Philco model offered only 13.6 cubic feet of space in its Supermarketer model, including its 180-pound freezer compartment. See "Only Philco Gives You New Custom-Tailored Cold," advertisement, *South Carolina Electric Co-Op News*, Little River Edition, July 1961, 7.

6. "It's Back to School!" *Living in South Carolina*, Pee Dee Edition, March 1963, 15. The Horry Electric Cooperative in Conway, South Carolina sponsored the event covered in this article.

7. Elizabeth Potter, "The Bride and Her Appliances," *Living in South Carolina*, April 1963, 4.

8. "Dishwasher Fights Spread of Germs Through Family," *South Carolina Electric Co-Op News*, York Edition, February 1962.

9. "Good Cakes Bake Better Electrically," *South Carolina Electric Co-Op News*, Lynches River Edition, April 1962, 4.

10. "Freeze Your Own Foods," *Living in South Carolina*, Coastal Edition, July 1963, 12.

11. See, for example, "Cook's Corner," *Living in South Carolina*, August 1963, 12. "Cook's Corner" was apparently edited for a time by Judy Weaver, listed as the "woman's editor" in Kirby Able's recurring column in May 1978. See Kirby Able, "Rambling," *Living in South Carolina*, Aiken Edition, May 1978, 4. Sadly, accepted submissions still garnered just two dollars in 1991.

12. "Fashions for the Ladies," advertisement, *Living in South Carolina*, Lexington Edition, March 1976, 18. These advertisements (which were an indexed section of *Living in South Carolina*) appeared monthly through the early 1990s.

13. "Electric Water Heater Is Quality in the Home," *South Carolina Electric Co-Op News*, Black River Edition, February 1961.

14. "This 1961 Frigidaire Range . . . ," advertisement, *South Carolina Electric Co-Op News*, Mid-Carolina Edition, April 1961, 10. For perspectives on turning women into modern consumers, see Victoria De Grazo with Ellen Furlough, *The Sex of Things: Gender and Consumption in Historical Perspective* (Berkeley: University of California Press, 1996).

15. "The Unbelievable Jones Girls," *South Carolina Electric Co-Op News*, Aiken Edition, October 1961.

16. "Beauties, Business, and Talent Highlight State Co-Op Session," *South Carolina Electric Co-Op News*, Broad River Edition, December 1961. One contestant in the talent competition—David Murphy of Beaufort—appears to have been a young man.

17. For two examples, see untitled photo spread, *South Carolina Electric Co-Op News*, Laurens Edition, January 1962; "Dorothy Lois Jones: Our Own Miss S. C. Electric Co-Op," *South Carolina Electric Co-Op News*, York Edition, February 1962. Both entries included photos of Miss Jones, including one in her bathing suit.

18. "Letters to the Editor," *South Carolina Electric Co-Op News*, Santee Edition, October 1962.

19. "Let's Talk Turkey," *South Carolina Electric Co-Op News*, Horry Edition, November 1962, 3.

20. For one such example, see Don Holcombe, "Mother," poem on front cover of *Living in South Carolina*, Santee Edition, May 1977. On page 4 of the same issue, Kirby Able's recurring "Rambling" column contained a lengthy "Tribute to Mothers." The same practice occurred less frequently for fathers in June. See, for example, Richard Brannon, "You Get What You Get Ready For," *Living in South Carolina*, Aiken Edition, June 1977, cover.

21. "Mother's Day 1961: Modern Madonna," *South Carolina Electric Co-Op News*, Tri-County Edition, May 1961, 1.

22. "Palmetto Personality: Mrs. Lois Myrick," *South Carolina Electric Co-Op News*, Black River Edition, February 1961.

23. "Ever Feel Like Screaming on Monday?" advertisement, *South Carolina Electric Co-Op News*, Santee Edition, October 1962, 10.

24. "Dillon Girl to Address NRECA Meeting," *South Carolina Electric Co-Op News*, Black River Edition, February 1961.

25. "Miss Ruth Rapin . . . ," *South Carolina Electric Co-Op News*, Little River Edition, July 1961, 7.

26. "German Girl Visits in Rural South Carolina Homes," *South Carolina Electric Co-Op News*, Little River Edition, July 1962. Established in 1927, 4-H is a national youth program, supported by the United States Department of Agriculture (USDA), that seeks to develop leadership and life skills in young people. The four "h" terms in their pledge and creed are head, heart, hands, and health. See two recent studies of 4-H: Kiera Butler, *Raise: What 4-H Teaches Seven Million Kids and How Its Lesson Could Change Food and Farming Forever* (Berkeley: University of California Press, 2014); and Gabriel N, Rosenberg, *The 4-H Harvest:*

Sexuality and The State in Rural America (Philadelphia: University of Pennsylvania Press, 2015).

27. "Are Girls Better Bus Drivers?" *Living in South Carolina*, Palmetto Edition, October 1963, 6. In South Carolina during this era, high school students were selected, trained, and paid to be school bus drivers.

28. "Downward Price Trend Makes Home Appliances Best Buys of the Year," *South Carolina Electric Co-Op News*, Black River Edition, February 1961. Potter later authored columns in the cooperative publications. See, for example, Elizabeth Potter, "The Bride and Her Appliances."

29. Dana Sawyer, "Horry Co-Op's First Director's Day," *South Carolina Electric Co-Op News*, Laurens Edition, May 1962.

30. Interview with "Recent Retiree" by Van O'Cain, December 17, 2014, transcript (ECSC).

31. Interview with Theresa Hicks by Van O'Cain and Lacy Ford, June 4, 2014, transcript (ECSC). Hicks later went on to serve on the Lynches River board after retirement.

32. Mrs. W. E. Dargan, "Garden Club Says: Conservation Is Vital," *South Carolina Electric Co-Op News*, Little River Edition, July 1961.

33. "About This Picture," *South Carolina Electric Co-Op News*, Mid-Carolina Edition, April 1961, 1.

34. Anne Bradford, "Job Opportunities in Cooperatives," *South Carolina Electric Co-Op News*, Mid-Carolina Edition, April 1961, 10.

35. Erma Angevine, "Women Can Help" and "Family Fare," *Living in South Carolina*, Horry Edition, June 1963, 8.

36. Erma Angevine, "Family Fare: Women Want to Know," *Living in South Carolina*, September 1963, 7.

37. Kirby Able, "A Bit of Ladylike Beak-Tweaking," *Living in South Carolina*, August 1963, 5.

38. "Hell Hole Swamp Welcomes Miss Rural Electrification," *Living in South Carolina*, Pee Dee Edition, April 1976, 12.

39. An advertisement for the 1987 Palmetto Electric Cooperative Annual Meeting makes no mention of a beauty or talent contest. Entertainment featured country music artist Stella Parton (younger sister of Dolly Parton). See "Palmetto Update," *Living in South Carolina*, Palmetto Edition, March 1987, 16.

40. R. D. Bennett, "Privilege or Obligation?" *Living in South Carolina*, Aiken Edition, May 1978, 30. Lest one think this was an oversight on Bennett's part, his article later that year about the election of cooperative trustees again focused repeatedly and exclusively on the male pronoun. See "Elected Officials," *Living in South Carolina*, Horry Edition, September 1978, 31.

41. "Co-Op Youth Vice President," *Living in South Carolina*, Aiken Edition, August 1976, 8–9.

42. "'Bud' Hennecy," *Living in South Carolina*, York Edition, March 1978, 24–25.

43. "It Still Happens!" *Living in South Carolina*, Laurens Edition, November 1978, 8–9.

44. Larry Cribb, "Or How to Save Money Couponing," *Living in South Carolina*, Aiken Edition, February 1980, 6–7.

45. "Now! Trim & Slim Any Figure Instantly," advertisement, *Living in South Carolina*, Aiken Edition, February 1980, 21.

46. "Social Security Facts for Women," *Living in South Carolina*, Little River Edition, March 1992, 11.

47. Larry Cribb, "She Plans to Be More Than Just the First," *Living in South Carolina*, Little River Edition, March 1988, 5, 14–15.

48. "WIRE President Is Honored," *Living in South Carolina*, Mid-Carolina Edition, January 1984, 5. Also unfortunate was the obligatory notice in the article that "Mrs. Bruce is the wife of Larry Bruce, general manager of Coastal Electric Cooperative," a line that simultaneously minimized the significance of Joan Bruce's contributions and evoked implications of nepotism. For more on WIRE's activities, see "1983 Annual Meeting: Cooperatives Must Fight in Order to Maintain Program, Congressman Says," at pages 12–13 in the same issue. Indeed, photos of the delegates in attendance at the 1983 NRECA Annual Meeting show a sea of men with no women to be found whatsoever. See "South Carolina Delegates Fight for the Program," *Living in South Carolina*, Lynches River Edition, March 1984, 8–9. On the key initiatives of WIRE, see Jan Bonnette, "Another Busy Year for the Women Involved in Rural Electrification (WIRE)," *Living in South Carolina*, Palmetto Edition, April 1984, 21–22. On the tenth anniversary of WIRE, see Larry Cribb, "WIRE Celebrates 10th Anniversary," *Living in South Carolina*, Berkeley Edition, January 1991, 8.

49. Larry Cribb, "Women Involved . . . ," *Living in South Carolina*, Little River Edition, February 1987, 8-9. Features covering fundraising efforts by WIRE were common throughout the 1980s. See, for example, Larry Cribb, "People Helping People," *Living in South Carolina*, Little River Edition, October 1987, 6–7 and 15; "We're All Proud of Wire!" *Living in South Carolina*, Little River Edition, March 1988, 4.

50. Larry Cribb, "SC Wire Takes Top National Honor," *Living in South Carolina*, Little River Edition, March 1988, 12 and 25. South Carolina WIRE groups continued to win numerous awards annually through the early 1990s.

51. Ilene C. Harral, "A Co-Op Member Speaks Out," *Living in South Carolina*, Palmetto Edition, April 1989, 12 and 25.

52. "Washington Plays Host to Co-Op Youth," *Living in South Carolina*, Pee Dee Edition, August 1984, 10. The 1989 Co-Op Youth Tour featured 22 rising seniors, 14 of whom were women. See "Co-Op Youth Tour Washington," *Living in South Carolina*, Pee Dee Edition, August 1989, 10.

53. Corey Keyes, "Co-Op Youth Tour Washington," *Living in South Carolina*, Aiken Edition, August 1992, 10.

54. Interview with Myrtle Faile by Van O'Cain, Jackson Shuford, and Lacy Ford, June 3, 2014, transcript (ECSC).

55. "Working with Members," *Living in South Carolina*, Lynches River Edition, March 1984, 16D.

56. Photos accompanied Larry Cribb, "SC Wire Takes Top National Honor."

57. Larry Cribb, "Electric Cooperatives Tackle Problem of Rural Economic Development," *Living in South Carolina*, Berkeley Edition, November 1988, 5.

58. Interview with Eunice Spilliards by Van O'Cain and Lacy Ford, June 4, 2014, transcript (ECSC).

59. Interview with Peggy Dantzler by Jackson Shuford, September 29, 2014, transcript (ECSC).

60. Interview with Charlene Haynes by Van O'Cain, March 18, 2015, transcript (ECSC).

Chapter 6: The Politics of Rural Electrification
in the 1950s and 1960s

1. For a good introduction to the way the defense build-up for the Cold War became an instrument for economic development in the American South, including South Carolina, see Kari Frederickson, *Cold War Dixie: Militarization and Modernization in the American South* (Athens: University of Georgia Press, 2013). On the displacement of Ellenton, South Carolina, by the construction the new atomic weapons facility, see Louise Cassels, *The Unexpected Exodus: How the Cold War Displaced One Southern Town* (Columbia: University of South Carolina Press, 2007). The latter book was first published in 1971. The 2007 version includes an introduction by Kari Frederickson.

2. See, for example, "Americans Turn Against Socialized Electricity," Carolina Power & Light Company advertisement, *Lake City Times Herald*, January 10, 1952, 2. For more on conservatism and debates about electric utilities, see "Countryside Conservatism and Conservation," in Christopher J. Manganiello, *Southern Water, Southern Power: How the Politics of Cheap Energy and Water Scarcity Shaped a Region* (Chapel Hill: University of North Carolina Press, 2015). For a state-level case study, see Conor M. Harrison, "Electric Conservatism: The Rise of North Carolina's Conservative Power Politics," *Southeastern Geographer* 57 (2017): 332–50.

3. "'Creeping Socialism' Gets Jolt" and "The High Price of Socialism," *Aiken Standard*, August 12, 1953, 4. The conservative critique of public power gained prominence when President Eisenhauer referred the TVA in connection with using the term "creeping socialism." See Matthew L. Downs, *Transforming the South: Federal Development in the Tennessee Valley, 1915–1960* (Baton Rouge: Louisiana State University Press, 2014), especially 162–65.

4. "Who Asked You?" Carolina Power & Light Company advertisement, *Florence Morning News*, September 19, 1951, 2.

5. For background on Reddy Kilowatt, see Kelly Kazek, "90 Years of Reddy Kilowatt: An Alabama-Created Icon Recognized around the World," *AL.com*, March 15, 2016, http://www.al.com/living/index.ssf/2016/03/90_years_of_reddy_kilowatt_an.html.

6. For information on the emergence of Willie Wiredhand, see Richard G. Biever, "Golden Boy: Willie Wirehand's Life Story: Perky Mascot Willie Wirehand Keeps Plugging Away for Electric Co-Ops and Consumers," *Indiana Connection*, January 27, 2015, https://www.indianaconnection.org/golden-boy. For more on Willie Wirehand memorabilia, art, and comic books, see Richard G. Biever, "65 & Pluggin' On: A Milestone of Service Reflected in the Things We Collect," *Indiana Connection*, June 20, 2016, https://www.indianaconnection.org/65-pluggin-on. *Indiana Connection*, formally *Electric Consumer*, is published by Indiana Electric Cooperatives.

7. "*Reddy-Kilowatt v. Mid-Carolina Electric Cooperative*," 142 F. Supp. 851 (1956). For full text of the decision, see "*Reddy-Kilowatt v. Mid-Carolina Electric Cooperative*," *Leagle*, https://www.leagle.com/decision/1956993142fsupp8511835.

8. Willie Wiredhand's legal battles with Reddy Kilowatt are nicely recounted in

Biever, "Golden Boy," cited above. See also Richard A. Pence, Patrick Dahl, and National Rural Electric Cooperative Association, *The Next Greatest Thing* (Washington, DC.: National Rural Electric Cooperative Association, 1984), 218. The decision in Willie's first legal case can be seen in "*Reddy-Kilowatt v. Mid-Carolina Electric Cooperative*," 142 F. Supp. 851 (1956).

9. "*Reddy Kilowatt, Inc., Appellant, v. Mid-Carolina Electric Cooperative, Inc., and National Rural Electric Cooperative Association, Inc.*, Appellees," 240 F.2d 282 (4th Cir. 1957). For full text of the decision, see "*Reddy Kilowatt, Inc., Appellant, v. Mid-Carolina Electric Cooperative, Inc., and National Rural Electric Cooperative Association, Inc., Appellees*, 240 F.2d 282 (4th Cir. 1957)," *Justia*, https://law.justia.com/cases/federal/appellate-courts/F2/240/282/119417.

10. "Uncle Sam's ahead again!" NRECA advertisement, *Living in South Carolina*, January 1963.

11. "This is Local?" *Living in South Carolina*, January 1963, 14.

12. "Private Enterprise?" and "Where the Money Goes...," *South Carolina Electric Co-Op News*, Broad River Edition, December 1961, 2.

13. "Power Company Rewrites Aiken City Contract," *South Carolina Electric Co-Op News*, Laurens Edition, January 1962.

14. "Here's How, Mister McMeekin" and "Who's Boss," *South Carolina Electric Co-Op News*, Salkehatchie Edition, August 1961.

15. Kirby Able, "Communism Is a Religion," *South Carolina Electric Co-Op News*, Salkehatchie Edition, August 1961.

16. Kirby Able, "Cooperation the Key," *South Carolina Electric Co-Op News*, Salkehatchie Edition, September 1961.

17. Raymond W. Mack, "Guest Editorial: Communication," *South Carolina Electric Co-Op News*, Mid-Carolina Edition, April 1961, 2.

18. W. V. Thomas, "Nothing in Common with 'Private' Enterprise," *Living in South Carolina*, Coastal Edition, July 1963, 14.

19. "Who Gets the Blame?" *South Carolina Electric Co-Op News*, Broad River Edition, December 1961, 3.

20. "Garden Club Says Conservation Is Vital," *South Carolina Electric Co-Op News*, Little River Edition, July 1961.

21. "The Debt Rural America Owes George Norris," *South Carolina Electric Co-Op News*, Little River Edition, July 1961.

22. "Area Redevelopment," *South Carolina Electric Co-Op News*, Tri-County Edition, May 1961, 6. By May 1961, a separate version appears to have passed the House already. See "Operation Crossroads" in the same issue cited in this note.

23. Kirby Able, "Rambling ... with Kirby Able," *Living in South Carolina*, Pee Dee Edition, February 1963, 3; "Rural Electrification is 97 Percent Complete," *Living in South Carolina*, Pee Dee Edition, February 1963, 11. A related advertisement appears on page 10 of this same issue, while an article on the recent connection of families in Saluda County is featured later in the issue.

24. "Power Companies Pipe $78 Million Overcharge," *Living in South Carolina*, Coastal Edition, March 1963, 6.

25. "The Case of the Busted Meter," *South Carolina Electric Co-Op News*, Salkehatchie Edition, November 1961, 1.

26. "Fair Play for Everybody," *South Carolina Electric Co-Op News*, Mid-Carolina Edition, January 1962, 1.

27. Terry Gunn, "The Elephant and the Mouse," *South Carolina Electric Co-Op News*, York Edition, February 1962, 1.

28. "The General Assembly," *South Carolina Electric Co-Op News*, Mid-Carolina Edition, March 1961.

29. "In His Lap," *South Carolina Electric Co-Op News*, York Edition, February 1962, 2. This editorial apparently ruffled some feathers, prompting the paper to issue a clarification the following month. See "To Clarify a Position," *South Carolina Electric Co-Op News*, Blue Ridge Edition, March 1962.

30. Kirby Able, "Fair Play," *South Carolina Electric Co-Op News*, Blue Ridge Edition, March 1962, 1.

31. Able, "Fair Play," 1, 3.

32. "Mayors, Town Councils, Chambers of Commerce Fight Fair Play," *South Carolina Electric Co-Op News*, Lynches Rivers Edition, April 1962, 4.

33. "The Farm Bureau Paper," *South Carolina Electric Co-Op News*, Laurens Edition, May 1962.

34. "Is This Fair Play?" *Greenville News*, May 12, 1962, 4.

35. The full text of the bills was published for cooperative customers in "Fair Play: Here's a Summary and the Complete Fair Play Bills as Presented," *Living in South Carolina*, Coastal Edition, March 1963, 12–13.

36. "S. C. Council of Farmer Co-Ops Endorses Fair Play," *Living in South Carolina*, April 1963, 4.

37. "'Logical Solution Is Coops'—Top Lawyer," *South Carolina Electric Co-Op News*, Tri-County Edition, May 1961, 2.

38. Able, "Fair Play," 3.

39. Clarence Cannon, quoted in "Consumer Must Pay," *Living in South Carolina*, Pee Dee Edition, February 1963, 22.

40. "The Savannah Valley," *South Carolina Electric Co-Op News*, Mid-Carolina Edition, March 1961, 4. For more on dams see, Manganiello, "Countryside Conservatism and Conservation," in *Southern Water, Southern Power* and Casey P. Cater, *Regenerating Dixie: Electric Energy and the Modern South* (Pittsburgh: University of Pittsburgh Press, 2019).

41. "Power Costs Vary Greatly," *South Carolina Electric Co-Op News*, Mid-Carolina Edition, April 1961, 2.

42. "The Savannah Valley," 4.

43. "The Savannah Valley Story," *South Carolina Electric Co-Op News*, Mid-Carolina Edition, March 1961, 2.

44. "Maneuvers by Duke Delay River Projects," *South Carolina Electric Co-Op News*, Horry Edition, November 1962, 2.

45. "By Their Words . . . ," *South Carolina Electric Co-Op News*, Little River Edition, July 1962, 2.

46. "It's Republican Versus Democrat in S. Carolina!!" *South Carolina Electric Co-Op News*, Santee Edition, October 1962, 1.

47. "One Analysis of the Vote," *South Carolina Electric Co-Op News*, Coastal Edition, December 1962, 2.

48. "The Savannah River Belongs to the People," *Living in South Carolina*, January 1963, 14.

49. "Why Mead Cannot Locate at Calhoun Falls," *Living in South Carolina*, Coastal Edition, March 1963, 6.

50. "Governor Russell Sides with Duke Power," *Living in South Carolina*, Horry Edition, June 1963, 14.

51. J. Strom Thurmond as quoted extensively in "By Their Words Ye Shall Know Them," *Living in South Carolina*, April 1963, 14.

52. Strom Thurmond, "A Letter to the Editor from Senator Thurmond," *Living in South Carolina*, Horry Edition, June 1963, 7.

53. "The Boy from Barker's Creek," *South Carolina Electric Co-Op News*, Coastal Edition, August 1961.

54. "Fighting Words," *Living in South Carolina*, August 1963, 14.

55. "Trotter [sic] Shoals Project Opposed by Wildlife Group," *Index-Journal* (Greenwood, SC), January 29, 1975, 16.

56. "Knights . . . in Somewhat Tarnished Armor," *Living in South Carolina*, September 1963.

57. Kirby Able, "Rambling with Kirby Able," *Living in South Carolina*, September 1963, 2; "Knights . . . in Somewhat Tarnished Armor."

58. "Who Owns the Power Companies?" *Living in South Carolina*, Pee Dee Edition, December 1963, 5.

59. "Co-Op Tax Bill Becomes Law," *Index-Journal* (Greenwood, SC), July 16, 1969, 24.

60. See S.C. Code Ann. § 58-27-610 through 670 (1976).

Chapter 7: Public Policy and Electric Power in the Late Twentieth Century

1. "Resolution," *Living in South Carolina*, Aiken Edition, January 1976, 14. For more on the Trotters Shoals project, see Christopher J. Manganiello, *Southern Water, Southern Power: How the Politics of Cheap Energy and Water Scarcity Shaped a Region* (Chapel Hill: University of North Carolina Press, 2015) and Casey P. Cater, *Regenerating Dixie: Electric Energy and the Modern South* (Pittsburgh: University of Pittsburgh Press, 2019).

2. United States Department of Energy, United States Energy Information Administration, *Annual Energy Review 2011* (Washington, DC: Government Printing Office, 2012), https://www.eia.gov/totalenergy/data/annual/pdf/aer.pdf.

3. "Makes You Wonder," *Living in South Carolina*, Aiken Edition, January 1976.

4. "Makes You Wonder."

5. Brantley Harvey and Charles Powell, "Advantages Demand Quick Building of Richard Russell Dam," *Living in South Carolina*, York Edition, February 1976, 6.

6. "Strom Thurmond: Long Time Rural Electric Friend," *Living in South Carolina*, York Edition, February 1976, 10.

7. "Hollings Leads Way for Energy Legislation," *Living in South Carolina*, York Edition, February 1976, 12.

8. "Fourth District," *Living in South Carolina*, York Edition, February 1976, 24.

9. "President Asks Russell Dam Allocation," *Living in South Carolina*, York Edition, February 1976, 26.

10. R. D. Bennett, "Think on This," *Living in South Carolina*, York Edition, February 1976, 31.

11. Lee Bandy, "Thurmond Bill Would Hike Russell Dam Power Output," *The State* (Columbia, SC), February 18, 1976. Article was reprinted in *Living in South Carolina*, Mid-Carolina Edition, March 1976.

12. B. H. Thurmond, Letter to the Editor, *Living in South Carolina*, Mid-Carolina Edition, March 1976, 30.

13. R. D. Bennett, "Now Hear This...," *Living in South Carolina*, Mid-Carolina Edition, March 1976, 31.

14. Robert W. Williams Jr., "Report from the Manager," *Living in South Carolina*, Pee Dee Edition, April 1976.

15. R. D. Bennett, "Standing Tall," *Living in South Carolina*, Pee Dee Edition, April 1976, 31.

16. R. D. Bennett, "More to Come...," *Living in South Carolina*, Mid-Carolina Edition, June 1976, 23; United States Army Corps of Engineers, *Final Environmental Impact Statement: Richard B. Russell Dam and Lake, Savannah River, George and South Carolina*, (Savannah: Corps of Engineers, 1974), 22–24.

17. R. D. Bennett, "The Greatest Threat...," *Living in South Carolina*, Pee Dee Edition, July 1976, 23.

18. Larry Young, "In the Public Interest?" *Living in South Carolina*, Aiken Edition, August 1976, 24–26.

19. William Park Jr., Letter to the Editor, *Living in South Carolina*, Aiken Edition, November 1976, 22.

20. "Those GIANT Reservoir Trout," *Living in South Carolina*, Mid-Carolina Edition, April 1977, 7.

21. Kirby Able, "Rambling," *Living in South Carolina*, York Edition, February 1976, 3.

22. "Republican—Democrat," *Living in South Carolina*, Tri-County Edition, October 1976, 8–9.

23. R. D. Bennett, "One More Time," *Living in South Carolina*, Mid-Carolina Edition, April 1977, 31.

24. "Friends All!" *Living in South Carolina*, Pee Dee Edition, October 1978.

25. "Vote Yes on Question 2," *Living in South Carolina*, Pee Dee Edition, October 1978, 25.

26. Linda Kuntz Logan, "Approval of Reserve Fund Disappoints Opponents," *The State* (Columbia, SC), November 9, 1978, 55.

27. "Dam Opponents, Supporters Offer Contrast," accompanying photo caption, *Living in South Carolina*, Santee Edition, May 1977, 17.

28. "Furbish WHAT?" *Living in South Carolina*, Horry Edition, July 1977, 10.

29. WSPA-TV and Radio, "Russell Dam," *Living in South Carolina*, Santee Edition, May 1977, 17.

30. R. D. Bennett, "Where Are We Headed?" *Living in South Carolina*, Santee Edition, February 1978, 38.

31. R. D. Bennett, "A Tragic Situation," *Living in South Carolina*, York Edition, March 1978, 30.

32. "Save 25 Percent on Energy," *Living in South Carolina*, Black River Edition, April 1978, 28.

33. R. D. Bennett, "Think Conservation" *Living in South Carolina*, York Edition, June 1978, 23.

34. "Food, Energy, and Poverty," *Living in South Carolina*, Laurens Edition, March 1977, 17.

35. "How Nuclear Energy Works," *Living in South Carolina*, Laurens Edition, November 1978, 22–23.

36. For more on Three Mile Island, see "14-Year Cleanup at Three Mile Island

Concludes," *New York Times*, August 15, 1993; Benjamin K. Sovacool, "The Costs of Failure: A Preliminary Assessment of Major Energy Accidents, 1907–2007," *Energy Policy* 36 (2008): 1807; and J. Samuel Walker, *Three Mile Island: A Nuclear Crisis in Historical Perspective* (Berkeley: University of California Press, 2004).

37. David Burnham, "Nuclear Experts Debate 'The China Syndrome,'" *New York Times*, March 18, 1979.

38. Tom Kapsidelis, "What's S. C.'s Role in Nuclear Industry?" *The State* (Columbia, SC), April 8, 1979.

39. "Co-Ops to Buy Catawba Plant," *The State* (Columbia, SC), December 22, 1979.

40. Richard M. Harnett, "Electric Industry Sees Nuclear Power Only Realistic Choice," *Living in South Carolina*, Aiken Edition, February 1980, 12.

41. Peter A. Bradford, "Delivering the Nuclear Promise: TVA's Sale of the Bellefonte Nuclear Power Plant Site," *Bulletin of the Atomic Scientists*, June 1, 2016, https://thebulletin.org/delivering-nuclear-promise-tvas-sale-bellefonte-nuclear-power-plant-site9524; Kurt Andersen, "Clinch River: A Breeder for Baker," *Time*, August 3, 1981, http://content.time.com/time/magazine/article/0,9171,949264,00.html.

42. Al Ballard, "The Bottom Line . . . People," *Living in South Carolina*, Aiken Edition, February 1980, 30. R. D. Bennett retired in late 1979 but later went on to serve on the South Carolina Public Service Authority, giving the cooperatives a prodigious ally on that board. See "R. D. (Bob) Bennett Named to PSA Board," *Living in South Carolina*, Mid-Carolina Edition, January 1984, 5.

43. Holly Gatling, "Judge Refuses to Plea-Bargain," *The State* (Columbia, SC), August 21, 1979.

44. "Wingard Sentenced," *The State* (Columbia, SC), October 4, 1979.

45. "Berkeley Aims High," *Living in South Carolina*, Little River Edition, October 1980, 4–6.

46. Lee Bandy, "Appropriation Sent to Carter," *The State* (Columbia, SC), September 1, 1979.; Mike Livingston, "Russell Dam Construction Progressing," *The State* (Columbia, SC), December 23, 1979.

47. Wallace C. Hitchcock, "Archaeologists Find Ancient Artifacts," *The State* (Columbia, SC), June 27, 1981.

48. "Judge Denies Bid to Halt Russell Dam," *The State* (Columbia, SC), April 30, 1982.

49. "Coalition to Appeal Lawsuit," *The State* (Columbia, SC), May 30, 1982.

50. "Abbeville Plans Lawsuit Over Reservoir Flooding," *The State* (Columbia, SC), August 5, 1982.

51. "Abbeville Reimbursed," *The State* (Columbia, SC), March 27, 1984.

52. "Army Corps Plans to Seal Leak in Russell Dam Section," *The State* (Columbia, SC), May 27, 1983.

53. "Russell Dam Completed," *The State* (Columbia, SC), September 16, 1982.

54. "Richard B. Russell Dam and Lake—History," US Army Corps of Engineers Savannah District, accessed June 15, 2021, http://www.sas.usace.army.mil/About/Divisions-and-Offices/Operations-Division/Richard-B-Russell-Dam-and-Lake/History/.

55. Al Ballard, "We Must Speak Out," *Living in South Carolina*, Little River Edition, April 1981, 3.

56. Larry Cribb, "How About Food?" *Living in South Carolina*, Little River Edition, April 1981, 4.

57. "1983 Annual Meeting: Cooperatives Must Fight in Order to Maintain Program, Congressman Says," *Living in South Carolina*, Mid-Carolina Edition, January 1984, 12–13.

58. "South Carolina Delegates Fight for the Program," *Living in South Carolina*, Lynches River Edition, March 1984, 8–9.

59. Al Ballard, "Administration Trying to Cripple REA Program," *Living in South Carolina*, Pee Dee Edition, August 1984, 3.

60. Patrick T. Allen, "Let's Work Together," *Living in South Carolina*, Mid-Carolina Edition, January 1984, 12–13.

61. "Campaign Designed to Save Textile Jobs," *Living in South Carolina*, Little River Edition, October 1984, 6–7.

62. See, for example, Al Ballard, "Electric Co-ops Can Meet the Challenge," *Living in South Carolina*, Palmetto Edition, March 1987, 3.

63. Larry Cribb, "South Carolina Congressional Delegation Solidly Supports Electric Co-Ops," *Living in South Carolina*, Coastal Edition, June 1987, 5.

64. Al Ballard, "Administration Appears to Have Little Concern for Rural America," *Living in South Carolina*, Lynches River Edition, July 1987, 3.

65. Larry Cribb, "Think Your Opinion Doesn't Count? Write Your Congressman . . . Here's How," *Living in South Carolina*, Lynches River Edition, July 1987, 5–7.

66. Al Ballard, "Rural Electrification Here to Stay," *Living in South Carolina*, Mid-Carolina Edition, November 1987, 3.

67. Larry Cribb, "Maintaining Loan Fund and Rural Economic Development Highlight Legislative Rally," *Living in South Carolina*, Aiken Edition, June 1988, 6-7.

68. "S. C. Congressional Delegation Assures Co-Ops of Continued Support," *Living in South Carolina*, Coastal Edition, June 1989, 6.

69. "Congressman Butler Derrick Backs Co-Ops' Call for Energy-Efficiency Incentive," *Living in South Carolina*, Palmetto Edition, April 1991, 5.

70. Larry Cribb, "Restoring REA Loan Cuts Tops Co-Op Congressional Agenda," *Living in South Carolina*, Coastal Edition, June 1991, 6.

71. Larry Cribb, "REA Is a Lending Program, Not a Spending Program," *Living in South Carolina*, Berkeley Edition, September 1991, 8.

72. Al Ballard, "We Must Speak Out," *Living in South Carolina*, Pee Dee Edition, February 1984, 3. See also, "Territorial Integrity Legislation Would Save State's Electrical Consumers Millions of Dollars," *Living in South Carolina*, Pee Dee Edition, February 1984, 5–7.

73. Al Ballard, "General Assembly Can End Costly Utility Territorial Struggles," *Living in South Carolina*, Lynches River Edition, March 1984, 3.

74. "Senate Passes Bill to Protect Consumers from Forced Sell-Outs," *Living in South Carolina*, Mid-Carolina Edition, May 1984, 8, 10; "Territorial Protection Bill Signed Into Law," *Living in South Carolina*, Berkeley Edition, July 1984, 8.

75. Al Ballard, "Who Pays for What?" *Living in South Carolina*, Aiken Edition, January 1989, 3.

76. Al Ballard, "Corporate Predator Stalks Electric Cooperatives," *Living in South Carolina*, Edisto Edition, February 1989, 3; "Let's Talk About Anti-Hostile Takeover Legislation," *Living in South Carolina*, Edisto Edition, February 1989, 8.

77. C. Richard Blackwell, "Members Talk About Their Cooperative," *Living in South Carolina*, Edisto Edition, February 1989, 6.

78. Al Ballard, "Living with a Mistake," *Living in South Carolina*, Lynches River Edition, March 1989, 3.

79. "Members Fight for Their Cooperative," *Living in South Carolina*, Lynches River Edition, March 1989, 5.

80. "Members Fight for Their Cooperative," 5.

81. Larry Cribb, "Charlie Walker's Opinion," *Living in South Carolina*, Palmetto Edition, April 1989, 4.

82. Interview with N. L. "Shorty" Caprell by Rachel Despres, June 26, 2013, transcript (in the possession of the Electric Cooperatives of South Carolina).

83. Interview with Oscar Sadler by Van O'Cain and Marc Howie, September 17, 2014, transcript (ECSC).

84. Interview with Bill Gibbons by Van O'Cain, March 16, 2015, transcript (ECSC).

85. Larry Cribb, "1,000 Co-op Members Assemble for House Committee Hearing," *Living in South Carolina*, Palmetto Edition, April 1989, 8.

86. Ilene C. Harral, "A Co-Op Member Speaks Out," *Living in South Carolina*, Palmetto Edition, April 1989, 10.

87. Interview with Robert Williams by Van O'Cain, September 17, 2014, transcript (ECSC).

88. "General Assembly Overwhelmingly Supports Electric Co-Ops," *Living in South Carolina*, Berkeley Edition, May 1989, 5.

89. Al Ballard, "SCANA Puts Profits Before People," *Living in South Carolina*, Pee Dee Edition, August 1989, 3.

90. "Aiken Co-Op, SCE&G Battling Over Serving New Customers," *The State* (Columbia, SC), August 16, 1989.

91. Larry Cribb, "Investor-Owned Utilities Have Declared War," *Living in South Carolina*, Black River Edition, September 1989, 8.

92. Cribb, "Investor-Owned Utilities Have Declared War," 8.

93. "Public Service Commission Rejects SCE&G's Claim to Serve Co-Op Territory," *Living in South Carolina*, Broad River Edition, January 1990, 5.

94. "Judge Stops Utility from Invading Electric Co-Op Territory," *Living in South Carolina*, Little River Edition, November 1990, 5.

95. See, for example, Larry Cribb, "Electric Cooperatives Hold Key to Rural Economic Development," *Living in South Carolina*, Berkeley Edition, September 1987, 5–7, 23.

96. "S. C. Congressional Delegation Assures Co-Ops of Continued Support," 7.

97. Al Ballard, "The Law Is Being Ignored," *Living in South Carolina*, Berkeley Edition, September 1990, 3.

98. Larry Cribb, "Electric Cooperatives Hold Key to Rural Economic Development," *Living in South Carolina*, Little River Edition, November 1990, 6.

99. Cribb, "Electric Cooperatives Hold Key to Rural Economic Development," 6–7, 17.

100. Public Service Commission Sees Duty to Uphold Territorial Integrity," *Living in South Carolina*, Broad River Edition, January 1991, 27, 34.

101. Al Ballard, "What If?" *Living in South Carolina*, Aiken Edition, May 1991, 3.

102. "Bennettsville to Get Electricity from Cooperative," *Living in South Carolina*, Lynches River Edition, November 1991, 7.

103. Van O'Cain and Jackson Shuford, Interview with Bobby Tuggle by Van O'Cain and Jackson Shuford, December 17, 2014, transcript (ECSC).

Chapter 8: From Water Closets to Weatherization

1. "From Outhouses to 'Snap-Ons' to 25,000 Home Loans," *The State* (Columbia, SC), June 16, 1996; "Gov. West Dedicates Bathroom in Carolina Drive for Plumbing," *New York Times,* June 4, 1972.

2. Herb Hartsook, "Governor John West, Poverty, and the 'Privy Project,'" *A Capital Blog,* South Carolina Political Collections, April 2, 2019, https://digital .library.sc.edu/blogs/scpc/2019/04/02/john-west-poverty-and-the-privy -project/.

3. Speech by Robert E. McNair to Annual Meeting of Carolinas Council Housing and Redevelopment Officials, April 21, 1969, Box 90, Robert E. McNair Papers, South Carolina Political Collections, University of South Carolina; Speech by John West to Carolinas Council of Housing and Redevelopment Officials, Francis Marion Hotel, Charleston, April 26, 1971, 3, Box 34, John Carl West Papers, 1922–2004, South Carolina Political Collections. Hereinafter, South Carolina Political Collections will be referred to as SCPC. West's April 26, 1971, speech will hereinafter be referred to as "CCHRO Speech."

4. CCHRO Speech, 4, Box 34, West Papers, SCPC.

5. CCHRO Speech, 16, Box 34, West Papers, SCPC.

6. CCHRO Speech, 4-5, Box 34, West Papers, SCPC.

7. CCHRO Speech, 4, Box 34, West Papers, SCPC; "From Outhouses to 'Snap-Ons' to 25,000 Home Loans."

8. Robert D. McFadden, "Ernest Hollings, 97, a South Carolina Senator Who Evolved, Is Dead," *New York Times,* April 6, 2019, www.nytimes.com/2019/04 /06/obituaries/ernest-hollings-dead.html.

9. *Nutrition and Human Needs, Part 4—South Carolina: Hearings Before the Select Committee on Nutrition and Human Needs,* 91st Cong. 1163, 1169 (1969) (statement of Hon. Ernest Hollings, US Senator from the State of South Carolina). The Select Committee on Nutrition and Human Needs was active from 1968 to 1977 and was often referred to as the "McGovern Committee" after its chairman, Senator George McGovern of South Dakota. For more on McGovern and the work of the committee, see "George McGovern: Serving the Plains and Beyond," in Peter J. Longo, *Great Plains Politics* (Lincoln: University of Nebraska Press, 2018), 57–71. For more on Hollings's efforts to address malnutrition and hunger, see "Hunger, USA" in David T. Ballantyne, *New Politics in the Old South: Ernest F. Hollings in the Civil Rights Era* (Columbia, SC: University of South Carolina Press, 2016), 88–107.

10. McFadden, "Ernest Hollings, 97, a South Carolina Senator Who Evolved, Is Dead."

11. Jack Bass, "The South Is Still Changing," *Washington Post,* October 30, 1983.

12. Interview with John Carl West by Herb Hartsook, February 1, 1996, transcript, p. 34, South Carolina Political Collections Oral History Project (SCPC), https: //digital.tcl.sc.edu/digital/collection/scpcot/id/31.

13. Ibid; Hollings, Ernest F. *The Case against Hunger; a Demand for a National Policy.* Cowles Book Co., 1970.

14. Derrick, Hope, "RE: Request for help on 'John's johns,'" Message to Lindsey Smith, January 28, 2021 (in the possession of Jared Bailey).

15. Barbara S. Williams, "West Tours Area and Sees Progress," *News and Courier* (Charleston, SC), August 3, 1973.

16. CCHRO Speech, 10, Box 34, West Papers, SCPC.

17. "From Outhouses to 'Snap-Ons' to 25,000 Home Loans."

18. CCHRO Speech, 20, Box 34, West Papers, SCPC.

19. CCHRO Speech, 17–18, Box 34, West Papers, SCPC.

20. CCHRO Speech, 21, Box 34, West Papers, SCPC.

21. CCHRO Speech, 22, Box 34, West Papers, SCPC.

22. "Gov. West Pledges Full Support of Stand Tall Commission," *Living in South Carolina*, April 1971, 16.

23. R. D. Bennett, "STANDING TALL: Bring Our Kids Home," *Living in South Carolina*, July 1970, 23.

24. Stand Tall Commission, *Sub-Committee on Housing* [Manual], May 4, 1971, 6–7, 16, Box 34, West Papers, SCPC. The Stand Tall Commission was part of the Industrial and Community Development Department of the South Carolina Electric Cooperative Association.

25. "Bennett Elected President Of RESMA," *Living in South Carolina*, June 1971, 14; Speech by John West to Meeting of Statewide Electric Cooperative Executives, Columbia, May 3–4, 1971, 3–4, Box 34, West Papers, SCPC.

26. "West: My Confidence in Co-op's Stand Tall Commission Program Has Been More Than Justified," *Living in South Carolina*, January 1972, 14.

27. Stand Tall Commission, *Sub-Committee on Housing*, 16.

28. "From Outhouses to 'Snap-Ons' to 25,000 Home Loans."

29. "Prototype Developed of Add-On Bathroom," *Greenville News*, July 8, 1973; *Oversight on Housing and Urban Development Programs: Hearings Before the Senate Subcommittee on Housing And Urban Affairs of the Committee on Banking, Housing, and Urban Affairs*. 93rd Cong. (1973) (statement of John C. West, Governor of the State of South Carolina).

30. "From Outhouses to 'Snap-Ons' to 25,000 Home Loans."

31. Walt Riddle, "Tri-County Electric Co-op Donates First Complete 'Add-on' Bathroom in Nation to Member-Owner," *Living in South Carolina*, July 1972, 16.

32. Riddle, "Tri-County Electric Co-op Donates First Complete 'Add-on' Bathroom in Nation to Member-Owner," 17.

33. United States Department of Housing and Urban Development, "First Add-On Bathroom," *HUD Newsletter*, August 21, 1972.

34. Riddle, "Tri-County Electric Co-op Donates First Complete 'Add-on' Bathroom in Nation To Member-Owner," 17.

35. Riddle, "Tri-County Electric Co-op Donates First Complete 'Add-on' Bathroom in Nation To Member-Owner," 17.

36. Derrick to Smith, email, January 28, 2021 (in Jared Bailey's possession).

37. West's testimony found in *Oversight on Housing and Urban Development Programs* (1973).

38. "Prototype Developed of Add-On Bathroom."

39. "From Outhouses to 'Snap-Ons' to 25,000 Home Loans."

40. "West Tours Area and Sees Progress."

41. Levona Page, "Toilets, Homes Please West on Poverty Tour," *The State* (Columbia, SC), August 4, 1973.

42. Stand Tall Commission, *Sub-Committee on Housing*, 3.

43. Interview with Mike Couick and Lindsey Smith by Jared Bailey, February 3, 2021, transcript (in possession of the Electric Cooperatives of South Carolina).

44. Keith Phillips, "The Power of Efficiency," *South Carolina Living*, October 1, 2010, https://scliving.coop/energy/the-power-of-efficiency/.

45. David Bookbinder, "Obama Had a Chance to Really Fight Climate Change. He Blew It.," *Vox*, April 28, 2017, www.vox.com/the-big-idea/2017/4/28/15472508/obama-climate-change-legacy-overrated-clean-power.

46. John M. Broder, "Obama Affirms Climate Change Goals," *New York Times*, November 18, 2008, www.nytimes.com/2008/11/19/us/politics/19climate.html.

47. Center for Climate and Energy Solutions, "Waxman-Markey Short Summary," *Center for Climate and Energy Solutions*, June 2009, www.c2es.org/document/waxman-markey-short-summary/.

48. Electric Cooperatives of South Carolina and the Environmental and Energy Study Institute, "Energy Efficiency: Serving the Cooperative Consumer/Owner," Presentation, May 20, 2011, 12, https://www.energy.gov/sites/prod/files/2014/01/f6/conf_whatsworking_7_coop_customer.pdf.

49. Phillips, "The Power of Efficiency."

50. "Resolution on Energy and Environmental Commitment," Central Electric Power Cooperative, September 4, 2007 (in the possession of ECSC).

51. Interview with Ron Calcaterra by Jared Bailey, January 22, 2021, transcript (ECSC).

52. GDS Associates, Inc. "Energy Efficiency and Renewable Energy Potential Study for Central Electric Power Cooperative, Inc.," Presentation, September 4, 2007 (in the possession of ECSC).

53. Patrick Keegan, Ron Calcaterra, et al. "Can On-Bill Financing Become a Replicable Solution for Rural Electric Cooperatives?", *American Council for an Energy-Efficient Economy (ACEEE) Summer Study on Energy Efficiency in Buildings*, 2012, 3, https://www.aceee.org/files/proceedings/2012/start.htm.

54. Couick and Smith, interview.

55. Interview with Mike Couick by Jared Bailey, March 15, 2021, transcript (ECSC).

56. Phillips, "The Power of Efficiency."

57. Couick, interview.

58. Phillips, "The Power of Efficiency."

59. Phillips, "The Power of Efficiency."

60. Keegan, et al. "Can On-Bill Financing Become a Replicable Solution for Rural Electric Cooperatives?" 2.

61. Couick and Smith, interview.

62. Phillips, "The Power of Efficiency."

63. Keegan, et al. "Can On-Bill Financing Become a Replicable Solution for Rural Electric Cooperatives?" 5.

64. Phillips, "The Power of Efficiency."

65. Interview with Mike Hacker by Jared Bailey, February 12, 2021, transcript (ECSC).

66. Phillips, "The Power of Efficiency."

67. Keegan, et al. "Can On-Bill Financing Become a Replicable Solution for Rural Electric Cooperatives?" 3.

68. Keegan, et al., "Can On-Bill Financing Become a Replicable Solution for Rural Electric Cooperatives?" 2.

69. Couick and Smith, interview.
70. Couick and Smith, interview.
71. Couick and Smith, interview.
72. Interview with Carol Werner by Jared Bailey, February 18, 2021, transcript (ECSC); Keegan, Patrick et al. "Can On-Bill Financing Become a Replicable Solution for Rural Electric Cooperatives?" 3.
73. Keegan, Patrick et al. "Can On-Bill Financing Become a Replicable Solution for Rural Electric Cooperatives?" 4.
74. Calcaterra, interview.
75. Calcaterra, interview.
76. Couick and Smith, interview.
77. Environmental and Energy Study Institute (EESI), "The Help My House Model," *EESI*, accessed April 30, 2021, www.eesi.org/obf/case-study/helpmy house.
78. Keegan, Patrick et al., "Can On-Bill Financing Become a Replicable Solution for Rural Electric Cooperatives?" 6.
79. Couick and Smith, interview.
80. Victoria A. Rocha, "First Loans for Energy Savings Program," *NRECA*, accessed April 30, 2021, www.electric.coop/help-my-house-for-rural-energy-savings -program-south-carolina.
81. Bookbinder, "Obama Had a Chance to Really Fight Climate Change. He Blew It."
82. Brook J. Detterman, et al., "D.C. Circuit Vacates Trump ACE Rule: What's Next for Power Plant CO_2 Regulation?" *National Law Review* 11 (2021), www .natlawreview.com/article/dc-circuit-vacates-trump-ace-rule-what-s-next -power-plant-co2-regulation.
83. Detterman, et al. "D.C. Circuit Vacates Trump ACE Rule: What's Next for Power Plant CO_2 Regulation?"
84. Couick and Smith, interview.

Chapter 9: Cooperative Principles and Member Services

1. National Rural Electric Cooperative Association, "Understanding the Seven Cooperative Principles," *NRECA*, December 1, 2016, www.electric.coop/seven -cooperative-principles%E2%80%8B.
2. R. D. Bennett, "STANDING TALL: Bring Our Kids Home," Living in South Carolina, July 1970, 23.
3. National Rural Electric Cooperative Association, "About the Youth Tour," *NRECA*, July 11, 2016, https://www.electric.coop/our-organization/youth -programs/about-the-youth-tour.
4. Rural Electric Cooperative Association, "President Johnson Welcomes 600 Rural Electric Youths," *Alabama Rural Electric News*, July 1965, 1–2; "Loris Beauty Will Host Washington Youth Tour," *News & Courier* (Charleston, SC), June 5, 1965.
5. Walt Riddle, "THOUGHTS FROM THE EDITOR'S DESK: HATS OFF TO THREE COOPERATIVES," *Living in South Carolina*, August 1971, 5.
6. Riddle, "THOUGHTS FROM THE EDITOR'S DESK," 5.
7. "Teenagers Converge on Nation's Capitol . . . They Marched, Carried Banners, Made Noise," *Living in South Carolina*, August 1971, 16–20.
8. Riddle, "THOUGHTS FROM THE EDITOR'S DESK," 5.

9. Mike Couick, "Dialogue: Voices of the New Generation," *South Carolina Living*, September 2020, 8.

10. Interview with Van O'Cain by Jared Bailey, April 1, 2021, transcript (in possession of The Electric Cooperatives of South Carolina).

11. The Electric Cooperatives of South Carolina, "Youth Tour 2014 Takes on Washington," *The Electric Cooperatives of South Carolina*, June 19, 2014, www.ecsc.org /content/youth-tour-2014-takes-washington.

12. O'Cain, interview.

13. Couick, "Dialogue: Voices of the New Generation," 8.

14. O'Cain, interview.

15. Couick, "Dialogue: Voices of the New Generation," 8.

16. O'Cain, interview.

17. Interview with Martha McMillan by Jared Bailey, January 27, 2021, transcript (ECSC).

18. Diane Veto Parham, "Small Change, Big Changes," *South Carolina Living*, October 1, 2014, https://scliving.coop/sc-life/sc-life-features/small-change-big -changes/.

19. Palmetto Electric Cooperative, Inc., "Operation Round Up: 30 Years of Commitment to Community," *Palmetto Electric Cooperative Annual Report*, 2019, 3.

20. Palmetto Electric Cooperative, "Operation Round Up," 3–4.

21. Jared Bailey, interview with Tray Hunter, April 7, 2021, transcript in possession of Jared Bailey.

22. Hunter interview; Matt Dillane, "Lowcountry Teachers Receive Classroom Grants from Berkeley Electric Cooperative," *ABC News 4*, October 1, 2020, https://abcnews4.com/news/education-news/back-to-school/lowcountry -teachers-receive-classroom-grants-from-berkeley-electric-cooperative.

23. McMillan, interview.

24. Parham, "Small Change, Big Changes."

25. Palmetto Electric Cooperative, "Operation Round Up," 3.

26. Parham, "Small Change, Big Changes."

27. Hunter, interview.

28. Palmetto Electric Cooperative, "Operation Round Up," 4.

29. Palmetto Electric Cooperative, "A Place to Call Home," *Palmetto Electric Cooperative Annual Report*, 2019, 4.

30. Interview with Lou Green by Jared Bailey, April 5, 2021, transcript (ECSC).

31. Parham, "Small Change, Big Changes."

32. Keith Phillips, ed., *Honor Flight* (Cayce, SC: Electric Cooperatives of South Carolina, Inc., 2012), 211. The cover page of *Honor Flight* reads, "These stories and photos were compiled by *South Carolina Living* magazine as part of the April 11, 2012, Honor Flight to Washington, D.C., sponsored by 19 South Carolina electric cooperatives." For a full list of contributing writers, see page 212.

33. Bernie Becker, "Long-Belated Homecoming for World War II Veterans," *New York Times*, September 27, 2009, www.nytimes.com/2009/09/28/us/28veterans .html.

34. "Regional Honor Flight Hubs," *Honor Flight Network*, accessed April 30, 2021, www.honorflight.org/regional-honor-flight-hubs.html; Philips, ed., *Honor Flight*, 211.

35. "Scene: Honoring South Carolina's 'Greatest Generation,'" *South Carolina Living*,

January 2012, 25; Mike Couick, "Honor Flight" Presentation, ECSC Board Meeting, October 6, 2011 (in the possession of ECSC).

36. "Scene: Honoring South Carolina's 'Greatest Generation,'" 25.

37. Interview with Mike Couick by Jared Bailey, April 12, 2021, transcript (ECSC).

38. Couick, "Honor Flight," Presentation, ECSC Board Meeting.

39. "Scene: Honoring South Carolina's 'Greatest Generation,'" 25.

40. "Scene: Honoring South Carolina's 'Greatest Generation,'" 25.

41. Mike Couick, "Honoring Our Homegrown Heroes," (speech and presentation, ECSC Winter Conference, December 5, 2011).

42. Interview with Keith Phillips by Jared Bailey, April 8, 2021, transcript (ECSC); Couick, interview.

43. Front Cover, *South Carolina Living*, January 2012.

44. "Scene: Honoring South Carolina's 'Greatest Generation,'" 22–25.

45. Couick, interview.

46. Keith Phillips, "We Honor Their Service," *South Carolina Living*, May 2012, 17.

47. Phillips, ed., *Honor Flight*, 211.

48. Phillips, "We Honor Their Service," 17.

49. Couick, interview.

50. Phillips, "We Honor Their Service," 17.

51. Phillips, ed., *Honor Flight*.

52. Mike Couick, "The Quiet Heroes of World War II," forward to Phillips, ed., *Honor Flight*, 3.

53. Phillips, ed., *Honor Flight*, 4.

54. Phillips, ed., *Honor Flight*, 108.

55. "Internet Access in South Carolina: Stats & Figures," *BroadbandNow*, March 11, 2021, https://broadbandnow.com/South-Carolina.

56. "Internet Access in South Carolina: Stats & Figures."

57. Interview with Bob Paulling by Jared Bailey, April 26, 2021, transcript (ECSC).

58. Paulling, interview.

59. Paulling, interview.

60. Paulling, interview.

61. Paulling, interview.

62. Paulling, interview.

63. Paulling interview; Jared Bailey, interview with Keith Avery, April 14, 2021, transcript in possession of Jared Bailey.

64. Bob Paulling, email message to Jared Bailey, April 27, 2021 (in the possession of the author); Stephanie Sullivan, email message to Jared Bailey, April 15, 2021 (in the possession of the author).

65. River Electric Cooperative, "About," *RiverNet Connect*, accessed April 30, 2021, https://rivernetconnect.com/about/.

66. Tri-County Electric Cooperative, "At-A-Glance," *Tri-County Electric Cooperative*, accessed April 20, 2021, https://tri-countyelectric.net/phase-1-sign-internet-service.

67. Couick, interview.

68. "Status Information: 2019-2020 Bill 3780: Growing Rural Economies with Access to Technology (GREAT) Program," *South Carolina State House*, accessed

April 30, 2021, www.scstatehouse.gov/sess123_2019-2020/bills/3780.htm.; See also S.C. Code § 58-9-3000.

69. Interview with Betsy Hix by Jared Bailey, April 8, 2021, transcript (ECSC).

70. Hix interview; "Status Information: 2019-2020 Bill 3780: Growing Rural Economies with Access to Technology (GREAT) Program."

71. Hix, interview.

72. Tali Arbel, "Broadband for All: Inside President Biden's $100 Billion Plan to Improve Internet Access," *USA Today*, April 5, 2021, www.usatoday.com/story/tech/2021/04/03/biden-infrastructure-plan-100-billion-broadband-internet-proposal/7074754002/.

73. Couick, interview.

74. Paulling, interview.

75. Couick, interview.

76. Paulling, interview.

77. National Rural Electric Cooperative Association, "Broadband," *NRECA*, accessed August 5, 2021, https://www.electric.coop/issues-and-policy/broadband.

78. Paulling, interview.

Chapter 10: Transparency, Accountability,
and the Power of Democracy

1. Avery Wilks, "SC utility's part-time board enriched itself while customers paid high power bills," *The State* (Columbia, SC), May 21, 2018.

2. Wilks, "SC utility's part-time board enriched itself while customers paid high power bills."

3. Tri-County Electric Cooperative, Inc., Minutes of the Regular Board of Trustees Meeting, June 21, 2018, 12–13 (in the possession of Tri-County Electric Cooperative). Hereinafter, referred to as "Tri-County Board of Trustees Meeting Minutes, June 21, 2018."

4. Avery Wilks, "Knives are out for Midlands utility board that gave itself high pay," *The State* (Columbia, SC), June 6, 2018.

5. Wilks, "SC utility's part-time board enriched itself while customers paid high power bills."

6. Interview with Chad Lowder by Jared Bailey, January 22, 2021, transcript (in the possession of The Electric Cooperatives of South Carolina).

7. Lowder, interview.

8. Tri-County Board of Trustees Meeting Minutes, June 21, 2018, 18.

9. Tri-County Board of Trustees Meeting Minutes, June 21, 2018, 17.

10. Lowder, interview.

11. Lowder, interview.

12. Lowder, interview.

13. Lowder, interview.

14. Tri-County Board of Trustees Meeting Minutes, June 21, 2018, 18–19.

15. Tri-County Board of Trustees Meeting Minutes, June 21, 2018, 19.

16. Tri-County Board of Trustees Meeting Minutes, June 21, 2018, 19.

17. Tri-County Board of Trustees Meeting Minutes, June 21, 2018, 19.

18. Tri-County Board of Trustees Meeting Minutes, June 21, 2018, 19.

19. Lowder, interview.

20. Interview with Joe Strickland by Jared Bailey, January 20, 2021, transcript (ECSC). There are two interviews with Joe Strickland, one in January 2021 and the other on June 18, 2021. References to Strickland interviews will specify the date and year.

21. Wilks, "SC utility's part-time board enriched itself while customers paid high power bills."

22. Interview with Barbara Weston by Jared Bailey, January 20, 2021, transcript (ECSC)

23. Wilks, "SC utility's part-time board enriched itself while customers paid high power bills."

24. Lowder, interview.

25. Wilks, "SC utility's part-time board enriched itself while customers paid high power bills."

26. Wilks, "SC utility's part-time board enriched itself while customers paid high power bills."

27. Wilks, "SC utility's part-time board enriched itself while customers paid high power bills."

28. Avery Wilks, "Customer sues Midlands utility that paid its board 'enormous and undeserved profits,'" May 23, 2018.

29. Lowder, interview.

30. Tanita Gaither and Caroline Hecker, "Midlands man sues utility company, says the co-op violated SC law in their 'excessive cost of doing business,'" WIS, May 24, 2018; See also SC Code § 33-49-630 (2014).

31. Wilks, "Customer sues Midlands utility that paid its board 'enormous and undeserved profits.'"

32. Wilks, "SC utility's part-time board enriched itself while customers paid high power bills."

33. Wilks, "Customer sues Midlands utility that paid its board 'enormous and undeserved profits.'"

34. Tri-County Board of Trustees Meeting Minutes, June 21, 2018, 2–5.

35. Tri-County Board of Trustees Meeting Minutes, June 21, 2018, 2, 13.

36. Tri-County Board of Trustees Meeting Minutes, June 21, 2018, 13.

37. Tri-County Board of Trustees Meeting Minutes, June 21, 2018, 14.

38. Tri-County Board of Trustees Meeting Minutes, June 21, 2018, 19–20.

39. Tri-County Board of Trustees Meeting Minutes, June 21, 2018, 8–9.

40. Tri-County Board of Trustees Meeting Minutes, June 21, 2018, 15.

41. Tri-County Board of Trustees Meeting Minutes, June 21, 2018, 6

42. Tri-County Board of Trustees Meeting Minutes, June 21, 2018, 18–20.

43. Tri-County Board of Trustees Meeting Minutes, June 21, 2018, 29–30.

44. Tri-County Board of Trustees Meeting Minutes, June 21, 2018, 29–30.

45. Avery Wilks, "Customers of Midlands power company move to fire board members who hiked their own pay," The State (Columbia, SC), July 9, 2018.

46. Wilks, "Customers of Midlands power company move to fire board members who hiked their own pay."

47. Avery Wilks, "'Cowardly and unethical:' Tri-County board thwarted in secret attempt to fire CEO," The State (Columbia, SC), August 17, 2018.

48. Avery Wilks, "'It's time you catch hell.' Tensions erupt as Midlands utility board refuses to resign," The State (Columbia, SC), August 19, 2018.

49. Wilks, "'It's time you catch hell.'"
50. Strickland interview, January 2021.
51. Wilks, "'It's time you catch hell.'"
52. Wilks, "'It's time you catch hell.'"
53. Avery Wilks, "High pay and expensive perks: Has 'absolute power' corrupted SC electric co-ops?" *The State* (Columbia, SC), August 9, 2018.
54. Wilks, "High pay and expensive perks."
55. Wilks, "High pay and expensive perks."
56. Wilks, "High pay and expensive perks."
57. Avery Wilks, "Electric co-op board enjoyed bonuses, high pay and dinner at Ruth's Chris, records show," *The State* (Columbia, SC), August 14, 2018.
58. Wilks, "Electric co-op board enjoyed bonuses, high pay and dinner at Ruth's Chris, records show."
59. Wilks, "Electric co-op board enjoyed bonuses, high pay and dinner at Ruth's Chris, records show."
60. Wilks, "Electric co-op board enjoyed bonuses, high pay and dinner at Ruth's Chris, records show."
61. Wilks, "Electric co-op board enjoyed bonuses, high pay and dinner at Ruth's Chris, records show," 8/14/2018; Tri-County Board of Trustees Meeting Minutes, June 21, 2018, 1.
62. Avery Wilks, "Tri-County co-op board stands up dozens of angry customers at meeting," *The State* (Columbia, SC), August 16, 2018.
63. Wilks, "Tri-County co-op board stands up dozens of angry customers at meeting."
64. Wilks, "Tri-County co-op board stands up dozens of angry customers at meeting."
65. Wilks, "'Cowardly and unethical.'"
66. Lowder, interview.
67. Strickland interview, January 2021.
68. Joe Strickland interview with Jared Bailey, June 18, 2021, transcript (ECSC).
69. Weston, interview.
70. Wilks, "'Cowardly and unethical.'"
71. Strickland interview, January 2021.
72. Strickland interview, January 2021.
73. Wilks, "'Cowardly and unethical.'"
74. Strickland interview, January 2021.
75. Lowder, interview.
76. Wilks, "'Cowardly and unethical.'"
77. Avery Wilks, "SC utility's board thrown out of office by more than 1,500 customers at meeting," *The State* (Columbia, SC), August 18, 2018.
78. Wilks, "Customers of Midlands power company move to fire board members who hiked their own pay"; Avery Wilks, "SC utility's board thrown out of office by more than 1,500 customers at meeting."
79. Wilks, "SC utility's board thrown out of office by more than 1,500 customers at meeting."
80. Avery Wilks, "SC co-op board resigns, won't challenge customers' historic vote to fire them," *The State* (Columbia, SC), August 21, 2018.
81. For more, see *G. Wayne Lorick, et al. v. Tri-County Electric Cooperative, Inc., et al* (Calhoun County Court of Common Pleas, 2018).

82. Electric Cooperatives of South Carolina, "Principles Developed by Governance Task Force," 2018 (in the possession of ECSC).

83. "Principles Developed by Governance Task Force."

84. Avery Wilks, "SC utility's directors got free power lines, landscaping work, employees say," *The State* (Columbia, SC), August 21, 2018.

85. Weston, interview.

86. Wilks, "SC utility's directors got free power lines, landscaping work, employees say."

87. Avery Wilks, "SC's electric co-ops under fire for high pay, lavish perks. Lawmakers may step in," *The State*, September 5, 2018.

88. Wilks, "SC's electric co-ops under fire for high pay, lavish perks. Lawmakers may step in."

89. Wendy C. Brawley, "Results of Tri-County scandal 'a testament to the power of an informed community,'" *The State* (Columbia, SC), November 29, 2018.

90. Brawley, "Results of Tri-County scandal 'a testament to the power of an informed community.'"

91. Wilks, "SC's electric co-ops under fire for high pay, lavish perks. Lawmakers may step in."

92. Avery Wilks, "After scandal and public pressure, SC's electric co-ops promise to change," *The State* (Columbia, SC), November 14, 2018.

93. Wilks, "After scandal and public pressure, SC's electric co-ops promise to change."

94. Avery Wilks, "SC utility's customers fired their board after pay scandal. Now, they're taking over," *The State* (Columbia, SC), December 28, 2018.

95. Wilks, "SC utility's customers fired their board after pay scandal. Now, they're taking over."

96. Avery Wilks, "Electric co-op reform bill advances in SC House but faces opposition," *The State* (Columbia, SC), February 27, 2019.

97. Avery Wilks, "SC House votes to give electric co-ops more oversight in wake of The State investigation," *The State* (Columbia, SC), March 20, 2019; Avery Wilks, "After board pay scandal, SC electric co-ops to get state oversight," *The State* (Columbia, SC), May 8, 2019.

98. Avery Wilks, "Scandal-scarred SC electric co-ops look to turn new leaf with new reform law," *The State* (Columbia, SC), May 17, 2019.

99. Wilks, "Scandal-scarred SC electric co-ops look to turn new leaf with new reform law."

100. For the full text of H.R. 3145, 123rd Sess. (S.C. 2019), see "A56, R76, H3145 Status Information," *South Carolina Legislature*, https://www.scstatehouse.gov/sess123_2019-2020/bills/3145.htm; See H.R. 3145, 123rd Sess. (S.C. 2019).

101. Lowder, interview.

102. See John Frick, email message to Lou Green, June 23, 2021 (in the possession of Lou Green, executive vice president of ECSC). Frick confirmed his statement via email.

103. See Mike Smith, email message to Jared Bailey, August 5, 2021 (in the possession of Jared Bailey). Smith confirmed his statement via email.

104. See Robert C. Hochstetler, email message to Lou Green, June 23, 2021 (in the possession of Lou Green, ECSC). Hochstetler confirmed his statement via email.

105. See Michael (Mike) N. Couick, email message to Lou Green, June 23, 2021 (in the possession of Lou Green, ECSC). Couick confirmed his statement via email.

106. Michael (Mike) Couick, "Letter to The Honorable Thomas C. Alexander, Chairman, Joint Oversight Committee on the S.C. Public Service Authority," March 3, 2016 (in the possession of ECSC).

107. Mike Couick, "Looking Back Ten Years: What's Trending?" presentation, ECSC Summer Conference, June 3, 2015, 1–17 (in possession of ECSC).

108. Sammy Fretwell, "SCE&G, Santee Cooper Abandon Nuclear Power Project," The State (Columbia, SC), July 31, 2017, https://www.thestate.com/news/local /article164544862.html.

109. Russ McKinney, "V.C. Summer Saga Continues Two Years After Collapse of the Project," South Carolina Public Radio, August 1, 2019, https://www.south carolinapublicradio.org/sc-news/2019-08-01/v-c-summer-saga-continues-two -years-after-collapse-of-the-project.

110. Seanna Adcox, "Billions down the Drain as New Nuclear Plants Scrapped," AP News, July 31, 2017, https://apnews.com/article/d4ca872ea6744a61bd3210d9df 3572c2.

111. Avery G. Wilks and Maayan Schechter, "Santee Cooper's Largest Customer Will Sue to Stop Charges for Failed Nuclear Project," The State (Columbia, SC), February 23, 2018, https://www.thestate.com/news/politics-government/article 201809254.html.

112. Interview with Mike Couick and Lindsey Smith by Jared Bailey, February 3, 2021, transcript (ECSC).

113. Santee Cooper, "Santee Cooper 2007 Annual Report," 11, https://www.nrc.gov /docs/ML0910/ML091060768.pdf.

114. Doug Pardue, "Pulling the Plug on Pee Dee Plant," Post and Courier (Charleston, SC), September 25, 2009. https://www.postandcourier.com/news/pulling-the -plug-on-pee-dee-plant/article_3372de17-64a1-5d91-aaea-84c83fcc792f.html.

115. Santee Cooper, "Santee Cooper board approves new generating station in Florence County to meet state's growing energy needs," Media Release, April 21, 2006. http://web.archive.org/web/20060502111156/http://www.santeecooper .com/aboutus/newsroom/releases/2006/news_2006_0421.html; Mike Couick and Lindsey Smith interview; Pardue, "Pulling the Plug on Pee Dee Plant."

116. Pardue, "Pulling the Plug on Pee Dee Plant."

117. Pardue, "Pulling the Plug on Pee Dee Plant."

118. Interview with Mike Couick by Jared Bailey, June 2, 2021, transcript (ECSC).

119. Pardue, "Pulling the Plug on Pee Dee Plant."

120. United States Securities and Exchange Commission (SEC), "Form 8-K/A Amendment No. 1 To Current Report Pursuant to Section 13 Or 15(d) Of The Securities Exchange Act Of 1934." SEC, May 23, 2008. https://www.sec.gov /Archives/edgar/data/91882/000075473708000032/amendedform8k.htm; Cindi Scoppe, "Timeline for SCE&G, Santee Cooper Nuclear Debacle at VC Summer," The State (Columbia, SC), September 20, 2018, https://www.thestate .com/opinion/opn-columns-blogs/cindi-ross-scoppe/article176539946.html; Power Technology, "Virgil C Summer Nuclear Station," Power Technology, accessed June 27, 2021, https://www.power-technology.com/projects/virgil -expansion/.

121. SEC, "Form 8-K/A Amendment No. 1 To Current Report Pursuant to Section 13 Or 15(d) Of The Securities Exchange Act Of 1934."

122. Couick, interview.

123. Pardue, "Pulling the Plug on Pee Dee Plant."

124. Couick, interview.

125. Pardue, "Pulling the Plug on Pee Dee Plant."

126. Couick interview; "Defendant Central Electric Power Cooperative Inc.'s Answer to Fifth Amended Class Action Complaint and Amended Cross-Claims Against South Carolina Public Service Authority and its Directors," in *Jessica S. Cook, et al. vs. South Carolina Public Service Authority (also known as Santee Cooper), et al.* (SC 14th Cir. Common Pleas Court, County of Hampton, 2017), filed August 9, 2019, 11, https://assets.sourcemedia.com/e8/88/ffbbf60647fab413071eb 296a3e4/central-electric-answer-cross-complaint-080919-claims-p10.pdf. Hereinafter, this August 9, 2019, filing will be referred to in endnotes as "Central's Answer to Fifth Amended Complaint and Cross-Claims Against Santee Cooper."

127. Couick, interview.

128. "Central's Answer to Fifth Amended Complaint and Cross-Claims Against Santee Cooper," 11.

129. "Central's Answer to Fifth Amended Complaint and Cross-Claims Against Santee Cooper," 12.

130. Couick, interview.

131. John Downey, "Duke Energy Negotiates to Gain Stake in S.C. Nuclear Plant," *Charlotte Business Journal*, June 10, 2011, https://www.bizjournals.com /charlotte/print-edition/2011/06/10/Duke-negotiates-to-gain-stake-in-plant .html.

132. John Downey, "Santee Cooper Looks to Sell More of the Summer Plant," *Charlotte Business Journal*, April 24, 2012, https://www.bizjournals.com/charlotte /blog/power_city/2012/04/santee-cooper-looks-to-sell-more-of.html.

133. John Downey, "Duke Energy Gets First Deal for Partner on S.C. Nuclear Plant," *Charlotte Business Journal*, February 11, 2011, https://www.bizjournals.com /charlotte/print-edition/2011/02/11/Duke-gets-first-deal-for-partner.html; Couick, interview.

134. Couick, interview.

135. John Downey, "Even amid CEO Controversy, New Duke Energy Is Taking Shape," *Charlotte Business Journal*, July 27, 2012, https://www.bizjournals .com/charlotte/print-edition/2012/07/27/even-amid-ceo-controversy-new -duke.html; John Downey, "Is DUKE Close to Buying Stake in SC Nuke Plant?" *Charlotte Business Journal*, October 17, 2013, https://www.bizjournals .com/charlotte/blog/power_city/2013/10/is-duke-energy-close-to-buying-stake.html.

136. "Central's Answer to Fifth Amended Complaint and Cross-Claims Against Santee Cooper," 12.

137. Howard Axelrod quoted in "Central's Answer to Fifth Amended Complaint and Cross-Claims Against Santee Cooper," 12.

138. John Downey, "Duke Energy May Again Push Back Plans for Nuclear Plant," *Charlotte Business Journal*, January 24, 2013, https://www.bizjournals.com /charlotte/blog/power_city/2013/01/duke-energy-may-again-push-back.html.

139. John Downey, "Dhiaa Jamil Remains Duke Energy's Point Person on Nuclear

Power," *Charlotte Business Journal*, April 30, 2013, https://www.bizjournals.com /charlotte/blog/power_city/2013/04/dhiaa-jamil-remains-duke-energys.html.

140. John Downey, "Duke Energy Ends Negotiations to Buy Share of SC Nuke Plant," *Charlotte Business Journal*, January 27, 2014, https://www.bizjournals .com/charlotte/blog/power_city/2014/01/duke-energy-ends-negotiations-to -buy-share-of-sc.html.

141. John Downey, "SCANA Sees No Need for More Partners in Summer Plant," *Charlotte Business Journal*, May 17, 2011, https://www.bizjournals.com/charlotte /blog/power_city/2011/05/scana-sees-no-need-for-more-partners.html.

142. John Downey, "Duke Energy Talks on S.C. Nuke Are Slow but Ongoing," *Charlotte Business Journal*, May 27, 2011, https://www.bizjournals.com/charlotte/blog /power_city/2011/05/duke-energy-talks-on-sc-nuke-are.html.

143. Couick, interview.

144. Couick, interview.

145. John Downey, "Planned SCANA Nuke Is First to Lay Construction Slab in 30 Years," *Charlotte Business Journal*, March 12, 2013, https://www.bizjournals.com /charlotte/blog/power_city/2013/03/planned-scana-nuke-is-first-to-lay.html.

146. David Roberts, "After Rising for 100 Years, Electricity Demand Is Flat. Utilities Are Freaking Out," *Vox*, February 27, 2018, https://www.vox.com/energy -and-environment/2018/2/27/17052488/electricity-demand-utilities.

147. "Central's Answer to Fifth Amended Complaint and Cross-Claims Against Santee Cooper," 11–13.

148. "Central's Answer to Fifth Amended Complaint and Cross-Claims Against Santee Cooper," 14.

149. "Central's Answer to Fifth Amended Complaint and Cross-Claims Against Santee Cooper," 15.

150. "Central's Answer to Fifth Amended Complaint and Cross-Claims Against Santee Cooper," 17.

151. John Downey, "Talks Heating up for Duke Energy Stake in V.C. Summer Power?" *Charlotte Business Journal*, January 24, 2014, https://www.bizjournals .com/charlotte/print-edition/2014/01/24/talks-heating-up-for-v-c-summer -power.html.

152. Couick, interview.

153. "Central's Answer to Fifth Amended Complaint and Cross-Claims Against Santee Cooper," 18.

154. "Central's Answer to Fifth Amended Complaint and Cross-Claims Against Santee Cooper," 20.

155. "Central's Answer to Fifth Amended Complaint and Cross-Claims Against Santee Cooper," 20.

156. Bechtel Power Corporation, "V.C. Summer Nuclear Generating Station Units 2 & 3 Project Assessment Report," *Bechtel Power Corporation*, February 5, 2016, 61–62. https://assets.sourcemedia.com/8c/d8/6686933e49518782cdc7cc1b577f /bechtel-report-on-v.C.%20Summer%20nuclear%20project%20020516.pdf.

157. "Central's Answer to Fifth Amended Complaint and Cross-Claims Against Santee Cooper," 21.

158. "Central's Answer to Fifth Amended Complaint and Cross-Claims Against Santee Cooper," 21.

159. Couick, interview.

160. "Central's Answer to Fifth Amended Complaint and Cross-Claims Against Santee Cooper," 24.

161. "Central's Answer to Fifth Amended Complaint and Cross-Claims Against Santee Cooper," 23.

162. Couick, interview.

163. Couick, interview.

164. David Boraks, "S.C. Utilities Abandon Nuclear Plant Expansion," *WFAE 90.7* (Charlotte, NC), July 31, 2017, https://www.wfae.org/energy-environment/2017-07-31/s-c-utilities-abandon-nuclear-plant-expansion.

165. Downey, John, "SCANA Pushes Back on Effort to Block Construction of V.C. Summer Plant." *Charlotte Business Journal*, July 21, 2017, https://www.bizjournals.com/charlotte/news/2017/07/21/scana-pushes-back-on-effort-to-block-construction.html; Andrew Brown and Tony Bartelme, "Documents: Failed South Carolina Nuclear Project Was Years and Millions of Hours Away from Completion," *Post and Courier* (Charleston, SC), September 7, 2017, https://www.postandcourier.com/business/documents-failed-south-carolina-nuclear-project-was-years-and-millions-of-hours-away-from-completion/article_9386379a-93dd-11e7-acf6-fbd8edabca48.html.

166. Sammy Fretwell, "SC Residents Pay Nation's Highest Electricity Bills, Report Says," *Greenville News* (Greenville, SC), February 20, 2018, https://www.greenvilleonline.com/story/news/2018/02/20/sc-residents-pay-nations-highest-electricity-bills-report-says/354524002/; "A Santee Cooper V.C. Summer Nuclear Disaster Timeline," *Charleston FYI*, July 30, 2019, https://charlestonfyi.com/2019/07/30/santee-cooper-timeline/.

167. Andrew Brown and Andy Shain, "Audit Highlighted Problems with South Carolina Nuclear Project a Year before Cancellation," *Post and Courier* (Charleston, SC), September 4, 2017, https://www.postandcourier.com/news/audit-highlighted-problems-with-south-carolina-nuclear-project-a-year-before-cancellation/article_9ac96112-9185-11e7-9979-977331ac2233.html.

168. J. Michael. Baxley to Governor Henry McMaster, September 3, 2017, from *Post and Courier* (Charleston, SC), https://bloximages.newyork1.vip.townnews.com/postandcourier.com/content/tncms/assets/v3/editorial/4/91/4916a960-91bc-11e7-babb-bf257e52714b/59adccc3ad266.pdf.pdf.

169. Brown and Shain, "Audit Highlighted Problems with South Carolina Nuclear Project a Year before Cancellation."

170. John McDermott, "Santee Cooper Customers Sue over Abandoned Nuclear Project," *Post and Courier* (Charleston, SC), August 29, 2017, https://www.postandcourier.com/georgetown/news/santee-cooper-customers-sue-over-abandoned-nuclear-project/article_fa3d8a4c-9b84-5a29-889d-718b21df93d3.html.

171. "Fourth Amended Class Action Complaint," in *Jessica S. Cook, et al. vs. South Carolina Public Service Authority (also known as Santee Cooper), et al.* (2017), filed March 27, 2018, 1, https://assets.sourcemedia.com/o2/ao/1cc1ced847-8f8ab3f8087e250c65/cook-class-4th-amended-complaint-032718.pdf; Avery G. Wilks, "SCE&G Renamed Dominion Energy South Carolina after Merger," *The State* (Columbia, SC), April 29, 2019, https://www.thestate.com/news/politics-government/article229799614.html.

172. Interview with Avery G. Wilks by Jared Bailey, June 4, 2021, transcript (ECSC).

173. Couick, interview.

174. Wilks, interview.

175. Daniel Tait, "Dominion and NextEra Takeover Bids for Santee Cooper Provide Little to No Benefit to South Carolina," *Energy and Policy Institute* (blog), February 18, 2020, https://www.energyandpolicy.org/dominion-and-nextera-takeover-bids-for-santee-cooper-provide-little-to-no-benefit-to-south-carolina/.

176. Wilks, interview.

177. Tait, "Dominion and NextEra Takeover Bids for Santee Cooper Provide Little to No Benefit to South Carolina."

178. Wilks, interview.

179. Wilks and Schechter, "Santee Cooper's Largest Customer Will Sue to Stop Charges for Failed Nuclear Project."

180. "Order Granting Preliminary Approval of Class Action Settlement and Continuing Stay of Pre-Trial Proceedings," in *Jessica S. Cook, et al. v. South Carolina Public Service Authority (also known as Santee Cooper) et al.* (S.C. 13th Cir. Court of Common Pleas, County of Greenville 2019), filed March 17, 2020, 3–4, https://arizent.brightspotcdn.com/a1/64/9635dfd747ca9665157c599858b1/order-granting-prelim-approval-santee-cooper-v-cook-settlement-031720.pdf.

181. Couick, interview.

182. Avery G. Wilks, "$520 Million Settlement for Santee Cooper, Electric Co-Op Customers Headed toward Approval," *Post and Courier* (Charleston, SC), March 17, 2020, https://www.postandcourier.com/business/520-million-settlement-for-santee-cooper-electric-co-op-customers-headed-toward-approval/article_44ee1268-6795-11ea-a11b-93b1ce04cb70.html.

183. Katherine Kokal, "Santee Cooper, Dominion Nuclear Plant Settlement Checks in SC | Hilton Head Island Packet," *Island Packet* (Bluffton, SC), December 21, 2020, https://www.islandpacket.com/news/local/article247915000.html.

184. Associated Press, "$520 Million Settlement Approved in Santee Cooper Lawsuit," *Washington Post*, July 21, 2020, https://www.washingtonpost.com/business/520-million-settlement-approved-in-santee-cooper-lawsuit/2020/07/21/12ce2642-cb86-11ea-99b0-8426e26d203b_story.html.

185. John Monk, "Ratepayers, Lawyers Are Winners in Santee Cooper Nuclear Case," *The State* (Columbia, SC), July 20, 2020, https://www.thestate.com/news/local/crime/article244355297.html.

186. Interview with John Frick by Jared Bailey, May 14, 2021, transcript (ECSC).

187. Couick, interview.

188. Couick, interview.

189. Wilks, interview.

190. Frick, interview.

191. Frick, interview.

192. Jason Raven, "SC Lawmakers Strike a Compromise on Future of Santee Cooper with Reform Bill," *WSPA 7News*, June 8, 2021, https://www.wspa.com/news/sc-lawmakers-strike-a-compromise-on-future-of-santee-cooper-with-reform-bill/.

193. Joseph Bustos, "Gov. McMaster Signs Santee Cooper Reform without Sale Plan," *The State* (Columbia, SC), June 15, 2021, https://www.thestate.com/news/politics-government/article252096773.html.

194. Video recording of Santee Cooper reform law signing ceremony on May 18, 2018, recording in possession of ECSC.

195. Video recording of Santee Cooper reform law signing ceremony on May 18, 2018, recording (ECSC).

Epilogue

1. Hersch, Diana. (2013), *HWE Cooperative celebrates 75 years of lighting the way* [Press release], March 26, available at: https://www.hwe.coop/media/2156/75thRelease3-27-13.pdf (Accessed: April 30, 2021).

2. Strom Thurmond, "On Address Before Newberry REA Meeting," News Release, October 22, 1955, https://tigerprints.clemson.edu/cgi/viewcontent.cgi?article=2222&context=strom.

3. Hope Derrick email message to Lindsey Smith, January 28, 2021 (in the possession of the ECSC).

INDEX